CONSTRUCTING
THE LIFE COURSE

THE REYNOLDS SERIES IN SOCIOLOGY
Larry T. Reynolds, *Editor*
by **GENERAL HALL, INC.**

CONSTRUCTING
THE LIFE COURSE

Jaber F. Gubrium
University of Florida
James A. Holstein
Marquette University
and
David R. Buckholdt
Marquette University

GENERAL HALL, INC.
Publishers
5 Talon Way
Dix Hills, New York 11746

CONSTRUCTING THE LIFE COURSE

GENERAL HALL, INC.
5 Talon Way
Dix Hills, New York 11746

Copyright © 1994 by General Hall, Inc.

Publisher: Ravi Mehra
Composition: Graphics Division, General Hall, Inc.

LIBRARY OF CONGRESS CATALOG CARD NUMBER: **93–81355**

ISBN:1–882289–15–3 [paper]
     1–882289–16–1 [cloth]

Manufactured in the United States of America

Contents

ACKNOWLEDGMENTS

Several friends and colleagues share our interest in interpretive practice and have taught us much, both through informal discussions and their published work. We express our thanks to Robert Emerson, Courtney Marlaire, Melvin Pollner, and Haim Hazan. Field research on biographical work done by four doctoral students was very helpful to the project in a variety of ways; we appreicate the work of Carol Ronai, Maude Rittman, Brandon Wallace, and Mary Kate Driscoll. We also appreciate the contributions of the many students, friends, colleagues, and family members who shared their insights into the life course with us. Glenna Holstein was a big help with the index, while Suzy Holstein bravely read the proofs. Cathy Reszka helped with some of the dirty work of typing materials for this book. Her assistance over the years has always been first-rate. We especially appreciate the ongoing support, encouragement, and inspiration of our friend Gale Miller, who is a living embodiment of being "old before his time."

INTRODUCTION

The concept of the "life course" has been extremely useful as a framework for studying human development and life change, providing a dynamic and comprehensive way of understanding the meaning of human experience in relation to time. The objective of this book is to develop a *social constructionist* perspective for life course studies. While the life course has been examined from a variety of disciplinary viewpoints — psychological, psychiatric, sociological, anthropological, and gerontological, among others — the constructionist approach is largely absent from the field. In many respects, then, our project is unconventional. Its aim is to introduce what for many readers will be a new way of thinking, simultaneously laying out the constructionist framework and showing how it can be used to understand human experience in relation to time.

Variations on the constructionist theme have been developing for several decades, yet for many who are more accustomed to the conventional approaches of the social sciences, the approach remains puzzling; for others, it is an anathema. Indeed, many constructionist assumptions and observations run counter to the way people generally understand commonplace phenomena. For example, when individuals think of the world of everyday life, they typically think of a reality that is "out there" — existing apart from our observations, perceptions, and descriptions of it. The meanings of actions and objects seem to emanate from those acts and objects. They are self-evident, something everyone knows or could possibly know. A constructionist approach holds that the reality that is seemingly so concrete is *socially accomplished* — that is, constructed as people interact with one another.

Commonsensically, persons believe that social interaction is mostly a matter of reacting and responding to reality's inherent meanings; it is a way of transporting, transmitting, or manipulating meaning. Language is typically considered to be a way of representing reality. Words convey meanings that issue from the things and acts that the words reference, correspond to, or stand for. Interaction helps us navigate reality, but its essential task is simple descrip-

1

tion—telling about reality. The constructionist approach, however, takes all forms of interaction and discourse to be reality producing and organizing activities. Talk and interaction are *reality work* through which the world of everyday life is structured and assigned meaning.

Following this theme, this book attempts to show how people in the midst of their ordinary activities constitute the meaningful realities of human experience in relation to time. The fundamental argument is that people assemble, articulate, and organize the meanings attached to life change, hence the title, *Constructing the Life Course*. The focus of analysis is on the interpretive activity that produces meaning.

People engage in interpretive practice in all aspects of everyday life. Whether they are medical or psychiatric professionals determining the onset of senile dementia or ordinary parents deciding which of their children is too old, or not old enough, to view a particular movie, individuals are constantly deciding the meaning of age. But chronological age alone is not determinative. Consider how it is, for example, that the same man could be called a "young Turk" in the corporate boardroom yet "over the hill" on the tennis court. Each description conveys a sense of where the man stands relative to others, and to the passage of time, yet neither depends solely on chronological age. Each reflects both the individual, creative agency behind the description and the interpretive orientation, demands, and resources of the situations in which the descriptions were accomplished. Our analysis emphasizes both aspects of interpretation: constitutive practice and interpretive circumstance.

As we demonstrate, individuals construct what it means to develop and change over time through the very mundane ways they talk about and describe objects and experiences. In conventional life course studies, stages and developmental sequences are treated as objective features of life as it unfolds and develops. But these "things"—developmental stages, maturity, immaturity, childhood, old age and the like—are also categories that people use to assign meaning. A constructionist approach treats them quite differently from conventional approaches, focusing on the ways in which people employ these categories and descriptions to make sense of life change. It treats the life course and related terminology as a descriptive *vocabulary*, a constellation of ways of talking about and meaningfully structuring experience in relation to time. This recasts the objects of conventional life course studies—phases, stages, and developmental sequences—as products of interpretive practice, not objectively meaningful "things" in their own right. The point is to analyze how these things are produced through interaction and how they are used to make sense of experience.

Because of its divergent assumptions and conceptualizations, the constructionist perspective suggests different questions from conventional sociological, psychological, or anthropological approaches. We ask our readers to set aside the conventional agendas for the moment and attend to the issues that our approach tries to raise. For example, the constructionist approach is more concerned with describing the dynamic processes through which reality is structured than with what conventional approaches might call social structures. The constructionist approach is not concerned with causal relations between the "variables" that ostensibly compose the social world. Instead, it is concerned with the social process through which those fixed variables are constructed through everyday interaction. While the constructionist and conventional approaches may deal with ostensibly the same phenomena, the alternate conceptualizations and emphases often lead to strikingly different observations. We hope to show readers how to appreciate the insights into everyday phenomena that the constructionist perspective offers.

Constructing the Life Course is a continuation of our ongoing interest in applying the constructionist approach to diverse aspects of everyday life—family, aging, mental health and illness, to name but a few. In 1977, J.F. Gubrium and D.R. Buckholdt published *Toward Maturity* (San Francisco: Jossey-Bass), raising some of the issues and discussing some of the materials contained in the present work. Since then, we have developed and elaborated the central theme and have moved to incorporate new and important concerns for interactional practice and circumstantial orientation. The data we have collected from a variety of sources and settings permit a rich examination of the diversity of life course depictions and practices that everyday life provides.

The first two chapters of the book present alternate perspectives on life course studies. Chapter 1 sets the stage for subsequent discussions by briefly presenting several conventional approaches to the life course. The purpose is to give a concise overview, providing a basis for contrast and comparison as we introduce our alternate approach. Chapter 2 outlines the analytic framework of the constructionist approach. Citing historical and cross-cultural evidence, we argue that persons in different times and places have different ways of representing experience in relation to time. We then specify the basic assumptions and procedures of the constructionist perspective.

The following four chapters take differing orientations to constructing the life course. Chapter 3 focuses on typification—the process by which we interpret objects and events as normal, typical, deviant, or strange. We examine the processes through which individuals' lives are interpreted to be typical or atypical, "on time" or "off time." Emphasis is on how everyday depictions of the life course are constructed.

Chapter 4 focuses on the future, examining how predictions of future growth and potential are accomplished. Our attention centers on how the future trajectory of a life course is discerned and projected.

Chapter 5 has a more present-time orientation. Here we examine common ways of describing human growth and development: competence and maturity. The analysis focuses on the interactional practices that produce documents of what are conventionally thought to be individual characteristics. We argue that the indicators of an individual's competence—often things like standardized test scores or organizational evaluations—are better understood as interactional accomplishments, labels fashioned and/or assigned by others as they deal with the persons whose competence is under consideration.

Chapter 6 looks at the personal past, examining how the life course of the past is retrospectively organized. Biography is framed as the work of constructing coherent pasts that make sense in relation to what is currently known.

Finally, Chapter 7 notes several practical and analytic implications for a constructionist analysis of the life course. We then raise a long-standing concern for the rationalization of experience as it is processed and made meaningful in the diverse organizations that dominate modern life. We conclude by discussing the diverse influences on how lives are represented and the implications this has for the public production of what are ostensibly private matters.

Chapter 1 PERSPECTIVES ON THE LIFE COURSE

We change as we get older. At least that is what we all say. The kids are "growing up" so fast. Parents "don't know where the time went" as their toddlers set off to school and the world beyond the front door. Later, these same parents cannot wait until their teenagers "outgrow" a defiant and obnoxious adolescence. We acquire maturity and responsibility in our "middle years," and the elderly become a valued repository, a wellspring of wisdom and tradition. Interest in the changes that seem naturally to accompany the passage of time — from birth to maturity into old age — is probably as old as self-reflection itself. Indeed, human groups, both across cultures and throughout history, seem to use various age stages or thresholds as landmarks indicating to one another where they stand and what they can expect to encounter next on life's journey.

The related notions of aging and life change are so central to the ways that members of Western societies think about human existence that it is hard to imagine life in any other terms. We view life as an unfolding sequence of events that individuals experience as they traverse the chronological terrain. The odyssey is developmental, almost evolutionary; we talk about growing into new traits, abilities, and outlooks as times in our lives demand them of us. We view aging as a natural process of change, and there are typical, predictable upshots of how old we are and how we have aged.

The theme of life change over time, and variations on the theme, usually refer to what happens to most people, not merely to a single individual. Life is viewed as a series of challenges or developments, events that are expected normally to present themselves in the experiences of all people. The notion of the "life course" provides us with an extremely useful way of conceptualizing and representing the process of age-related change as we interpret the contours of everyday life. It allows us to formulate the trajectories of our lives, revealing the relatedness of different phases, explaining how we have developed, and anticipating our futures. As a practical matter, representing experience in terms of a life course helps us convey where we are in relation to others and where we, ourselves, have been. It makes life a little more understandable, more predictable. We know what we should expect from one another as time passes and we grow older.

It seems that people have always conceived of their lives in terms of a familiar order or sequence. Throughout recorded history, accounts of human experience abound with images and metaphors of some sort of life course. Life has often been called the "journey" from birth to death. For some, life unfolds like the seasons of the year; the ancient Greeks believed that childhood was warm and nurturant like the springtime, youth was hot like the summer, adulthood cool like autumn, and old age cold and harsh as the winter. Others hold that life resembles the times of the day, the cycling of planets, or the phases of the moon. In the "All the world's a stage" speech from *As You Like It*, Shakespeare tells us that people live through seven stages, while Hindu scriptures predating Shakespeare by centuries describe four distinct life stages in terms of their incumbents' obligations and expectations. Even the "riddle of the Sphinx" ("What walks on four feet at dawn, two feet at noon, and three feet at dusk?") suggests the stagelike progression of human development.

Groups of people who share a common way of life are likely to have common beliefs and behaviors that reflect themes of general, expected life changes for their members. On a more abstract level, researchers and professionals have found the life course to be a profound analytic resource for systematically explicating the aging process. Social scientists and scholars interested in the human condition have a long-standing concern for this process; biologists, psychologists, psychiatrists, sociologists, anthropologists, and gerontologists, among others, have developed distinctive approaches to the phenomenon of aging, building complementary, yet often unrelated, literatures. The life course perspective, however, represents a relatively recent convergence of viewpoints on aging that has become the principal theoretical scaffolding for contemporary studies of human development (Hagestad and Neugarten 1985; Kertzer and Keith 1984).

Concern with life change and the life course, then, is socially and historically widespread within the lay, academic, and professional communities. The difference between lay and academic interest is not that one is more important than the other. Instead, lay interest tends to be viewed as practical, part and parcel of thoughts, words, and actions related to the routine concerns that life change poses in people's mundane lives. Academic concern, in contrast, typically claims to focus more abstractly either on laypersons' attitudes and orientations concerning matters of life change or on more general social or maturational forces that may affect life change but may be only dimly recognized by laypersons. While laypersons are conceived as affected by, and oriented to, their location in a life course, theorizing about development, change, and the life course as an abstract organizing framework is thought to reside within the "scientific" jurisdiction.

This book is about human experience and the life course in everyday life. Its focus is on how persons in ordinary circumstances and settings use practical reasoning about the life course, and changes associated with it, to make sense of the experiences they encounter. In one respect, the book deals with some very commonplace phenomena—topics with which we are familiar from both our technical readings about maturation and aging and our own real-life efforts to deal with, and make sense of, life change. But the book proposes an alternate way of understanding experience that asks readers to suspend the commonsense understanding of the life course as a distinct entity, as a feature of lives that exists over and above, or separate from, everyday acts of living. The perspective also blurs the typical distinction between lay, scientific, and professional viewpoints. Our analysis puts aside many conventional notions in order to conceptualize the life course as something that is *socially constructed*. We treat the life course as the product of the situated interpretive work we all do—social scientists, laypersons, and professionals—to give meaning and pattern to individual experience in relationship to time.

In anticipation of presenting our constructionist perspective, this chapter briefly outlines some familiar, conventional approaches to life change. Using the familiar as points of contrast, we then elaborate in subsequent chapters our alternate approach to constructing the life course. As we show from a constructionist viewpoint, the conventional approaches not only contrast with each other, as well as some commonsense understandings, but are also *used* by all concerned as they abstractly represent life change.

SOME CONVENTIONAL APPROACHES
TO LIFE CHANGE

The social and behavioral sciences have developed a variety of approaches to understanding human change and development that incorporate the concept of the life course. Psychological approaches are perhaps the most explicit and long-standing, although sociological and anthropological versions have flourished since the 1960s. There is considerable diversity within the general framework. Psychologists, for example, stress patterning and continuity in life change through the use of such terms as development, stage, and maturation. Sociologists and anthropologists, in contrast, are more likely to address the subjective problems of structured continuity or discontinuity in socialization across the life span.

In order to illustrate the variety of concerns and emphases that emerge in life course analysis, we consider the following prominent approaches: behavioral, psychoanalytic, cognitive, covert personality, symbolic interactionist, functional, and psychocultural. Some of the approaches respect traditional disciplinary boundaries; several are basically psychological (behavioral, cognitive, covert personality), while others are sociological (symbolic interactionist, functional). Some are more interdisciplinary; the psychoanalytic approach, for example, might be categorized as either psychiatric or psychological, while the psychocultural approach draws on anthropology, psychology, and psychiatry. The approaches also vary in terms of their central issues and focus, as well as their empirical bases. For example, psychoanalytic interest in the life course grew from a concern with the affective, psychosexual dynamics of the psyche. The symbolic interactionist approach, in contrast, grew from a sociological concern with a "social" self and role-mediated social perception; its life course focus emphasizes the processes by which the self is socially structured. Each approach has its pioneers, elaborators, and revisionists, including (but not confined to) Pavlov, Watson, Hull, Miller, Skinner, and Bandura (behavioral); Freud and Erikson (psychoanalytic); Piaget, Loevinger, and Kohlberg (cognitive); Neugarten and Gutmann (covert personality); George Herbert Mead, Cooley, Blumer, Becker, Strauss, Zurcher, and Rose (symbolic interactionist); Durkheim, Parsons, and Merton (functional); and Kardiner, Benedict, and Margaret Mead (psychocultural).

The list of well-known names and approaches serves merely to identify and locate the perspectives. We provide only brief sketches of each, giving a flavor for the more general enterprise each represents.

Behavioral Approach

The behavioral approach may have been poorly named, since it cannot be defined simply in terms of an exclusive concern with observable behavior. Certainly, some behaviorists eschew the products of mind as subject matter for scientific study. For them, only outward, visible conduct can be studied objectively. Others expand the empirical referents of behavior to include symbolic activity, such as modeling (Bandura 1969). The critical distinguishing feature of the behavioral approach is the kind of treatment that behaviorists give to these and other empirical referents. Behavior, to the behaviorists, is any activity, directly visible or otherwise, that can be treated as objective and predictably reactive to various kinds of stimuli; these stimuli may, in turn, also be behavior. Stimuli may be anything that objectively and predictably affects the activity of those who behave.

The empirical world of the behavioral approach has two prime components: behaving entities and stimuli. The former (whether human or some other species) exist as real entities that may or may not be changed, while the latter are taken to be concrete sources of change or stability. Actions in the empirical world are governed by operant conditioning and reinforcement; in brief, stimulus is thought to provoke response.

Given this treatment of behavior, how do behaviorists make sense of life change or the life course? Individuals respond to a variety of stimuli in their daily lives, becoming virtual products of reinforcement contingencies. When reinforcement is patterned— that is, it is not random—over an individual's lifetime, there is a perceivable course of development. Life progresses in a linear fashion if reinforcement contingencies change continually to produce new behavior patterns, altering what has already been established. Life appears to cycle, in contrast, if reinforcement contingencies re-create conditions and behaviors that previously existed. Other variations may occur, depending on reinforcement schedules. When reinforcement contingencies are not well patterned, for example, ensuing lives appear to be without a recognizable course; they have neither linear nor cyclic patterning, though they still undergo change.

Behaviorists make no claims about the normality of a life course or cycle apart from the reinforcement contingencies that affect living. Life may or may not cycle; it may or may not follow a linear course. Theoretically, there is no stipulation that life should do either, since cycling or pursuing a steady track are products of basic behavioral principles. The behavioral approach is thus theoretically indifferent to whether a particular normative life course or cycle exists.

Psychoanalytic Approach

The psychoanalytic approach differs considerably from the behavioral perspective. Although deeply concerned with change in individual lives over time, the psychoanalytic approach specifies basic, normal patterning. Behaviorists contend that individuals do not initiate or effect change themselves; the source of change is located in reinforcement contingencies. Psychoanalytic theorists, however, locate the sources of change within the individual, although the specific source varies over the normal lifetime of the person. Initially, change results from inherent psychobiological growth, but it subsequently becomes a product of the meaningful relations between dynamic components of the developing psyche.

Following Sigmund Freud (1933), psychoanalytic theorists assume that the newborn infant is a biological entity with structurally undifferentiated psychological energy. He or she does little that is noticeably patterned except the activity associated with fulfilling biological needs. The neonate is active until its basic demands are satisfied; satiation is presumably experienced as pleasurable. Not much can be said about the psychic state that exists in this newborn, other than it appears to be closely tied to the infant's biological apparatus and that its driving force seems to be the attainment of pleasure and avoidance of pain. It is a kind of psychobiologically gratifying, psychosexual organism. Freud called the original psychological entity and mechanism an "it" or "id"—rather appropriate, it seems, for something that is minded and yet not consciously known to itself.

Given the bond between infant psychology and human biology, changes in one are affected by changes in the other. What the infant becomes over time, psychologically, is a function of changes in the psychosexual state of the body. Psychic growth is considered to be sequentially patterned such that, at or about particular chronological ages, different areas or zones of the body provide the focal point for psychosexual development. As the child grows bodily, its psychic apparatus develops in parallel. Since the former is generally sequential, so is the latter.

The psychosexual relevance of body zones emerges in the following sequence: oral, anal, and, finally, phallic. Concerns for gratification follow in step. When the infant "realizes" that gratification is contingent on the affairs of a world beyond its immediate body, the original psychosexual apparatus is partially transformed into an entity that deals with contingencies external to itself. Part of the id becomes rational and, in the process, becomes self-reflective, increasingly aware of itself—an "I," or "ego." Thus, biological growth spawns the growth of consciousness.

At this point, human life has undergone major changes. The behaving organism has been transformed from a self-gratifying entity to one that has the capacity to rationally act upon itself and its world, to consider the experiential contingencies of gratification. Subsequently, objects of pleasure shift from those that satisfy bodily needs, such as food and elimination, to those that serve the ends of a genitally activated (phallic) desire for sexual possession. Freud assumed that a male child's normal desires for possession were most readily focused on his mother, while a female desired her father. Certainly, Freud was aware of the variety of other possible familial sources of sexual gratification, but, in the psychoanalytic approach, these are considered aberrations.

With the classic completion of these early stages of development, a mind emerges, ready to deal with the world, potentially able to become one of its normal adult members. For Freud, the blueprint for development is essentially in place by the age of five or six.

While growth and changes ensue, later psychic progress basically reflects patterns laid down in the early years.

Erik Erikson's *Childhood and Society* (1950) popularized a psychoanalytic version of the life course that partially supplanted biological determinants with distinctly social considerations and extended the approach beyond infant sexuality. It detached psychic development sufficiently from early biological demands to provide for a lifelong psychosocial treatment. Erikson suggested that mature ego qualities continued to emerge out of critical periods of growth long after childhood. In each of "eight ages of man," the individual ego is challenged to integrate the timetable of the human organism with the structure of social participation.

Erikson saw the life course unfolding as a sequence of turning points, or "crises," each representing a crucial period of vulnerability and simultaneously heightened potential. At each juncture, personal growth could gain or lose ground. In the initial adult stage, for example, the central issue is intimacy versus isolation. If steps are taken to enhance the capacity for intimacy, positive development continues; if one proceeds in isolation, future growth is compromised. The course of life is determined by how such crises are resolved.

Taking the approach in still other directions, Elizabeth Kubler-Ross (1969) has used psychoanalytic theory to specify an additional developmental sequence at the end of life, tracing adaptations to death. Her well-known conceptualization is based on interviews with approximately two hundred hospitalized patients in the Chicago area and other patient interviews across the nation. From these, she outlines a developmental sequence through which dying persons typically advance. Kubler-Ross argues that the stages are normative, using the familiar psychoanalytic notion of defense mechanisms to analyze adaptations at each stage.

The dying person, for example, begins with a stage of denial, which is a refusal to acknowledge the impending possibility of death. The person then moves to anger, which marks the resentment at being chosen for this fate. Next follow stages of bargaining, which is a way of dealing with fate; depression, where symptoms are too evident to ignore; and finally acceptance, which represents a resignation to what is forthcoming. This stage-wise approach has been widely applied by both professionals and laypersons as a model for adapting to other crises—for example, the onset of Alzheimer's disease.

Cognitive Approach

Jean Piaget (1947, 1952, 1957) provides the foundation for a cognitive approach to the life course centered on the development of intelligence and reasoning and informed by two general principles. First, Piaget argues that there are different, basic kinds of thinking about the world: that is, different forms of cognitive orientation. The second principle is that the orientations develop sequentially over the life course. Piaget was chiefly concerned with the cognitive development of children, considering and delineating the structures of children's intelligence and elaborating the structures as epistemological systems. Others, most notably Lawrence Kohlberg (1984), have focused on moral development extending further across the life span.

Piaget's research on cognition involved careful observation of children's behavior in relation to their verbal descriptions of objects and events. He conducted a variety of informal experiments to uncover the sense that children of various ages make of commonplace intellectual challenges. In one famous demonstration, water is poured from a short, squat beaker into a tall, thin one in front of a child. The child then is asked which beaker holds more water. According to Piaget, the young child (aged two to seven years) regularly responds that the beakers differ in quantity, sometimes claiming that the tall one holds more and sometimes the short one, depending on whether the child's attention centers on the relative height or breadth of the beakers. In contrast, the older child (about seven to eleven years) is more likely to say that the beakers hold equal amounts of water.

In another experiment, a child is seated at a square table around which there are three other seats. On the table are three adjacent cones, one of which is larger than the other two. The experimenter places a doll in one of the three empty seats and asks the child to draw the "mountains" (the cones) as the doll sees them. The younger child cannot draw them from the doll's perspective, but portrays the cones as seen from his or her own vantage point. The older child can systematically represent the perspective of a doll seated in each position around the table.

From these and other studies, Piaget concluded that there is a developmental aspect to cognition. The younger child orients to the world as a vessel of objects without an operational logic. A quantity of water that changes shape is a different amount. Others' mountains are the same as the child's own. Such ostensible mistakes can occur only if thought is attached to a particular, personal viewpoint. It is as if the young child thinks about objects and events without being aware of his or her own perspective. This mode of cognition is called *preoperational*; the "mistakes" produced in the experiments are correct responses, given the child's mode of comprehension.

The older child in Piaget's experiments sees as well as notices the transformation in a constant amount of water, concluding that the volume remains the same. He or she also distinguishes the doll's perspective in positions other than the child's own. The ability to do so is a matter of virtual re-cognition. This is called a *concrete operational* mode of cognition.

As the child grows older (twelve years and beyond), he or she enters yet another cognitive stage. Attention to, and consideration of, objects and events are not limited to their concrete presence. The child is increasingly capable of abstract reasoning. Thinking is more hypothetical than before; alternative strategies of action are considered in relation to diverse possibilities. In effect, the child becomes capable of theoretically addressing the world by means of what is called *formally operational* cognition.

To the extent the cognitive approach treats early life changes in intelligence as stagelike, it has affinities with the psychoanalytic approach. But movement from stage to stage in the psychoanalytic approach is a psychosexual process, while movement from one stage of intelligence to another in the cognitive approach is a matter of practical intelligence, a dual process of intellectual equilibration between the developing individual and the environment. On one side is an assimilation process by which new objects and events are integrated into an existing cognitive scheme. On the other side is accommodation, a process of cognitive adjustment in which schemes of thought are altered to reconcile with new experiences. As the child grows, new experiences of all sorts challenge his or her cognitive orientation, which is adjusted by assimilation or accommodation.

Assimilation is perhaps the easier form of adjustment. Although the child may be momentarily annoyed by cognitive anomalies, he or she accepts the challenge and works them into an existing mode of thinking about the world. Indeed, this process may be somewhat forced. With an increasing number of anomalies and their challenges to cognitive orientation, assimilation becomes a trying tactic. The child is likely to begin to see the world as having another, more general character governed by more comprehensive principles. Full accommodation is achieved when the child becomes comfortable with a new mode of cognition.

The equilibration argument is reminiscent of Thomas Kuhn's (1962) theory of scientific revolution. Kuhn calls basic scientific perspectives on the world "paradigms." Paradigms constitute related theoretical and methodological principles that derive from a particular set of assumptions about the universe (see Gouldner 1970; Friedrichs 1970). According to Kuhn, most scientific activity occurs as normal science. Theoretically and methodologically, a paradigm generates and assigns meaning to data according to a process of assimilation. This persists even while anomalous facts challenge the existing paradigm's assumptions and explanations. When anomalies are too intellectually costly to assimilate, a crisis occurs. Science moves to accommodate the anomalies by questioning whether there is a more comprehensive way to account for all the facts. This is the beginning of scientific revolution and imminent paradigm shift, comparable to Piaget's process of accommodation.

Covert Personality Approach

The covert personality approach is another psychologically oriented perspective on life change, focused on middle and late adulthood (see Neugarten 1968). Two levels of personality dynamics are distinguished. Overt processes are conscious and subject to direct personal control. Covert processes are unconscious and are not readily controlled by the actor. Indeed, covert processes may be difficult to detect and must be assessed through projective techniques such as the Thematic Apperception Test used by David Guttman (1967) to explore age-related changes in "interiority."

Three distinct covert processes, called "mastery styles," have been identified as ways that individuals deal with late adulthood. One is *active* mastery, which emphasizes the controlling force of self over the outer world. A second is passive mastery, in which one comes to terms with the world through accommodation. A third style is *magical*, most common among the eldest, which features denial and projection, the person orienting in a reality-distorting fashion to his or her world. Development from one style to another is not based on early psychosexual experience, nor is it a matter of equilibration or contingencies in relation to the outside world. Instead, changes in mastery style are assumed to be intrinsic to the aging personality.

Projective studies have been conducted in a variety of societies, from seminomadic to urban/industrial, the results of which have been interpreted to show that the three covert mastery styles accord with age despite cultural differences. The relationship exists regardless of the person's overt activity or the levels of prestige associated with holding particular roles. There are also important gender differences, men growing in passive mastery and women in active mastery with the passing years. As Gutmann (1987) notes in his "new psychology for men and women in later life," aging men and women have potential for growth denied them in earlier adulthood, but later years afford men the opportunity to become more contemplative and expressive, while women can become more assertive and competitive as they age.

Symbolic Interactionist Approach

Symbolic interactionism offers a social-psychological approach to life change based on the notion that the world is composed of actors whose behavioral scripts are formed from relations with others. Herbert Blumer (1969:2) offers three basic premises for the approach: [1]

1. Individuals act toward objects, events or situations on the basis of the meaning that the objects, events or situations have for them.
2. The meaning of objects, events or situations emerges out of social interaction.

3. Meanings are interpreted and modified through interactional processes.

To understand life change from this perspective, one examines how persons occupying diverse social locations interact with one another as they interpret and respond to social messages about the meanings of age (Karp and Yoels 1982). A social self is central to the process. Following George Herbert Mead (1934), this self is conceived as an entity that constantly searches and tests the interpersonal environment for significant direction. Individuals actively seek others' interpretations of their actions. Through symbolically mediated interaction, one learns to take the attitudes, values, and affect appropriate to the social circumstances one encounters. Similarly, the reflected evaluations of others provide the basis for formulating assessments of one's own behavior and serve to organize courses of action.

Definitions of self typically implicate notions of age and a life course. Put simply, individuals glean the meaning of the life course and life change through others' definitions. If a person senses that others treat him or her as an "adult," then he or she takes on the identity of an adult. If, however, one is consistently viewed as immature, then immaturity comes to dominate one's self-definition. As David Karp and William Yoels (1982:18) suggest, "you are as young or old as *others* make you feel."

For symbolic interactionism, the expression of self or identity involves role enactment (Zurcher 1983). Roles associated with the self provide guiding principles and expectations that shape behavior, informing persons what they should do and how they should act in different situations. Roles may be formal or informal. In either case, they are internalized as guides for the individual's behavior; while roles specify normative behavior, they do not dictate conduct. Persons have more than one role, so they must arrange their role repertoires hierarchically. Some roles are preferred to others; some are more or less dominant. Those that are highest in the preferential hierarchy are the most central to the self concept (Zurcher 1983).

From this point of view, an individual's life course is made up of the roles he or she may occupy across time. Through participation in a particular role, or set of roles, one's experience is shaped so as to provide a particular outlook located in a distinctive social world that is shared by those interacting in similar or complementary roles.

A life course, then, may coalesce as one passes from one role to another; life change is a matter of role change. One might, for example, view one's life in terms of membership in an "adolescent subculture" (Schwendinger and Schwendinger 1985), an adult occupational role (Zurcher 1983), or a "community of grandmothers" (Hochschild 1973). Life's distinguishing features derive from the ways that the various roles are enacted, while life changes take the form of transitions between roles.

Arnold Rose (1965a, 1965b) has extended this notion to suggest that people arrange themselves into distinctive age "subcultures," separate ways of living within the wider cultural context. Youth gangs, for example, represent subcultures at one end of the aging spectrum (Berger 1991), while "social worlds of the aged" (Unruh 1983) characterize experience at the opposite end. Rose suggests that the social meaning of aging may be tied to the changing age subcultures that people enter as they grow older. What is thought of as a life course is a matter of lifelong adjustments in roles and self-definitions that proceed with age. For most people, this results in a discernibly patterned life.

While roles, subcultures, and assessments by others give the symbolic interactionist approach a socially deterministic tinge, the process of self-expression and role enactment is complex and subject to individual discretion, as Kathy Charmaz (1991) describes the self in relations to chronic illness and time. Both active and socially formed, the self produces a multifaceted awareness of the meanings of action as it moves between roles. Biographies are worked up in the process (Couch 1982; Maines 1983). In one role, the self may be mirrored as a particular kind of entity, while in another it may reflect something different.

In the process of gaining knowledge of, and dealing with, itself from one situation to another, the self "invests" itself. For example, as a by-product of being billed as a brand new Ph.D. ready to be launched into the academic and intellectual world, a person is likely to invest in the "side bets" (Becker 1960, 1964) of such a role. She may cultivate academic friendships, which may replace her predoctoral ones. She may settle down in "respectable" academic housing, rather than graduate student quarters. These side bets or self-investments are part of the value one places on an academic life. In time, the gradual, often unwitting accumulation of side bets generates what appears to be personal consistency in relation to those others significantly involved in the process. A life *course* forms out of such social adjustments and interpersonal investments.

Still, some areas of social life are more structured than others, despite the activity of the subject. Entry into some roles or career lines may entail a rigidly specified life course in its own right. This is perhaps most evident in careers that are integral to bureaucratic institutions. Academic careers, for example, require a progression from bachelor degree to doctorate, into a faculty position where one climbs a career ladder through the ranks of assistant professor, then associate, before eventually reaching full professorship. Changes in role and life style often accompany career advancement. In such cases, the notion of "structured" side bets captures the process of life patterning better than self-investment (Becker and Strauss 1956).

The emergence of a life course is clearly a product of socialization and investments. But the process is not one-sided or strictly determined. Anselm Strauss (1959) draws on the metaphor of "coaching" to elaborate the development of a discernible life course. In the process of building a career, a person submits to a variety of agents—individuals or teams—who, in effect, coach or guide the person into socially appropriate attitudes and responses. Coaches' expectations allow for the reasonable mistakes of a novice, while encouraging the backslider to live up to accepted standards. Yet coaching treads a fine line between the autonomy of the person being socialized, on the one side, and social definition, on the other. Life change, in this respect, emerges out of socially situated and mediated learning experiences in which both teacher and learner are active participants.

As we noted earlier, symbolic interactionism provides a more social view of the life course than other conventional approaches. Inasmuch as the approach stresses activeness and reflectiveness, it eschews the vision of a strictly deterministic shaping of life change like that proposed by the behavioral and psychoanalytic approaches. Reinforcement schedules or unconscious motivations are supplanted by the roles and interpretive activities that mediate behavior and its meaning. The life course itself is a consensual reality built up from shared understandings, role enactments, and role transitions, experienced through the dynamic processes of social interaction (Karp and Yoels 1982).

Functionalist Approach

Sociological functionalism, particularly the variety associated with Talcott Parsons (1951), differs from the symbolic interactionist approach to life change in that functionalism does not give separate but equal warrant to self and society. Instead, functionalism builds on the idea of value-integrated social systems. Society is likened to a living organism. Every element of the system that persists over time serves some distinctive function for keeping that system in a state of equilibrium, or optimal functioning. Various elements of the system are functionally integrated to produce and sustain order in the society.

Unlike symbolic interactionism, which examines how the self manages to work through the web of social life, functionalism's interest in the individual centers on how the web, as a dynamic system of parts, shapes people into socially functioning actors. There is little personal autonomy or reciprocity between the self and the social order (Gouldner 1959b). The self is passive, the product of social influences. If the individual is spoken of as an "actor," his or her agency is not readily apparent.

With regard to aging, functionalism suggests that social system viability rests on normative patterning in personal life change. A viable system relies on the contributions of each of its actions. The young are not required to be productive because they are still learning to be contributing members, but as they mature, they are expected to become productive members. A typical life course thus exists, with maturing adults providing for system needs being rewarded accordingly. As individuals grow into old age and their productivity allegedly wanes, the system requires that they disengage from their roles for the sake of the community as a whole (Cumming 1963; Cumming and Henry 1961). Those with declining abilities yield their roles to others and sever social ties, providing opportunities for younger, more productive persons.

Commonly know as *disengagement theory* as it applies to aging and life change (Cumming and Henry 1961), the functionalist approach stresses that the process of withdrawal in later life is both functional and inevitable; disengagement represents life change benefiting both individual and society.

> [There is] an inevitable mutual withdrawal or disen-
> gagement resulting in decreased interaction between
> the aging person and others in the social system.... The
> process may be initiated by the individual or by others
> in the situation.... When the aging process is complete,
> the equilibrium which existed in middle life between
> the individual and his society has given way to a new
> equilibrium characterized by greater distance and an
> altered type of relationship. (Cumming and Henry
> 1961:14–15)

Society clearly benefits by replacing persons who can no longer make the requisite contributions. Aging individuals benefit because they escape the stress of coping with diminished productivity. They are allowed to maintain a sense of worth by performing decreasingly demanding roles, say within the family. Persons grow old "grace-fully" when they do so in a manner that promotes the stability or equilibrium of the social system. Functional changes occur as a result of the socially defined course of life. Other responses to aging — ones that refuse disengagement — are dysfunctional for the system.

Psychocultural Approach

The psychocultural approach to life change maintains that there is an intimate relationship between what human beings become and a society's way of life or culture. The approach varies according to whether emphasis is placed on the "becoming" or the "way of life" side of the equation. Emphasizing the former, Geza Roheim (1950) considers the psychosexual conditions of early life, as described by Freud, to be human universals; culture is merely an expression of these conditions. As Robert LeVine (1973:50) explains, "culture patterns are, for the most part, seen as expressions of motives, emotional constellations, and preoccupations that are pan-human; the emphasis is more on universal themes and symbols than on variations along psychosocial dimensions." Studies of "cultural character" (M. Mead 1928, 1930, 1935, 1954; Benedict 1934, 1938), in contrast, emphasize the importance of a people's "way of life."

They suggest that "in every culture a typical personality is transmitted to the young which more or less corresponds to the dominant configuration of that culture" (Singer 1961:49).

An intermediate position holds that personality mediates two aspects of culture: primary institutions composed of environmental and child-rearing constraints on the development of personality, and secondary institutions consisting of symbolic expression such as religion and art (Kardiner 1939, 1945; Linton 1936, 1945). "Basic personality structure" actively integrates various aspects of culture but is not causally related to culture.

Notwithstanding the varied emphases, the psychocultural approach treats personality and culture as separate entities having important influences on human development. Persons may be *reflected products* of cultural configurations, cultural configurations may be *rooted in* the psychobiological contingencies of early life, or persons may *articulate* varied aspects of culture. Accordingly, the course of an individual life, from birth to death, both presents and represents larger shared understandings of growth and aging.

Differences and Similarities

The various approaches discussed differ significantly, particularly regarding the primacy of life patterning. The behavioral approach represents one extreme where, in principle, no definite patterning is basic to life change. The other extreme may be found in the covert personality approach where a definite gender-related pattern exists in the formation of mastery styles; the pattern is claimed to be a universal feature of adult development. The psychocultural approach, for one, falls in between, as its conception of patterning is both individual and cultural. Pattern exists, but within cultural bounds. Life change may have a typical course in one society and a different course in another.

Another important difference is the extent to which the approaches emphasize what, in a broader epistemological context, might be called the "discourse of the individual" as opposed to a "discourse of the social" (Silverman 1987). While the behavioral approach elides patterning, it is nonetheless highly individualistic in its orientation to life change; the psychoanalytic and psychocultural approaches, while underscoring patterning, can be highly individualistic. The symbolic interactionist approach has been individualistic but, in particular versions, can be outright socially deterministic, as is typical of functionalism. Taken together, the conventional approaches differ in how they constitute the life world, more or less individualistically or socially.

Still, the conventional approaches share a basic premise regarding the nature of social life and the way to conceptualize life change. Each takes for granted — that is, does not subject to question — the objective existence of commonplace entities of the life world that shape experience and age-related transitions, entities such as behavioral contingencies, mastery styles, cognitive orientations, roles, and system needs. The approaches are conventional in that the taken-for-granted entities or commonplace "conventions" are accepted as the objects of analysis (Pollner 1987) as specified by their respective discourses.

The behavioral approach, for example, accepts the objectivity of stimuli and responses, reinforcement schedules, and the reinforcement value of whatever is considered to be personally profitable or costly, considering them to be sources of behavior change. The psychoanalytic approach assumes the existence of powerfully motivating psychosexual (and psychosocial) orientations and specific modes of psychobiological growth through which people normally develop. The approach contrasts these with abnormal forms, which are equally concrete and recognizable. The cognitive approach considers certain modes of thought to be sequentially ordered; the means by which persons experience their world evolve as persons grow older. The covert personality approach defines certain inherent styles of inner experience that serve to organize people's sense of mastery as they age. The symbolic interactionist approach accepts the existence of varied scripts of meaning; while socially mediated, they are nonetheless taken for granted by participants. The approach treats the life course as an external "thing" to be experienced, even if it has social origins. The functionalist approach conceives of personal development as a product of the operating needs of social systems — societies, institutions, families and the like — which are considered social facts or objects in their own right. Finally, the psychocultural approach considers culture to have an observable relation to individual growth and development. Some adherents suggest that social life grows out of personality, while others maintain that personality is a replication of culture. In either case, both personality and culture shape what one is and what one does as time passes.

PUTTING ASIDE THE CONVENTIONAL

Clearly, life change and the life course can refer to many objective things, commonly patterned over time as phases, stages, transitions, and the like. These objects of experience are of a very special sort, however; they are *meaningful*. While they may defy our physical grasp, they appear very real to us. Lives traverse time, and changes occur, but to understand the notion of a life course or life change requires the assignment of meaning to experience. Meaning does not flow directly from objects of experience themselves, but is secured through words, actions, and interpretation. As a social object, the life course takes the form of what Durkheim (1961) called a "collective representation." It is an abstract image or notion evident in particular vocabularies and social rituals that is taken to stand over and above lived experience and simultaneously represents experience to those concerned. In practice, persons establish the meaningful reality of the life course by articulating the collective image with its concrete or behavioral referents. Like "community," "personality," or "social role," "life course" is a concept that provides a means of structuring and apprehending lives. It is distinctive in that it serves to represent and make sense of the things persons experience *in relation to time*.

Of course, this is not the way we conventionally think about our lives. We do not think that we *produce* the meanings of things; we *encounter* them. In the course of our daily affairs, we take things like the life course, old age, childhood, and maturity to be entities or definite phases that, in principle, stand apart from our references to them. We experience them as separate and distinct from interpretive processes. From a commonsense standpoint, "growing up" or "being at the peak of your career" are descriptions of stages or places in life, real locations that we might confront, engage, or depart from. Such a view assumes a correspondence theory of meaning in which words are believed to convey the meanings that lie inherently within objects or that have been socially established, permanently attached, and accepted. Language and social interaction are believed merely to convey meaning. From the standpoint of everyday life, the life course and related entities are treated as having an objective reality of their own.

But the panoply of ordinary and professional depictions of life change implies that meaning is somehow related to usage. While the conventional approaches considered earlier all orient to objective things—objects of age-related change across the individual's lifetime—there seems to be little consensus on just what these things are. Imagine the responses we might generate if we asked proponents of each of the approaches to answer the question "what is the life course?" Some might say that it was a stagelike, unfolding pattern through which individuals pass as they move from youth to middle, then old age. If pressed for greater detail, agreement would dissolve. While several might agree that there was something called a life course, each would describe it differently. One would say it included anal, oral, and phallic stages of psychosexual orientation, while another would distinguish between preoperational, operational, and formal stages of cognitive development. Still others would concentrate on functional capacity, with stages corresponding to societal demands on individuals of particular ages. While the notion of a course or progression might persist, the portrayals of change would scarcely coincide.

Nor would they necessarily be recognizable to persons who, in ordinary circumstances, are just as certain that they know what the life course is, due in part to the diverse images and metaphors of growth and change that laypersons typically use to interpret their lives in relation to time. Mothers and fathers may convey the life course in terms like "the terrible twos" (a phase of emerging independence and obstinacy used to characterize toddlers) or the "teen" years, meanings and usages that correspond to parenting experiences. Their own adolescent children might relate the life span in terms of being a "kid" or an "old guy," that is, anyone over, say, thirty. And the sixty-five-year-old grandparents might talk about the volunteer work they do with the "elderly" at the local nursing home. The point is not that laypersons are unsophisticated or inconsistent. Instead, it is that ordinary people in the course of everyday life use a variety of images to make sense of experience in relation to time, quite apart from professional formulations.

Rather than try to impose some comprehensive framework from the outset, then, analysis of the life course might consider how the very notion of life change and images of a life course and its components, including the various conventional approaches, are used to describe and organize personal experience in relation to time. In this regard, life changes and transitions are understood in terms of the way people, from laypersons to professionals, present change to one another. Life change becomes an object of interpretation whose sense and substance emerge through language-mediated interaction. In practice, the life course consists of a configuration of abstract meanings, categories, and labels that are attached to experience through everyday methods of interpretation. In this context, the key to understanding the courses and changes that are said to characterize our lives lies in deciphering how, through words and actions, experience is given developmental shape and meaning.

In putting aside conventional notions of life change — shifting our focus of analysis from objects of experience to the construction of those objects — this book becomes a description of people's descriptions of their lives in time. It examines the myriad ways that images of the life course are invoked to provide pattern and meaning to lives in progress, considering the ordinary conditions that affect usage. Because talk and interaction provide the constructive basis for life change, the analysis centers on descriptive practice, the mundane interpretive work through which conventional terms such as "childhood," "maturity," "developmental stage," "the golden years," and "act your age" constitute the realities of life change. The analysis also considers how aspects of life change — like stages, courses of growth, competence and maturity — are mediated by the ordinary interpretive contingencies of time and place (see Smith 1987). Practice, then, is composed of both discourse and circumstance.

Finally, we do not want to ignore the conventional approaches we have summarized. They are far too prevalent and useful as aspects of everyday interpretation to be set aside completely. Instead, we analyze the conventional approaches as well as lay formulations as practical resources — ideas and categories that people use in everyday circumstances to make sense of life in relation to time. Rather than abandon the conventional approaches, we treat them as part of our topic.

NOTE

1. It is possible to understand Blumer's (1969) programmatic statements on symbolic interactionism in a way that is complementary with, if not indistinguishable from, the constructionist arguments that appear throughout this book. Most symbolic interactionist theorists, however, have not developed or exploited the connection.

Chapter **2**   **THE CONSTRUCTIONIST APPROACH**

Ask a six-year-old child to describe what it is like to "grow up," and she might tell you something like this.

> First you're born and you're a baby and you can't do anything but cry and lay in your crib. Then you get to be a toddler and learn to walk and talk and eat things. Then you are a child and it's more fun because you can run and play and do things and play with other kids. You have to go to school but it's okay because you have art and science and gym. When you're a big kid, maybe eight or nine, you have more homework and it's not so much fun, but it's okay because you still get to be a kid and play around and stuff. After that, you're just a grown-up. It's not as much fun because you have to work.

Compare this to a brief portion of a "life story" told by a forty-nine-year-old woman.

> I was just a child when I got married. I was so excited about being a good wife and mother. That was all that really mattered to me and I never really thought about anything else. It never occurred to me that I would do anything else—ever. . . . Well the marriage just wasn't working out and we finally separated, even though I didn't really want to. There I was, a middle-aged house-wife without any skills, any way to support myself except child support and I wouldn't take welfare. . . . I don't know how we survived that phase, but the kids are all grown up and gone now and with this heart problem I can't work. So I'm as good as retired. A regular senior

citizen. [Laughs.] I guess I'm looking forward to being
a grandmother now.

Both accounts offer versions of the life course, as divergent as
they may be. But what do they actually tell us about the experience
of life change? Vernacular usage and commonsense notions about
life and its transitions offer pictures that hardly coincide with one
another, much less the conventional theories of life change discussed in chapter 1. Moreover, vantage point, or perspective, brings
disparate aspects into play. We may be tempted to dismiss accounts
such as these as merely interesting, naive reports or theoretically
unsophisticated observations. Conventional approaches, to be sure,
favor conceptual frameworks and abstractions developed at a dis-
tance from empirical settings. The frameworks can then be applied
to the experiences of people like our informants above in order to
describe and understand their lives in abstract, methodic, and
generalized terms. The life course, in these terms, is a systematically
conceptualized, objective reality, something that gives shape to
persons' lives in terms of time. Employing this approach, the stories
told here represent sincere, yet conceptually underdeveloped assessments.

There is another way to appreciate vernacular depictions. Instead of thinking of them as faulty versions of the analytic constructs
professional analysts employ to characterize experience, we might
conceptualize the life course and its various stages as descriptive
resources that ordinary people use in the course of their everyday
lives to "make sense" of what they encounter as they, and those
around them, orient to issues of age and change. From this perspective, the life course, life phases, stages of aging, and the like are terms
and categories that people use to describe and interpret their worlds.
They are not just things experienced or encountered; they are
interpretations assigned to experience. In application, age-related
phases and stages descriptively *accomplish* life change, both literally and figuratively, to produce meaningful interpretations of pasts,
presents, and futures.

For example, both the six-year-old and the "senior citizen" who
tell us about the life course use phaselike images to characterize lives
in progress. While they designate distinctly different patterns, each
uses the framework of "stages-in-a-sequence" to help convey the

meaning of their lives (Bruner 1986; Cohler 1982). The life courses that emerge are not mere representations of inherent patterns of experience as much as they are formulations of just what the tellers understand their experience to be. Describing one's self as a "child" helps the six-year-old convey the carefree fun associated with a particular chronological period, fun that is tempered by the advance of time and responsibility as one becomes a "big kid." She interprets "growing up" for us in vernacular life course terms that both constitute the periods she speaks about and supply the stages with their practical meaning. From her perspective, she makes the span of life that she knows into a distinct period—childhood—and leaves the rest—being grown up—undistinguished.

Our forty-nine-year-old also constructs a life course, albeit a distinctly different one. She uses images of "child," "middle age," and "senior citizen" to convey sequential changes in her outlook on life and the challenges she has encountered. She, too, establishes the meaning of her varied experiences with terms characterizing distinctive periods or phases. She divides her life into segments in order to differentiate the qualities, challenges, and priorities that distinguish the various times in her life. Calling herself a "senior citizen" does more than indicate chronological age. Indeed, it may *mis*represent it in terms of most literal standards. Yet it imparts the sense of enervation that the woman feels as a result of her advancing years, declining health, and changes in domestic and employment circumstances. Saying that she is a "regular senior citizen" is more than a simply descriptive act; it is a rhetorical claim about the quality of her life and thus persuades us that her description reflects another vantage point.

The use of the category "child" in the two accounts is particularly interesting and noteworthy. Clearly, its meaning is established in the way the term is used in the alternate depictions. For the six-year-old, it conveys a relative maturity; the capabilities and options of one characterized as a "child" certainly supersede those of a "baby" or "toddler." To be a "child" bride, however, means much the opposite; it is a mark of innocence and immaturity. The point is not that the two depictions differ or that someone is misusing a descriptive category. Instead, each uses life stages to construct the meaning of their lived experiences, but they use the same term to impart different meanings. The term "child" thus derives its meaning, in part, from its respective narrative contexts. Its meaning is neither an objective feature of a particular chronological time in life nor a property of the term itself (Saussure 1960).

Viewing the life course as a social construction requires a distinctive analytic stance. We need to consider aspects of everyday reality in an unaccustomed way. Rather than take the social objects of our world for granted as being "out there"—objects such as the stage "child"—we must ask how such objects are *brought into being* as meaningful realities. The task in analyzing the life course is to discern how it is constructed through everyday interpretive practices such as our informants' narratives.

This chapter provides the groundwork for such analysis. It introduces and elaborates a constructionist framework for analyzing life change, outlining the assumptions and methods of describing how the life course is socially accomplished.

THE ANALYTIC FRAMEWORK

The constructionist approach is informed by several sociological traditions. In their distinctive ways, ethnomethodology (Garfinkel 1967; Heritage 1984; Pollner 1987), social phenomenology (Berger and Luckmann 1966; Schutz 1967, 1970), and particular versions of symbolic interactionism (Blumer 1969) each conceive of everyday realities as interactively constructed and sustained. Taken together, they suggest that persons' depictions of, and dealings with, their social worlds create or constitute those social worlds as meaningful phenomena. From this perspective, interaction in general and, more specifically, talk and language use are not mere ways of conveying meaning. Instead, they are ways of *doing things with words* to produce meaningful realities and formulate the social world. In a sense, the orderly and recognizable features of social circumstances are "talked into being" (Heritage 1984:290) as interpretive practice organizes, manages, and transforms reality. Descriptions, such as when we portray someone as old or middle-aged, are not disembodied commentaries on ostensibly real states of affairs. Rather, they are *constructive actions*, applications of categories and assignments of meaning that are consequential within specific situations and inter- actional contexts. In this respect, descriptions are virtually "reality projects." The life course may be viewed as one such project, similar in this regard to social projects such as family or community (Gubrium 1988b; Gubrium and Holstein 1990; Hazan 1990).

The world that we construct is generally a familiar one, a reality interpreted in terms of commonsense categories and ideas. The categories and ideas are conceptual resources for interpreting matters at hand, grasping the intentions and motivations of others, achieving intersubjective understandings, coordinating actions, and more generally constructing meaning. Both natural and social objects are interpretively constituted and continuously updated through our constantly evolving stocks of knowledge (Schutz 1967, 1970)—our interpretive frameworks for making sense of experience.

While interpretive practice is sensitive to larger social, cultural, and historical contexts, these are highly localized and artful in application (Garfinkel 1967). The specific knowledge we use to characterize our worlds and experience reflects the interpretive orientations, goals, and contingencies of the situation at hand. Life change is interpreted with reference to circumstantially available and acceptable images. While we may have knowledge of many means of conveying and construing life change, situations inform us of how to select from, and apply, what we know. Consequently, the life course as an object may have as many practical realities as there are vocabularies, categories, and circumstances for assigning its shape and substance. Indeed, we might argue that our sense of life change and the life course is *organizationally embedded*—that is, grounded in the diverse descriptive domains in which change and the life course are addressed.[1] This is not to say that circumstance dictates interpretation. Instead, socially organized context provides distinctive discourses, interpretive resources, and structures of normative accountability to which persons orient as they produce situationally adequate accounts and descriptions. We take it that individuals draw from these, but never yield authorship of realities to deterministic structural imperatives.

Whereas the life course is constructed, it is not ephemeral, mere words without substance. The images, terminology, models, and theories of the life course and its phases and stages are known-in-common resources for both naming and making sense of life change. As they are applied to aspects of experience, they attach meanings that, for all practical purposes, are attributed to the objects of interpretation. If, for example, we describe someone as undergoing a "midlife crisis," we convey a set of understandings about the person, his or her circumstances and responses, and the meaning this has in relation to the person's past, present, and future. Those hearing the characterization apprehend an urgent *reality* behind the discourse in terms of what it actually conveys about the person described, glossing over the descriptive activity itself that constitutes and conveys meaning. The interactional processes through which we "accomplish" the life course, then, are "seen but unnoticed" (Garfinkel 1967), while their artifacts appear to us as concrete and "real."

By virtue of its concern for socially mediated meaning, the constructionist approach has some affinity with the more conventional symbolic interactionist approach discussed in chapter 1. Indeed, Blumer's (1969) programmatic directives for symbolic interactionism can be assimilated to the more ethnomethodologically oriented version of constructionism we offer here. But there are some important differences. Symbolic interactionism shares several principles with structural functionalism, for example, that are incompatible with our constructionist framework. While, in its fashion, symbolic interactionism holds reality to be socially constructed, it also frames reality as a set of enduring, consensually shared constructs that exert causal influence over everyday behavior. The influence is evident in the symbolic interactionists' reliance on such constructs as self, identity, and roles as real features of the everyday world that shape individual's behavior. In this sense, the concepts are used much as functionalism uses them, especially as norms, social scripts, or roles are treated objectively and particularly as the social self-as-agent is placed at the center of experience.

From the symbolic interactionist perspective, roles exist to be "played" or "enacted," eventually to be assimilated into a more or less integrated personal identity—a kind of role internalization. Our constructionist approach stresses role-use rather than role playing (Gubrium 1988a). "Role" is construed as an interpretive resource that persons use in the course of everyday activity to explain behavior. It may be used in conjunction or in competition with other resources, such as personality (cf. the covert personality approach) or shared values (cf. the functionalist approach), to account for everyday occurrences. Where symbolic interactionism takes social reality for granted and attributes behavior to roles, social selves, or socially instigated motives, our approach examines how people articulate diverse concepts as part of their own explanations that construct a sense of order. We thus take "role," "self," and "identity" to be aspects of reality-constructing discourses, parts of vocabular-ies of motive (Mills 1940) used to describe experience.

The constructionist approach is broader than symbolic interactionism in the sense that it focuses on vernacular explanatory resources that are not limited to what Silverman (1987) calls "the discourse of the social," whose terms such as "roles" and "social selves" characterize symbolic interactionism. The constructionist perspective accepts the equal force of what might be labeled "the discourse of the individual," whose signal language—personality, id, ego, cognition, temperament, mastery—is featured in other conventional approaches. As far as usage is concerned, any and all of the conventional approaches discussed earlier, including sym-bolic interactionism, can serve as vernacular explanatory resources and thus become the focus of constructionist analysis.

THE LIFE COURSE ACROSS CULTURE AND HISTORY

Some of the most vivid illustrations of the social construction of the life course are those depicted cross-culturally and historically. Cultural anthropologists seem to agree that the life course—or something like Western notions of it—is recognized in all societies (Fortes 1984; Hagestad and Neugarten 1985; Myerhoff 1984). They are similarly convinced, however, that specific features such as cycles, age categories, stages, and the like are culturally defined. The familiar American life course, for example, cannot be found in many non-Western settings. The notion that lives begin at birth, proceed through stages of a developmental process, and end in death is a relatively recent, Western intellectual development (Hogan 1989). Nevertheless, this view of progressive, stagewise life change as the "natural" course of life has been sustained by the tendency in Western social science to grant the aging process a "universal linearity" and a "seeming objectivity" that ignores cultural variation in conceptions of time and age (Ostor 1984).

Western notions of an aging process are based on several fundamental assumptions about chronology. We organize our temporal perceptions by connecting the past to the present, and this to the future, in linear terms. References like "stream of experience," "the march of time," "time flies," and so on, convey the progression. We divide and mark our days with units of time, seemingly orienting our every activity to clock or calendar. Life change and a linear chronology implicate one another, as our phenomenological understanding of aging and life change is circumscribed and propelled by our view of time passing—irresistibly, irreversibly, irretrievably, inevitably. The linear, progressive life course is an artifact of this chronology (Rubinstein 1990).

Contrary to the familiar Western conception, time in other societies may be experienced as cyclical, plural, reversible, nonlinear, nonmeasureable, or open-ended (Ostor 1984). Or it may be unimportant, virtually nonexistent for all practical purposes. Clifford Geertz (1973), for example, argues that the Balinese have a "detemporalized" sense of time. The Balinese employ both a twelve-month, solar-lunar calendar and one that is permutational, consisting of ten different cycles of day names. The importance of time in the latter system is not durational but punctual. The calendar is not used to divide or measure the passage of time in the Western sense, nor does it accent the uniqueness and irrecoverability of moments of time-in-passing. Instead, it is used to mark and classify noteworthy experiences—to describe and characterize them, formulating their differential social, intellectual, cultural, and religious significance. The cycles and supercycles that the two systems combine to produce are endless, unanchored, uncountable. They do not accumulate and are not consumed. They do not tell one what time (date) it is; they indicate what kind of time it is. The effect is to strip time of its cumulative, developmental, and transformative features, replacing it with a series of recurrent cycles linking family, person, production, ideology, and ritual without being aggregated linearly. Notions of chronological aging as Westerners conceive it are virtually meaningless within this system (Ostor 1984). Time lacks a forward motion. Social life goes on in a culturally grounded "present." Individuals do not relate to one another as consociates, successors, or predecessors as much as merely contemporaries. Any sense of biological aging is blunted, as Geertz (1973) puts it.

Other cultures experience and depict time in still different fashions. In a well-known example, Benjamin Whorf (1956) argues that the Hopi of the American Southwest have no verb tenses indicating past, present, or future, but merely indicate the duration of an event. One grammatical category represents fleeting events, like lightning, while another indicates long-term events, like a lifetime. The Hopi do not interpret time as a series of discrete occurrences following each other in succession. Instead, they conceive of it as a "getting later" of everything that has ever been done. Events are cumulative through time. Alternatively, Troibrianders (Lee 1949) do not really order events so much as name them. They are concerned mainly with "being" and do not describe sequential progressions through time. Consequently, for them there is little sense for progressive "history," an orientation apparently shared in traditional India (Lannoy 1971).

The sense of time varies even among Westerners. Haim Hazan (1980) describes a group of elderly Jews in London who have collectively constructed a social world outside of time, a virtual temporal limbo. Past events are considered irrelevant to the present; indeed, they are unspeakable. The accomplishments and failures of earlier times do not matter. According to Hazan (1980:183), "change is arrested and progress and planning are eliminated." Group members depict time as neither cyclical nor linear, but as literally and figuratively inconsequential, living their lives in the collective present.

Conceptions of time, then, may vary from group to group. Some report that it passes relentlessly or cycles repeatedly as an endlessly renewing flow. It may be a central organizing principle of social life or virtually unimportant as a feature of lives in progress. These diverse understandings provide frameworks within which persons interpret aging and life change, formulating the shape and meaning of their lives. The linear life course is merely one variant, as across cultures we find depictions of aging and life change aligning with local notions of time.

Villagers and irrigation rice farmers in western Taiwan, for example, interpret life in terms of various cycles, rather than as a "life course" (Thompson 1990). At one level, there is a prevalent belief in reincarnation; life is viewed as cyclically renewed. Villagers also orient to a sexagenary cycle (sixty-year periods made up by aligning the twelve Animal Years with five "phases"). While the sixtieth year may indicate passage into old age chronologically (from a Western standpoint), from the cyclical perspective, it marks the beginning of a "second childhood," a concept that is not used disparagingly.

Villagers also orient their lives to the growth, fertility, and recycling of plant life and the flow of water, reflecting their concern for conditions affecting the production of the rice crop. Their orientations provide schemes for interpreting individual lives within the succession of generations. Life is said to stem from ancestral roots that nurture successive generations, virtually living on in them. The passage of time is likened to the growth cycle. A man does not grow old while his parents are still alive, and he has a duty to ensure the continuity of the family or he is out of phase with the stream of time, and the harmony of persons, nature, and the cosmos. Thus, the imagery of aging and life change yields a pattern of cyclical growth and rejuvenation, ultimately resulting in the veneration of the old (Thompson 1990). This stands in stark contrast to the imagery of progressive decline or disease (Sankar 1984) used by Americans to characterize the life course.

The Venda of southern Africa also constitute their lives in terms of cycles, but their imagery depicts spiritual aging as separate from biological aging (Blacking 1990). Spirits of departed ancestors are considered the guardians of the land and people. All persons are thought to begin life as reincarnations of the deceased and to continue after death as ancestral spirits. Infants and old people — being at the extremes of earthly life — are thus closest to the purity of the spiritual world. As a child grows, the ancestral spirit lodged in the child's body is gradually modified by social experiences so that the person begins to develop a strong and independent soul. As the body grows and ages, the spiritual perfection of the baby is lost. By adolescence, the body is growing strong, but the spirit is still immature and weak. From this point, continued maturation of the personality is seen as the development of the spirit, which will move on into the community of ancestors after death, there to assume responsibility for returning to guide a living successor. Biological maturation, then, is not synchronized with spiritual development; indeed, those at the most "frail" extremes of physical being are considered the most spiritually "mature." The Venda "life course" transcends a living person's earthly experience, with spiritual development cycling in diametric opposition to physical or chronological aging.

There are, of course, many other examples across cultures of alternate life course constructions. We can even see changes in the way Western societies have formulated life's phases and stages. Childhood, for instance, was not a distinct life course stage until fairly recently (Aries 1962). Indeed, during the Middle Ages, there is no mention of periods corresponding to our contemporary notions of childhood or adolescence. Persons labeled "children" today were then considered "adults" on a smaller scale. In descriptions of the aging process, individuals proceeded from infancy to little adulthood to adulthood. Activities and social worlds were not taken to be the separate spheres they are portrayed as today; daily contact between adults and children revealed few age-related distinctions. As Phillipe Aries (1962:37) writes, "children mingled with adults in everyday life, and any gathering for the purpose of work, relaxation, or sport brought together both children and adults. . . ." Participation was not restricted to members of certain age groups, and linguistic divisions were not clear-cut as they are today.

More recently, we find the middle portions of the age spectrum being elaborated in greater detail, distinguishing it in heretofore unnoted ways. Historically informed life course studies, for example, reveal complex patterns of personal and familial development in relation to social and economic change (Elder 1974, 1979; Hareven 1978), especially regarding the changing course of men's and women's lives (Degler 1980; Mintz and Kellog 1988; Coontz 1988). Corresponding to these patterns, new life stages are being constructed as we employ new age-grading categories—the "young-old" versus the "old-old" (Neugarten 1974, 1978), for example—to describe persons as they advance through the later parts of progressively longer life spans.

Cross-cultural and historical variation in the way life change is formulated allows us to see how different groups and eras construct and interpret the temporal contours of personal experience. The point is not so much that biological aging proceeds differently from place to place, although the experience of that process is surely apprehended differently. Instead, alternate, culturally grounded conceptualizations of a life course or cycle reveal the ways that various societies draw upon different categories, images, and inter-pretive templates to represent their lives.

Consequently, we might consider the life course (or any other representation of a life span) as a "cultural unit." Its definition and meaning are specified by cultural beliefs and assumptions (Keith 1985). Age is calculated differently in different cultures, with varying emphasis on chronology versus function, with different categories and signposts. The number of classifications may range from the two (young and old) used among the St. Lawrence Eskimos to ten or more named age-grades (Keith 1985). What becomes evident is that there is no single "natural" life course segmentation inherently characterizing people's lives. The "life course" itself is a formulation that constitutes a particular understanding of aging that is different from that conveyed by a "life cycle" or the image of life that does not pass with linear time.

Even the idea of a *personal* life course may not be a relevant unit in all societies for characterizing one's existence and experience in time. As Mark Luborsky explains:

> . . . the ethos of individual independence and *autonomy* (vs. individuation within a group) that typifies current Western culture, . . . emerged only with the onset of industrial economic-political conditions that reduced individuals' control over the conduct and course of their public life (e.g., Dumont 1965, 1986). The ideal disre-gards interdependence in social life and growth (cf. myths of nuclear households as independent, Segalen 1986), and underlies Western psychological models of the self as a single, autonomous, coherent whole (Marsella and White 1982; Geertz 1986). One conse-quence is that Western thought equates the biographical unit with the biological body. (n.d.:4–5)

The image of an individual life course or life history, then, is informed by Western notions of personal interiority, agency, and privacy, so that the independence of one life from another is a cultural construction.

We might think of the life course and other ways of depicting life change as *metaphors*—devices for understanding and experiencing one kind of thing in terms of another (Lakoff and Johnson 1980). We use metaphors to borrow or transfer meaning between interpretive domains. They allow us to attach familiar meanings to what might otherwise seem uninterpretible. But metaphorical usage does not merely enrich description; our thoughts, sentiments, and actions are known to us through metaphor. In effect, metaphors constitute the reality we experience and how we perceive it.

Metaphors capturing life change — the life course, life cycle, life stages, and the like — literally provide ways of seeing. They are paradigms through which complex, abstract, or unformulated experience can be interpreted (Thompson 1990). As a metaphor, the Western notion of a personal life course composed of phases or stages reflects distinctive social, cultural, and historical conditions and assumptions. It aligns images of aging and life change with historically and socially appropriate concepts of time, history, and change. The result is a cultural vocabulary that reflects an aging process in collectively representative terms (Durkheim 1961).

The Western life course, for example, "progresses" through adulthood, but old age marks a distinct downturn in life's trajectory. A lifetime is finite; time "marches on" irresistibly and irretrievably. Individuals "strive" for maturity, then get "spent." In contrast, the Taiwanese villagers' "plant life" metaphors that convey their life patterns liken various life experiences to phases in the growth of crops. The metaphor of cyclical growth and rejuvenation is used to construct a "life cycle" that contrasts with the linear, clocked life course that Westerners experience.

Individuals, then, are guided by culturally grounded commonsense theories about their lives. They use these theories to sort their experience, to display continuities or breaks between the past and present, and to predict the trajectory of the future. Cross-cultural differences in the way lives are represented show us that age and time are not universal and objective conditions with the same meanings for all persons or groups. Life course depictions rely on locally indigenous, socially assembled constructs, subject to broad cultural and historical editing.

CONSTRUCTIONIST ASSUMPTIONS

Analyzing the life course as a social construction requires a radical departure from the conventional approaches we outlined in Chapter

1. Rather than attempting to describe what are believed to be the objective features of life change, we examine how persons engaged in ordinary activities *constitute* the life course through interpretive practice. Interpretive practice is the situationally sensitive interactional process through which people construe and represent reality. The focus of our approach is on how experience is made meaningful in relation to the passage of time. Our analysis of everyday construction relies upon distinct assumptions and procedure. We turn to these in the following sections.

Bracketing the Life World

Assuming a constructed reality and analyzing the practices through which it is accomplished requires us to "bracket" the life world (Schutz 1970), setting aside people's everyday assumptions about its factual, objective character. In practice, this means that we assume that the life course, and life change more generally, are ontologically problematic; their reality status is uncertain. We avoid a priori judgments regarding the correctness or appropriateness of persons' practical reasoning and interpretations. For example, we make no evaluative distinction between "normal" and "deviant" behaviors for persons of any age. Instead, we let people speak for themselves, paying attention to how they represent their lives (and those of others) as members of particular groups with "normal" or "abnormal" characteristics, among other native distinctions. This approach is quite different from, say, the psychoanalytic and functional perspectives on aging, which take for granted the early psychosexual experiences and later social roles and statuses that are said to affect the course of lives.

In bracketing the social world, we orient to speaking members as its principal agents—persons who use available categories and vocabularies to address the life world's conventional objects as real, to-be-dealt-with things.[2] Within this frame of reference, when members refer to such things as a "stage" of life that they have or have not reached, or a "crisis point" or "milestone," we treat the stage or point as a practical feature of talk—not some place or entity in a course of life at which they may arrive. Our aim is to document how talk about everyday life *constructs* the realities that are referenced.

Consider, for example, a family whose members are heatedly discussing whether or not the teenaged son, Johnny, is really old enough to take his girlfriend on an unchaperoned camping trip. Amid the deliberating, arguing, yelling, making of exceptions, crying, pleading, and explaining, it turns out that Johnny's father once boasted that when he was Johnny's age, he did as much with most of the girls in town and, what is more, "made it" with each of them. In his own defense, the father claims that times were different then and he was "already grown up" at his son's age. At this point, the issue of maturity — as both a practical and theoretic concern — is thrust center stage.

Bracketing this social scene means that we approach it without prejudging who or what is mature. We take maturity to have no absolute or concrete standing in members' lives. Instead, we treat maturity as a practical outcome of the interpretive work done by members as they present maturity as a topic for discussion and come to some conclusion about what it is in the situation at hand. We take it that, for all practical purposes, Johnny's maturity is constituted out of the occasion of its consideration.

From this perspective, social life is continuously being constructed by its members. Whatever is real about the life world is made so through the talk and interpretive work that members do to constitute it. They may, for example, talk and work themselves or others into being "grown up" or immature, middle-aged or "over the hill," or myriad other things related to age. Analytically, reality is nothing more or less than what members make of it. Being mature is a matter of the *sense* of maturity that members come to have about someone, or about themselves, on occasions when maturity is a topic of consideration. Members come to know the sense of their own and others' maturity by talking about it or by having it conveyed in some other discursive or representational form. When the discourse is locally validated, we take it that they or others feel and become mature. When it is not validated, maturity remains problematic. As interpretation flows, so does maturity.

Returning to our example, if Johnny manages to convey the view that he is grown up enough to act responsibly, his maturity is discursively established. But if Johnny's father succeeds in convincing the family that what he did in his youth was "different" or "an exception," and that Johnny is not yet "ready" for what is proposed, then for all practical purposes, Johnny is immature.

To argue that reality is constructed is not to suggest that the life world is made up by conscious schemers. Far from it. For the most part, members remain unaware of the construction process, naturally attending instead to the ostensible realities at hand. They speak, as members of Johnny's family do, of stages, developmental progressions, levels of maturity, roles, and life courses with every assurance of their actual, objective reality. Suspending commonsense assumptions about reality, however, allows us to view and analyze these acts of everyday construction as entities in the making.

Bracketing the life world thus establishes an analytic indifference toward the phenomena being studied (Garfinkel and Sacks 1970), creating what Schutz (1970) called a presuppositionless or "scientific" attitude. It does not mean that we lose interest in the phenomena or disregard them because they are insubstantial or subjective. To the contrary, it means that we adopt a perspective outside and apart from, the objects of our inquiry, dispassionately examining the practical activities that constitute the objects. Analytic indifference allows us to respect and topicalize members' constitutive practices, to discern and describe how members produce and manage the myriad objects of their lives without judging their actions against some transcendent standard of what the life world is "really" like. In this context, there is no basis for invidiously comparing commonsense practices with idealized standards, no warrant for pointing out errors in members' interpretations. As far as our example is concerned, we are not interested in judging whether or not Johnny is actually mature, but in how his maturity or lack thereof is socially manifested and accomplished.

Situated Rationality

When human scientists speak of rational behavior, they do not all mean the same thing. Some evaluate rationality in terms of a standard they, as scientists, take to be independent of particular subjects and applicable to all, regardless of circumstance. For instance, they might suggest that to act rationally is to maximize one's gains and minimize one's losses. In contrast, our construction-ist approach treats rationality as a practical or situationally condi-tioned matter. The rational in any situation is mediated by the local working assumptions that define reasonableness.

Every situation or occasion is built on background expectancies or "life-as-usual" assumptions (Garfinkel 1967). The assumptions make certain talk and actions reasonable to those who observe or engage in them. What is glossed over also depends on background expectations. On some occasion, certain talk or particular gestures may be construed as irrational by members who in other circum-stances would assume them to be quite rational. Comparing what people treat as "perfectly reasonable" on one occasion with what they treat as equally "reasonable" on another occasion suggests that what allows them to behave the way they do from place to place is their ability to gloss over the apparent inconsistency by naturally attending to the taken-for-granted realities at hand. Rationality is practical because it is locally bound and interpreted.

Take the practical rationalities of the occasions described in the following example. A new father is eager to see and hold his daughter in the nursery of a hospital's obstetrics ward. As he enters the nursery, one of the nurses rushes toward him and cautions him first to don a hospital gown, mask, and cap. She provides him with the clothing, which he dutifully puts on, and he proceeds into the nursery among the cribs toward his daughter. Meanwhile, the nurse politely reminds him of the need to take precautions because "people can bring any kind of germ into the nursery."

The next day, we find the same father walking toward the nursery. As he approaches, a man dressed in janitor's overalls and carrying a screwdriver and pair of pliers precedes him into the nursery. The nurses look up, notice who it is, and nonchalantly ask the janitor what he is going to fix. He answers while prying open a window. The nurses perfunctorily turn to other matters, glossing over the fact that the janitor is not wearing sanitary clothing. Though it is not formulated, one background expectancy of this occasion is that janitors are not included in the category of people who infect nurseries. As the scene with the janitor unfolds, the father is once again handed his gown, cap, and mask. As before, he enters the nursery and proceeds toward his daughter's crib, which is near the janitor. Things seem as routine and "rational" as ever.

Later, as the nurses gather to chat on one of their breaks, one of them recalls the "gall" of a father who "walked right in there [the nursery] in street clothes and all," reminding herself and others that "you have to watch those eager beavers or they'll contaminate the whole place." The others concur. At the moment, those present are attuned to fathers who are likely to contaminate the premises, the nurses' exasperation "justifiably" and "reasonably" centering on such fathers. In the circumstances at hand, this is "perfectly reasonable" talk. The nurses take the reasonableness of their complaints for granted and get on with their affairs. When one of them interrupts to remind the others of "what it *really* means to watch for contamination," noting that the janitor also might contaminate the nursery, her comments are dismissed. As one of the nurses later remarks, "What a know-it-all she has suddenly become!" The background assumption of the gathering is that it is a place to share complaints about eager fathers, not haughtily castigate co-workers. Whether the "know-it-all" nurse is right in the final analysis may be important on formal grounds, but in practice, it may be peripheral to the circumstantial understanding of what and who are reasonable. In this instance, the foreground issue is fathers' improper infringements on the obstetrics ward's tone of cleanliness, layered with the co-workers' shared sense of the trouble that eager fathers can present on such premises.

The point in relation to our analysis of the life course is that rational argument and description regarding matters such as maturation or development are bound to the working rationalities of circumstances. The commonsense reasoning through which members of situations establish the realities of everyday life is not accountable in principle to universal or objective standards regarding the "facts" of the life world—unless, of course, universal standards are locally invoked as part of the statuted rhetoric used to depict the occasion. The rationality of depictions or claims must be made evident to those concerned at relevant junctures. Not all claims about the meaning of experience will be honored. Establishing the situational realities of the life course requires that interpretive practice display locally apparent rationality—practical accountability to what is known to be true and reasonable.

Documenting the Construction Process

From a conventional standpoint, the "things" of the life world are objective. For example, when life is said to change, it suggests that from some point in time to another, things such as a view of the past or hope for the future are different. From a constructionist point of view, change's referent is the *sense* that members have of life having changed, not objective differences. The sense of things like change has its most obvious expression in talk. When people suggest that change has taken place in their lives, they talk about it; its practical existence is rhetorically established.

Expanding on our example concerning Johnny, we see his maturity being publicly considered by members of the family. The father suggests that Johnny is "not really ready for that sort of thing," since Johnny is only sixteen. Johnny, in turn, invokes the developmental chronology of which he once heard his father boast, concluding that maturity arrives at sixteen. His father responds with a "theory" that sexual maturity has a historical component, claiming, "We grew up faster in those days." Unconvinced, Johnny counters with evidence of his own, which, according to Johnny, shows that Johnny is actually far ahead of where his father was at the same age. As Johnny points out, "Look at all the things I've done that you said a lot of times you never even thought of doing till after you married Ma." Johnny soon zeroes in on his exceptional precociousness, demonstrating by way of a discourse of individuality that his father's more decidedly sociohistorical reasoning does not apply in this case, using vernacular forms of conflicting conventional approaches to life change. As their reasoning flows back and forth, so, in practice, does the working status of Johnny's maturity.

In time, the children leave; mother and father are alone. She brings up the maturity question again, asking her husband whether he really stopped to think about what he said, gently reminding him of what she states were inconsistencies in his argument. For the moment, the mother ignores her son's attempt to stack his own case. The husband considers the wisdom of his statements in view of his boasts about himself and the "obvious" evidence of his son's self-reliance. What seemed so clear-cut earlier now seems less so. He concludes that he will speak with his son about it later, hinting that the son might be old enough at that.

The objects of the life world — Johnny's maturity, for example — appear strange indeed when they are considered as practical accomplishments, realized through occasioned talk and interaction. There is a profound difference between treating maturity, growth, and the life course as part and parcel of the life world within which people are located and treating them as constituent aspects of references to that world. Considered from the latter point of view, what is thought to be solid and external to working experience becomes an integral part of it, something emerging from everyday constructive activity.

METHOD, EMPHASIS, AND SOURCES

The methodological implication for constructionist analysis is to shift attention away from things such as life stages and statuses to the situated, interpretive processes through which things are constructed. The analytic focus on the family scenario we have been describing would not be on Johnny's maturity per se, but on how a sense of his maturation is achieved. Interpretive *practice* is our field of data.

If the life course is socially constructed, then our analytic task is to "de-construct" (Derrida 1977) its various versions into the diverse discourses, processes, and situations that constitute it. Deconstruction is a way of working backward from the taken-for-granted realities of everyday life to the contexts and practices that constitute them, documenting the production process. The goal is to make visible the methods by which the realities of life change are accomplished. While this does not discount those things that might conventionally be considered facts or data — for example, mortality statistics, life graphs indicating the chronological ages at which children reach varied behavioral stages, or the sections of students' school records that presumably track their academic progress along, or deviations from, a course of normal development — our willing appreciation for them changes. A constructionist orientation leads us to examine the ways such "facts" are assembled in the first place, and how they are used by those who deal with them in the course of everyday life.

In focusing on members' interpretive practices, we address the issue of social order. As we noted in chapter 1, there are a number of approaches to the topic. Functionalists, for example, locate order in the shared values that motivate individuals to act as socially responsible persons. Behaviorists conceive of order as habits contingent on a profit principle. Such habits continue undisturbed as long as returns on behavioral investments profit individuals. For constructionists, social order is the work that enters into the constitution of the life world. As such, order is never fixed; it is continuously precarious, structured and maintained through members' talk and interaction.

The construction of order becomes apparent when we attend to how people use words in everyday interaction. Documentation necessitates being on the scene and explicating members' practices when facts are assembled, managed, or made salient and consequential. It means paying close attention to interaction on the occasions it unfolds. It means "listening in order to see" how the life world and its objects are constructed (Gubrium and Holstein 1990).

In the chapters that follow, we use the constructionist perspective to empirically examine various aspects of life change. Several conceptual emphases characterize our approach to interpretive practice and everyday construction processes. First, the processes ① are socially constitutive. The life world is constructed through talk and interaction. Consequently, we examine language-mediated social exchanges, focusing on how the life course and its components are interactionally accomplished. Second, while interpretive activ- ② ity organizes our understanding of actions, objects, and circumstances, it is itself conditioned by circumstance. Context and local interpretive culture provide commonsense resources for depicting and understanding everyday experience. Interpretive practices must articulate interpretive categories and schemas with the concrete circumstances at hand. Practical interpretive activity thus brings culturally understood images of the life course, human development, and aging to bear on aspects of experience as ways of making concrete sense of them. Interpretive practice and social circumstance, then, stand in a reflexive relation to one another, each providing the basis for the other. Third, the constructive process is ③ *ongoing*. Reality is locally managed and thus requires people's continuing participation in its maintenance, even while local cultures provide categorical resources for what is managed.[3] Finally, ④ interpretation is *as much rhetorical as it is descriptive*. Reality construction is practical activity that brings partisan interests to bear on what is produced. Because alternate versions of reality compete, interpretive activity must be persuasive if a particular version is to be validated. Even when persuasion is not consciously intended, descriptions are implicitly rhetorical because, with the natural tendency of words to "realize" things, words advocate as much as convey particular versions of reality.

The material we present to illustrate the construction of the life course comes from a variety of everyday settings. One source is the myriad instances where life change or the life course has been a topic of discussion in our own lives. Some of these instances have been recounted to us by friends, colleagues, and associates. Some were gathered as part of university teaching activities, mostly in relation to students' lives. Some were found in public documents, institutional reports, and newspapers.

Another source is existing studies of social interaction where human development, aging, or both have been the focus. While many of the studies were not originally intended to be analyses of interpretive practice or the life course per se, considerations of life change are nonetheless prominent and offer valuable material for constructionist analysis.

In addition, all three authors have collected life course data through qualitative research in a variety of human-service settings. This includes fieldwork in nursing homes (Gubrium 1975, 1980a, 1980b, 1991a), a residential treatment center for emotionally disturbed children (Buckholdt and Gubrium 1985), a physical rehabilitation hospital (Gubrium and Buckholdt 1982), support groups and self-help organizations for the caregivers of Alzheimer's disease victims (Gubrium 1986a, 1986b), family therapy agencies (Gubrium 1992), involuntary mental hospitalization proceedings (Holstein 1984, 1987, 1988a, 1988b, 1990, 1993), and a variety of other community mental health settings (Grusky et al. 1986, 1987; Holstein and Staples 1992). Data also were drawn from life narratives collected from residents of nursing homes (Gubrium 1991b).

We turn in the next four chapters to evidence from these sources. Chapter 3 addresses the process of typification by which the undistinguished minutiae of the life world are sorted into more or less coherent versions of objects and occurrences. Chapter 4 takes a future orientation to life change, describing constructions of growth and development. Chapter 5 adopts a present orientation to deconstruct competence and maturity. Chapter 6 orients to the past to make visible the biographical work that constructs who and what people were. We conclude by discussing the prospects and implications for a constructionist analysis of the life course.

NOTES

1. We use the term "organizational" here in its most general sense, referring to any socially structured circumstance. While our examples are typically drawn from formal organizations, the analysis would also apply to circumstances organized along different lines, say, by reference to gender or race. The point is that alternate social contexts serve to realize different domestic orders according to their varied descriptive options, constraints, and agendas.

2. Our use of the term "member" implies that, in their behavior, people take into account the practical meaning of belonging somewhere, at some time, in what they do and say there. Talk and interaction index membership in particular situations. Within specific circumstances, members speak the vocabulary of particular, taken-for-granted realities, assuming a "natural attitude" (Schutz 1970) toward things. To be a member of a collectivity is to proceed, together with other members, to use its tacit orientations and understandings.

3. This emphasis on the ongoing management of the life world is characteristically ethnomethodological and should be distinguished from other "constructionist" approaches. For example, Berger and Luckmann's (1966) version of constructionism is primarily concerned with the cognitive *principles* governing the world of meaningful objects and the normative convergences that sustain our sense of its reality. The focus is on how that world is collectively constituted as a stable entity and how meanings shape it and are shaped by it. Emphasis is on the normative dynamics of "universe maintenance."

   In contrast, our ethnomethodologically informed approach highlights the ordinary and practical process of reality construction located in situated talk and interaction. For Berger and Luckmann, social objects such as the life course, or, say, marriage, once constructed, are virtually self-maintaining in the absence of problems or challenges; institutions "tend to persist unless they become 'problematic'" (1966:117; see also Berger and Kellner 1970). Ethnomethodology, however, construes institutional realities as ongoing managed accomplishments. Rather than treat objects such as the life course as self-sustaining, ethnomethodology underscores the constitutive activity that continually and reflexively produces social order (Heritage 1984).

   At the same time, our version of constructionism is not singly ethnomethodological. The local management and enactment of the life world takes place within concrete premises (as interpretively mediated as they might be), with their available interpretive resources and categories. The emphasis on "established" realities orients to the substance of what is interpreted as well as to the (ethno) methods of doing so.

Chapter **3**   TYPIFYING LIFE CHANGE

Listening closely, we hear lives described in many ways, especially in terms of having a course of change. We heard this in the six-year-old's story of "growing up" at the beginning of chapter 2. We hear it in the account of a fifty-year-old attorney, anticipating a federal judicial appointment:

> I practiced law for ten years, then was elected Municipal Court judge. Four years later I was elected to the County Circuit Court. Then the governor appointed me to the State Court of Appeals. I've moved up each step of the way. I guess this appointment is the next move up the line.

Whether it is conveyed in terms of childhood stages or steps up a career ladder, an expectable course points the way, providing guideposts for typical development.

Of course, people use a variety of images and metaphors to convey the shape and character of change. We can see distinct contrast to the imagery of the life course, for example, in the following depiction provided by an eighty-three-year-old nursing home resident who describes her life as a "tangle" :

> My life has been a tangle. But after all my troubles, I've had a pretty good life. Been able to take care of myself . . . until now. [She had recently broken her hip.] Well, getting there and separating [her first marriage ended in divorce] and God gave me one good marriage. [My life] would be such a tangle you couldn't read it and I couldn't either. I've always been happy, I don't know why, until my son died and my husband died in seventy three. . . ."

Nonetheless, the idea of the life course is a powerful and widely shared design. We encountered it frequently in the conventional approaches to life change presented in chapter 1. If a conventional approach posited a particular order to life change, it took a developmental contour, hardly as complex or indeterminate as a "tangle." Similarly, in everyday circumstances, courses are conveyed, at least partly, in terms of common or characteristic sequences or progressions, with their distinguishing tasks and crises. The typical course for any particular life—whether it is good, bad, confused, or even tangled—provides the standard against which the ups and downs of daily living are represented.

In considering events or developments related to life change, people often distinguish those believed to be normal, expectable, or appropriate from those considered abnormal, unexpected, or extraordinary. Speaking metaphorically, yet popularly, they may wonder whether a life is "on or off course." Is life, one might also ask, "on time," or is it somehow "out of sync?" This chapter deals with the social construction of normal patterning and alignment. Our concern is with what people do and say when the proper progression of life becomes an issue, with how life is then represented, repaired, or reproduced.

THE TYPIFICATION PROCESS

Alfred Schutz (1970) conceived of the way people orient to events in their own and others' lives as a process of *typification*. In their day-to-day relations, people are confronted with a multitude of events or displays of behavior that they make sense of in order to get on with their affairs. Events are interpreted by casting them as elements of one or another ideal category or type that is part of a stock of knowledge at hand:

> All forms of recognition and identification, even of real objects of the outer world, are based on a *generalized* knowledge of the *type* of these objects or of the *typical* style in which they manifest themselves. . . . Each of these types has its typical style of being experienced, and the knowledge of this typical style is itself an

element of our stock of knowledge at hand. This same holds good for the relations in which the objects stand to one another, for events and occurrences and their mutual relations, and so on. (Schutz 1970:118–19)

Events are encountered by people who, either through delibera-tion or instantaneously, conclude that such-and-such occurrence is typically this-or-that. An event, in its own right, makes no sense until it has been categorized as evidently an instance of some known type of occurrence, at least for the time being. To make sense of an occurrence is not just a matter of discovering its meaning. The process is more active and constructive than this. Events are typified as a very part of the process of responding to them. The experiential reality or sense of events does not exist before typification, but emerges within the process of interpretation itself.

Needless to say, this places the study of life change in the very midst of representational work. This work, as ordinary as it is, parallels traditional notions of scientific practice. Scientific practice is said to be two-sided. It is empirical in that scientists focus their attention on some facet of a world tacitly accepted as real, consid-ered in principle to be separate and distinct from observation. Scientific practice also is analytic in that the real world is not simply *perceived* but is also *conceived*; the design of reality is constituted through conceptualization, using hypotheses, theories, models, and other formulations.

Scientific theories, hypotheses, and analytic schemes may be thought of as typifications. They are the formal schemas the scientist uses to make meaningful the events encountered in a world of interest. They constitute the scientist's set of categories, to which he or she is committed as a systematic way of representing subject matter, whatever that might substantively be.

Both scientists and laypersons rely on typifications, but there are two important differences traditionally noted about their practices. First, scientists formally commit themselves to the systematic elaboration of typifications, within the bounds of a field or disci-pline. Second, conventional scientific protocol urges scientists to make public their typifications. Professionals, such as psycholo-gists, psychiatrists, social workers, and counselors, who do not as much study as they assess and treat life change, are similarly engaged in typification. They, too, stand in parallel, yet differ from lay and scientific practitioners. Like laypersons, professionals categorize and classify — typify — in order to represent and understand. But as the widespread use of the *DSM-III* (the American Psychiatric Association's diagnostic and statistical manual) and other algorithms suggest, their typifications have become increasingly formal and extensively formularized. Human-service professionals, however, are bound by standards of privacy and confidentiality in ways that scientists are not. Professionals' clients' lives are at stake in more immediate and consequential ways than the lives of scientists' "subjects," "respondents," and "informants." Hence the typification process is not as fully, publicly disclosed.

Recent social studies of science show that, in practice, scientists act more like laypersons in the way they orient to and report their work than has been traditionally thought (Knorr-Cetina and Mulkay 1983). Even more convergence may be the result of trends that popularize the findings of human science, providing laypersons with increasingly scientific and formal ways of describing and typifying their own experience. Still, because of the difference in formal commitment to systematic elaboration distinguishing scientists and professionals from laypersons, and the formers' commitment to comprehensive organizing frameworks, the life course may be a more compelling representational device for scientist and professionals.

Typification in Practice

How does typification work in practice? Consider those who typify people's acts as being either those of frauds or those of honorable persons. A fraud may have typical undesirable characteristics such as hypocrisy, being deceitful, and being untrustworthy, suggesting a set of acts that are logically and obviously related. Likewise, honorable persons, being what frauds are not, are defined as typically unhypocritical, honest, fair, and open-minded. Now, consider those who make this distinction as they encounter behavior that they define as tricky. Such behavior may be seen as the acts of a fraud. The category "fraud" suggests a number of reasonable inferences that could be made about the person so categorized. Tricks, if not "dirty tricks," are generally distasteful because they are understood to be typical of the behavior of a kind of person who is obnoxious in that he is also, by implication, untrustworthy and hypocritical. Of course, this may be only a momentary response. With further evidence, tricks may become typical of something else, more innocent or less pernicious. For example, emerging circumstances may suggest that the trickster is not a fraud, but merely has a "warped" sense of humor. With this categorical turn, the related acts under consideration take on different meanings. The acts become different "things" as they are attributed to different types of people.

Depending on the occasion of their use, typifications differ in their functions. All types serve to organize events and courses of action, to give them meaning. Sometimes, types are used as ordering devices. For example, to conclude that an event is trivial represents it in relation to more significant ones. At times, types serve to explain events. For instance, to suggest that an act — say, petty vandalism of school property — is the normal immature behavior of an adolescent accounts for the behavior as the manifestation of a common developmental process. At still other times, types serve rhetorical purposes, not only naming but aiming deliberately to persuade. The particular emphasis in typification cannot be understood separate from its actual use. On one occasion, typifying an act as normal, immature behavior may be used to deny a boy or girl the privileges of adulthood ("You're still too young to stay out past midnight!"), while on another occasion, it may serve as a means of dissuading others from chastising the child—for the same "misadventure" ("He's just a kid. He didn't mean any real harm.").

It is important to note that, in practice, there is much more at stake in the typification process than categorization and representation. Typification elaborates understanding, guides and justifies action. In representing a particular occurrence as typical of a larger category of occurrences, all features of the category reasonably accrue to the occurrence, each suggesting its respective course of action. For example, if an incident is typified as the act of a normally "childish" or "immature" adolescent, it can safely be concluded that, for all practical purposes, the event is not unusual. There is no good reason to look further into the matter, say, for signs of abnormality. Instead, one might conclude that the adolescent will "grow out of such things in time." This further normalizes the behavior and sustains the commonplace notion of developmental change. Slightly annoyed, we might conclude, "It's only natural, isn't it? What can you do but live with it?"

In turn, the categorization of the adolescent as basically normal is corroborated as the incident is interpreted as one typical of a normal, if immature, child. The typification of the person and the definition of the act reciprocally document and sustain one another (Garfinkel 1967). The type of person involved makes the act understandable in a particular fashion, while the act thus defined provides further evidence that the person is acting in accordance with the specified type.

Defining the "same" event as a typical *abnormal* act, however, suggests an entirely different course of action. It would be reasonable to search for more evidence suggested by one's theory of abnormality, attending very carefully to the individual involved for clues that would lend further credence to the theory. Dismissing this type of behavior, under the circumstance, would be unreasonable, and remedial or punitive responses might be in order. The abnormality would become more "apparent" as its concrete signs were actively sought and located, again reciprocally documenting the occurrence and the category.

Typifications persuade and convince. A woman may discover, for example, that her husband has spoken too frankly to his friends about their marital relationship. When she confronts him with this, she is, in effect, taking issue with the sense of order that she thought both agreed governed their lives, namely, an understanding that their intimacies were private matters. She is visibly shaken by the breach of faith, shouting, "How could you?" When her spouse explains, "Something must have come over me" or "I had to say those things in order to show my openness so they'd open up with me," he frames the alleged betrayal to typify it as reasonable or excusable, given the circumstances, attempting to persuade her of something forgivable.

Certainly, the order at stake in this small example is only a brief moment in the larger order of this couple's everyday life. Nonetheless, on this particular occasion, it is the order at stake, for all practical purposes. The nature of that order eventually comes to rest on what kind of event the alleged breach of intimacy is convincingly defined to be. In retrospect, the typification settled on will offer a "vocabulary of motives" (Mills 1940) or an "account" (Scott and

Lyman 1968) for what was said and done, giving order to the past in relation to an alleged breach of faith.

Typification is both retrospective and prospective. It serves to explain events that have already occurred and are considered to be in need of repair. It also predefines impending untoward events through "disclaimers" so that the upcoming events are presaged positively (Hewitt and Stokes 1975). For example, rather than risk the definition of one's statements as being those of a racist, a person may preface them with "I'm not prejudiced. Some of my best friends are Jews, but..." This suggests to an audience that, while what he or she is about to say would otherwise be construed as anti-Semitic, the audience should typify the speaker as an ethnically tolerant person who is simply commenting on a related ethnic matter.

Typification Shifts

Typification may be quite fleeting, even if particular categorizations are supported by local organizational or cultural interests. Take people confronted with a simple incident having no apparent meaning involving a friend of theirs named Charlie. One of the group suggests that the occurrence was just another instance of Charlie's typical behavior: "That's just the kind of thing Charlie does." Others may agree and nod in ostensible certainty. A friend may glibly explain, "That's probably true" because of what Charlie did yesterday. Another comments, "That's Charlie," implying that Charlie will be Charlie, over the normal course of events. Perhaps, finally, one concludes, "Well, you know Charlie. That's to be expected." The matter is treated as part of the nature of things, in this case, Charlie's nature. Fleeting as they are, the exchanges offer a history of the occurrence, a prognosis of things to come, and a philosophy by which to understand what happened. An interpretive frame is built up rather suddenly as the reality of the situation emerges on the spot.

Now, suppose someone refers to another event, relates it to the preceding incident, and suggests that the original occurrence is something different from what it appeared to be. It might be suggested, for example, that "what happened, somehow, just doesn't jibe with how Charlie acted last fall at the same time." It raises the possibility that what occurred may not be "natural" or "just Charlie." Thinking about Charlie and knowing how to respond to him necessitate resolving the issue. Which way it is resolved is not the significant point of our analysis. Instead, we focus on the conversational participants' need to resolve the issue in order to engage in a course of action, typification rightly or wrongly being an integral part of the action.

If the occurrence is defined as out of the ordinary, a search is in the offing. Are there other events that support the "hypothesis" that the occurrence may be an expression of an unnatural or abnormal process? Given a "theory" of abnormality, what and where should one look for further evidence for or against the "theory"? The past? The future? Is the occurrence typical of normal or abnormal events given the circumstance and person under consideration? A world is being constructed and elaborated, centered on the occurrence at hand. Its conceptual framework is being developed, and its logical conclusions are being drawn. Contrary to popular advice against "jumping to conclusions," which suggests that such jumps be avoided for the sake of being reasonable, "jumping to conclusions" is at the very heart of meaningful interaction, organizing it and in turn being organized by it.

Should the occurrence be redefined again as something other than previously thought, once more, another whole world is opened to elaboration. Such qualitative shifts in the meaning and understanding of occurrences are analogous to quantum leaps or gestalt shifts. Typification shifts abruptly alter the meaning of an occurrence from one reasonable scenario to another. Such scenarios are parts of worlds but are not logically reducible to one another. Persons experience the shifts as ordinary and generally overlook them in practice. Should they become aware of them as reality shifts per se, they would likely be shocked, to say the least.

Acknowledging the significance of the typification process radically challenges conventional analyses of life change. Rather than treat change as an objective feature of development, growth, maturation, and the like, we view it as a product of the way people typify—elaborate, assess, and compare—experience in relation to time. While the life course is conventionally presented as linear and continuous, the pattern is an artifact of everyday typification processes, not an inherent feature of lived experience.

DOMAINS OF TYPIFICATION

Typification is a pervasive component of interpretation. Consider how it figures in articulations of life change in two domains of everyday life: the casual experiences of laypersons and professional assessments of troubled lives.

A Lay Example

The following is a familiar scene reconstructed for one of the authors by a graduate student, who is the mother involved. The scene opens as the woman is hurriedly preparing for an afternoon get-together of the members of her charity organization. Her son, aged thirteen, is in the midst of what the mother considers to be a normal spell of the summer "blahs," puttering around the house and complaining that there is nothing to do. Mother halfheartedly listens as he follows her around the house. She begins to feel harried as time runs out and the guests' arrival approaches. Her son continues to complain, whining occasionally and intruding on his mother's fastidious preparations. The two are gradually getting on each other's nerves, but Mother forges on.

Suddenly, having heard enough of her son's complaints, Mother turns to him and yells bitterly, "You are such a child!" She caustically reminds him that kids like him grow up to be pests, never knowing what to do with themselves, always hanging on to other people. He shouts back, blurting that he's not a child and reminding her of how "grown up" she said he was just yesterday. She ignores the comment as she dwells on what children like her son grow up to be. She calls him a "pantywaist" and exasperatedly concludes that, at this rate, he will never make it on his own.

The mother becomes thoroughly enmeshed in the way she has typified the son. She hurries about the house muttering to herself, addressing him in curt phrases: "you good-for-nothing," "lazy," "no mind." He, in turn, eggs her on, sneakily reversing every characterization and repeatedly touting his maturity. She asks herself, in a voice loud enough for her son to hear, "What could possibly have made him like this?" She half blames herself for overprotecting him as a child. Finally shouting, she concludes, "Yes. That's why you're still such a child!"

What are we witnessing here? Is this merely a fleeting exchange centered on a mother's preparation for a social gathering and a son's meddlesome intrusion? In typifying her son and assembling an explanation of his behavior, the mother, in effect, constructs a theory of life change. She casually invokes the image of an abnormal early life as the source of the son's dependence and childishness. The son responds with a more flattering portrayal, denying his childishness, stressing his maturity. Ignoring him, the mother elaborates her typification. She retrospectively invokes evidence of overprotection, evidence that, she surmises, explains the son's dependency. In the process, she invokes a linear pattern for understanding both her son's current behavior and his apparent immaturity.

Returning to the scene, the doorbell beckons and the mother politely greets the first guests to arrive. The son helps welcome the guests, asking them to be seated in the living room. They chat for a while, then the son interrupts his mother to say that he is going to see if he can "round up some guys to play ball." Mother urges him out and returns to her guests. One of the guests then comments on what a "nice young man" the son is, adding that he certainly is "the gentleman" and is obviously more mature for his age than many adolescents she's known. The others agree. Mother does, too, and recounts several examples of her son's resourcefulness. She even hints at what transpired immediately before the guests' arrival, noting that when he wants something, he can be persistent, even "hardheaded." Then again, she reminds the group, such hardheadedness is a sure sign of independence. The guests concur and compliment their hostess on what a fine boy her son is. She responds that he is, indeed, a fine boy.

The conversation then turns to other boys the son's age, casually elaborating their normal, developmental life courses. One of the guests asks the mother about the "self-reliance training" she provided her children when they were growing up. Mother comments at length. Some time later, another guest concludes, "Well, I guess that explains it, doesn't it?" As time passes, the conversation about childhood development becomes serious. Some guests, as well as their hostess, are visibly proud of their offspring, what their children have been and what they are becoming. Two guests, however, express disappointment with their own children and for what lies ahead, given, they say, what the normal course of life for children and adolescents holds in store.

Consider what this conversation has accomplished. The typical course of childhood and adolescent development has been mapped and elaborated. Children have been described and assessed accordingly. The mother's original characterization of the son has been radically transformed. Her son is now typical of a different kind of person, less characterized by dependency than promise. Discursively, his life has shifted from one course of growth to another. Something different is being done with words and evidence than before the guests arrived. Such events are so ordinary as to seem trivial, hardly noticed by those involved. Nevertheless, they produce and re-produce the everyday realities of life change.

A Professional Example

Turning to another domain, consider how a group of professionals view life change. Despite the differences in orientation and purpose at hand, parallels in the interpretive process are striking.

One of the authors (see Gubrium 1975) conducted fieldwork on the social organization of care in a nursing home called Murray Manor. (The names of all persons and places have been fictionalized throughout this book.) Common to such facilities, the professional administrative or top staff of the home conduct weekly meetings or "patient care conferences." Top staff include the administrator, medical director, director of nursing, assistant director of nursing, social worker, chaplain, occupational therapist, in-service director, activity director, and dietitian. Most regularly attend staffings, which some say is unusual for a nursing home, a sign of the high quality of this home's care. Less frequently, a member of the home's floor staff, such as an LPN or a nurse's aide, or an interested outsider, such as a patient's clergyman, participates. Staffings are occasions for discussing patients' current care, their families, their medical and emotional status, and for formulating care plans.

Although top staff members spend little time on the units, they have four sources of information about patients' daily lives: nurses notes on patients' charts; "serious" interviews that staff members occasionally conduct with patients, typically lasting five to ten minutes; anecdotes about events in patients' nursing home lives that are widely shared by staff members; and casual observation. The nurses' notes are commonly written by nurse's aides, usually at shift change. They consider this an annoyance at best, but it is made less bothersome by formulaic entries. The notes virtually homogenize variations in patients' daily lives. Chats with patients centered on the weather, how "good" the patient looks today, upcoming nursing home events, and whether the patient plans to attend them may be presented later as "serious interviews." Patients mostly orient to the interviews as visits. Staff members share anecdotes about patient romances, boisterous quarrels, escapes or near escapes from the home, and other unusual activities. While casual observation provides top staff with surface information about the decorum of a floor, it also may be taken as an indicator of patients' emotional status, a quiet floor, say, indicating contented occupants.

As far as typification is concerned, the proceedings of a patient conference have much the same dynamics as in the foregoing lay example, even while context, purpose, and vocabulary differ. Following the documentary method of interpretation, the practical relationship between top staff's knowledge of patients' lives and conference participants' typifications is mutually informing. On one side, bits of information about patients are treated as documents of a wider scheme of things, including personality types, disease syndromes, and vernacular explanations of daily life. Recollected anecdotes may suggest that someone is "obviously" this or that type of person. The results of a "serious interview" might imply that a particular theory of behavior is "certainly" applicable in the case at hand. On the other side, once typifications are formed, they in turn are used to warrant and elaborate the meaning of the available information. The documents can be arranged into a general pattern, while the pattern makes sense of the individual pieces of information. Each elaborates the other.

Typification comes in different vocabularies. Information on a patient's behavior may typify him or her as "really [mentally] sick, you know what I mean" or as "a real leader [on the unit]." Meaningfully framing a patient's behavior in this way, staffers are prompted to look for, or recollect, other evidence about the patient who is "really sick" or the one who is "a real leader." Typifications may be offered in rather technical language. For example, staff may define one patient's behavior as an example of "typical regression" and portray another as a "typical introvert."

Typifications are tacit directives for how to talk and act in the deliberations at hand. Events assume an increasingly rational character as they become evidently typical. Certain reasonable considerations follow from the application of one type, while other reasonable concerns flow from another. A staffer who suggests that a bit of information shows someone to be a "leader" virtually implores others to search for, recollect, and interpret information about the patient in such terms, or, alternatively, to attend to how the individual is not a leader. A staffer who suggests that someone is "really" mentally ill tacitly conveys that a "theory" of mental illness is relevant for understanding the case at hand. As we noted earlier, typification is both descriptive and rhetorical, in this case inviting the staff not only to use, but to do things with, words in conveying patients' life worlds.

Typification also provides grounds for glossing over or reinterpreting "atypical" information, selectively sifting through varieties of "facts" and integrating them into reasonable portraits of "perfect leadership," "perfect insanity," and the like. The mother in our lay example virtually followed and elaborated the working logics of two separate occasions—the shouting match with her son and the discussion with her guests—to produce evidence first for her son's dependence, then his independence. Similarly, staff members construe the life changes of patients by documenting patterns in their daily lives with "data" that are meaningful in light of the patterns to which they are assimilated. In practice, discrepant "facts" are then "obviously" irrelevant in light of the typifications that are in place.

Below, we present excerpts from two staffings to illustrate the use of typifications in making practical sense of patients' lives in the service of care planning. The following is a list of regular staffing participants:

Staffing Participants

Mr. Filstead	Administrator
Dr. Cosgrove	Medical Director
Miss Timmons	Director of Nursing
Mrs. Singer	Assistant Director of Nursing
Mrs. Boucher	In-service Director
Mrs. Smith	Activity Director
Miss Erickson	Social Worker
Reverend Edwards	Chaplain
Mrs. Walsh	Occupational Therapist
Mrs. Hoffman	Dietitian

The first excerpt is from patient Joan Borden's staffing. Note the shifts in typification as the staff interpretively transform Borden from being independent to being mentally deteriorated, next agitated, then self-sufficient and a leader, and, finally, to being subject to "spells." Each typification is elaborated with anecdotes, casual and formally recorded information recounted as documentary evidence of who and what Borden "really" is. As a practical matter, the reality of Borden's daily life and changes in it lie not so much in her objective experience as in the typification process itself. The interpretation of Borden's life is complete, again for all practical purposes, when the staffing ends and care goals are formulated.

The contrast with our lay example is not in the typification process as such, but in the organizational context of the process. While all manner of ordinary theorizing is done in the staffings, there is a distinct orientation to clinical reasoning and medical concerns. Just as the mother in our lay example theorized in her own way about her son's life course, guided by the practical circumstances of a household and special occasions, professional conference participants respond to care planning using a specialized vocabulary and locally available interpretive resources.

Staffing of Joan Borden, Seventy-two years old

SINGER: Joan's a very independent lady. She's quite active and participates in all the sing-alongs. The reason we decided to discuss Mrs. Borden is that she's recently had two strokes. She was watched closely. Dr. Savoy [Borden's personal physician who is not present] feels comfortable at this point that she remain on the first floor. [The first floor of the home is for "residents" who are considered in need only of personal care while the other floors are for "patients" who are considered in need of various levels of skilled nursing care.]

Singer proceeds to review Mrs. Borden's medical history,
frequently glancing at Dr. Cosgrove. Then Father O'Brien
speaks.

FATHER O'BRIEN [Borden's priest]: She's been very active at St. Barbara's. I saw her in bed here and then I saw her later when she was up and around.

TIMMONS: Mentally, also, she has deteriorated. She doesn't continue with her personal care. She has trouble with putting her clothes on.

   Several participants nod in agreement as Timmons' charac-
   terization is elaborated by others.

SMITH: She has trouble with crafts. She can't see the calendar right. She seems confused.

   At this point, a number of side conversations take place
   noting Borden's physical symptoms as evidence of her
   "mental deterioration," whereupon Dr. Cosgrove offers a
   suggestion.

COSGROVE: We should try to limit the demands on her. We should try to lighten an already taxed mind. This is not a time for new things for her.

SINGER: I'm worried about her activities outside the building. [Borden has planted and cares for a flower bed next to the building, among other activities.]

COSGROVE: We should limit her outside activities. But I don't want you to take this as final. This recommendation is only for discussion.

SMITH: I find her considerably agitated. You know Joan.

TIMMONS: Her hearing must be getting worse. She picks up certain things and interprets them wrong and then spreads them. You remember . . . like she spread the rumor that someone had died and spread that. [The alleged death was reported incorrectly to the home's receptionist. Borden overheard correctly.]

Timmons chuckles.Others recount various aspects of the rumor. Erickson continues.

ERICKSON: You're not thinking of moving her to the third floor, are you?

COSGROVE I think that that would be too sudden.

REVEREND EDWARDS: Well, I saw her helping someone in the parking lot.

COSGROVE Well, this indicates that she thinks of herself as a leader.

Staffers begin to elaborate a differenttypification.

ERICKSON: That's why we better be careful about moving her, because we'd threaten her and she'd flip out.

FATHER O'BRIEN: Joan, to my knowledge, has been very alert.

COSGROVE: I think if we should look at this over a period of time . . . maybe we should lighten the burden.

ERICKSON: The family has noticed these trends also. She's also a leader. When I first came here, Joan gave me my first sock in the stomach. [Several staffers ask for details.] She said that nursing homes are not for her. [Other participants recount similar comments they have heard from Borden.] Now, she's a real promoter of Murray Manor [the nursing home].

There is more reminding and recounting of events that typify Joan as a leader and alert. Then Timmons suggest another characterization.

TIMMONS: Miles [Borden's roommate] says that her personal hygiene has gotten worse.

SMITH: I think she knows that she can't do the things she used to do. She's had a few seizures . . . .

COSGROVE By the way, we should get out of the habit of calling these things "seizures." Maybe "spells." That's bad, too. Let's call them "thing." Someone is having their thing.

FILSTEAD [*interrupting to change the subject*]: Father O'Brien, do you think that these things [patient care conferences] are helpful to you?

FATHER O'BRIEN: Yes. I think that this is very helpful. We have a real practical problem in any church. When they go into a nursing home, we lose contact with our older members. So when a funeral comes up, because of changes in personnel in the parish, we don't know who this member of the parish was who was here ten years ago.

FILSTEAD: We do want you to be here at the meetings. You may agree or disagree with us, but at least you know what we're doing. You can get an insight into what we're trying to do here. We are trying to do what we profess to do when I first talked to you. *Considerable public relations talk ensues. Borden's care plan is lost in it. Finally, the social worker interjects*

ERICKSON [*rushed*]: Then the goal for Borden is to curb burdensome activities and encourage realistic independence. Right? *Everyone nods in the midst of side conversations about other matters. Time is running out. The next case is introduced.*

The second excerpt is taken from Eileen Radke's staffing. Here again, note the typification shifts, the practical reasoning, and the flow of acceptable "facts" that elaborate alternative characterizations. The course of Radke's life shifts from being aimless and morbid to being withdrawn and, finally, to being religious, "philosophical," and concerned for others' needs. As in Borden's staffing, Radke's ends with the formulation of a care goal.

Staffing of Eileen Radke, Eighty-six years old

ERICKSON: First patient to consider is Eileen Radke. Dr. Resnik [Radke's personal physician] can't make it.

JANE SCHUMAN [floor nurse]: Trying to find things out from her is like pulling teeth. If she can develop a need to report symptoms to us, then we've something accomplished. She speaks of dying. She doesn't have a goal.

SINGER [*introducing a competing "theory of the "real" Radke*]: I disagree with that. She has a very definite interest in maintaining herself at her present level. Jane, why don't you go on and give a patient profile.
Schuman continues briefly, whereupon Erickson introduces yet another characterization of Radke.

ERICKSON: She's an introvert. She's very family-oriented and withdrawn. I don't want to put a psychological emphasis on it.

WALSH: She really wants to stay by herself. I think we really have to draw her out.

Other participants offer personal anecdotes about Radke that "confirm" her alleged introversion. Then, Smith invokes another characterization.

SMITH: She doesn't really feel depressed about being alone. It's a problem for us, but may not be a problem for her.

ERICKSON: That's right.

REVEREND EDWARDS: When I interviewed her this morning, I found no depression. She was really being very philosophical about her life.

Staffers now recount evidence for Radke's "philosophic" character, which Timmons eventually places in a religious context.

TIMMONS: I see her as a very religious person. She takes a very existential role about "you die to live."

HOFFMAN: I've interacted with her at lunch. She's very concerned with the other patients' needs . . . whether they get their trays or not and so on.

ERICKSON: I don't think we should try to force our lifestyle upon her.

WALSH: Yes. I feel that if she wants to be alone, then that's her choice and we should respect it. Don't you?

COSGROVE: She may not think in terms of her body. The other possibility is that she understands very well what you're trying to do and is simply not clinically oriented.

ERICKSON: We have to think of her generation as different than ours. Her generation never learned to relax. Her life is empty because she has no work to fill it.

COSGROVE: Let's just treat her like she wants to be. That'll be our care goal.

FILSTEAD: What's the meaning of "treating her like she wants to be"?

All staffers sigh and exasperatedly assure him that he knows very well what that means, glossing over his question.

COSGROVE: I think that these conferences are good. They enable us to get away from our bird's-eye view of things.

INTERPRETING "STRANGE" ACTIONS

Typification cuts across the normal and abnormal, the familiar, the extraordinary, and the strange. An interpretive framework can sustain a particular understanding of persons, acts, and occurrences as normal, even in the face of potentially contradictory evidence. Should the framework be supplanted, however, that evidence may take on completely new meaning and importance, documenting instances of entirely different, abnormal forms.

Distinguishing the unusual from the ordinary often implicates the timing of occurrences, with the unusual being more likely than the ordinary to implicate the person's past in explanations. Interpreting a "strange" occurrence often requires the construction or reconstruction of a past to render the present understandable — a practice we discuss in greater detail in chapter 6. Recall, for example, how the mother in our example of lay typification made sense of her son's current childishness and dependency by depicting his past as "overprotected." Lives, both present and past, are thus subject to constant reconsideration and reconstruction.

Consider the following report of occurrences that came to be retrospectively seen as quite strange, despite having been considered only eccentric at various present-time junctures. The account details the observations of a Mrs. F. concerning her husband, Robert F., a thirty-five-year-old taxi driver, who was eventually admitted to a mental hospital with a diagnosis of schizophrenia (Yarrow et al. 1955). From early in their marriage, Mrs. F. had noted that her husband intermittently behaved in peculiar ways. For example, he began to work sporadically at his job as a taxi driver, then hardly at all. At first, Mrs. F. thought this was the reaction of a romantic, if poorly disciplined, newlywed who simply wanted to spend time at home with his wife. The behavior was understood to be typical of the early course of marriage. Later, she started to see him as being "like other cab drivers," that is, a member of a group that typically was not inclined to work very hard. Inconsistent work habits were considered typical for cab drivers at her husband's career point. As time passed, Mrs. F. noticed other things that she thought were not characteristic of her husband: his complaint that the TV set was "after him"; talk about his grandfather's mustache and a worm growing out of it; his statement that his genitals had been blown up and that little seeds covered him; and his report that he had killed his grandfather, accompanied by pleas that his wife forgive him, and then wondering if his wife were his mother or God.

The husband's talk and actions did not immediately lead Mrs. F. to conclude that he was being "strange." The occasions on which these events were recounted were interspersed with times when Mr. F. was believed to be well and working, when Mrs. F. "never stopped to think about it." When she heard them, Mrs. F. was surprised and always somewhat puzzled at why her husband should say such things. In trying to understand his behavior, she continued to integrate it into what she knew and felt would be normal for a person with his typical background and character, as she had come to define them. After she gave the matter some thought, she dismissed his reference to the worm growing out of his grandfather's mustache as just a kind of confusion that he "must" have experienced after watching little worms in the fishbowl in their home. She normalized his shaken cries about killing his grandfather as "probably due" to the fact that wartime experiences like her husband's would, understandably, lead most people to talk like he did.

For a few years, Mrs. F. considered her husband's intermittent peculiar behavior and talk to be the kinds of things that any *normal* person might do under the circumstances. She continued to provided her husband with a motivational history that helped assimilate his peculiarities to the typification of a basically normal husband. She construed them as minor "imperfections," "troubles," or "mistakes," not thinking they were at all strange. Her long-standing knowledge of his actions, some of which she considered not unlike, or at least understandable antecedents of, the present ones, sustained her commitment to his normalcy. An ostensibly general knowledge of what people like her husband must go through because of the typical experiences of soldiering, for example, corroborated his normalcy. What Mrs. F. knew about her husband, as well as what she believed about typical people like her husband, meant that her husband was really normal but had occasional "troubles."

A few days before Robert F. was admitted to the hospital and after a number of episodes of untoward behavior, the following was reported:

> Three days before admission, Mr. F. stopped taking baths and changing clothes. Two nights before admission, he awakened his wife to tell her he had just figured out that the book he was writing had nothing to do with

science or the world, only with himself. "He said he had been worrying about things for ten years and that writing a book solved what had been worrying him for ten years." Mrs. F. told him to burn his writings if they had nothing to do with science. It was the following morning that Mrs. F. first noticed her husband's behavior as "rather strange." (Yarrow et al. 1955:15)

Now defining her husband's behavior as "rather strange," a whole new framework emerged for making sense of her husband, one that typified him as abnormal, indeed, crazy. The new framework led Mrs. F. to reinterpret her husband's unusual past behaviors, now reconstructing his life history in a fashion that eventually served to document a "long-standing" abnormality.

In practice, there is no particular sequence to the interpretation of either normality or abnormality, although the reconstruction of interpretations may be well patterned, as the preceding report seems to suggest. In the case of the F. family, an entire life history changed from having had a normal course to one that had been abnormal from the start. It is not unreasonable to conclude that the reverse also occurs when "strange" people come to be seen as having been "normal all along," as in the case of some convicted criminals who are later proved innocent of the crimes of which they had been accused.

DISCERNING THE ADEQUATELY NORMAL

The normal, too, is subject to social construction, in relation to the past, the anticipated future, and in conjunction with what is believed to be normal for persons of certain ages. Earlier in this chapter, we stated that all people, including scientists, professionals, and laypersons, practice typification. Indeed, psychiatric, psychological, sociological, and other scientific theories and their applied counterparts—such as the conventional approaches described in chapter 1—are kinds of typification. Much of the work of human service professionals consists of producing or constructing the persons, backgrounds, family lives, and behaviors about which the professionals are ostensibly concerned, and for which they will eventually care (Gubrium 1992; Holstein 1992; Miller 1990, 1991). Some of the work seeks to discern the shape and substance of recovery, of a return to the near or fully normal. As this is done in the context of professional understandings and sensibilities, those behaviors and occurrences that align with the understandings and sensibilities are those most likely to be typified as recovered or normal.

Consider exchanges that took place in patient staffings at a mental hospital studied by Robert Perrucci (1974). Perrucci writes that in these staffings, "becoming mentally ill, being mentally ill, and becoming normal again are related to communal definitions and relationships" (p. xiii). The following transcriptions display how "becoming normal" is specified not only by the hospital staff's sense of change but also by its professional sensibilities.

When a patient, the family, or the patient's physician desires the patient to be discharged or given a leave of absence (L.A.) from the hospital, the patient is required to appear before the hospital's disposition staff, which is composed of all physicians having responsibilities for a particular treatment service. This is called "going to staff." On occasion, staffers may include additional professionals, such as a social worker, minister, or a nurse who has a special interest in a case. The disposition staff decides whether or not the patient being staffed is well enough to be discharged or to go on leave.

Staffers take for granted that all who come before them for disposition have been abnormal and now, after hospitalization and treatment, are possibly ready for discharge. The life of the typical patient is believed to run a course from developing illness through institutionalization and rehabilitation to release. The staff discusses discharges and leaves within this framework, resisting discussions framed in other terms.

It is evident in the following transcriptions that the matter of "structuring," as Perrucci calls it, is important in obtaining a discharge or leave. Structuring refers to the way patients present themselves to the staff as far as their illness is concerned. When a patient does not structure his or her behavior and talk in accordance with the staff's illness and recovery framework—such as the patient insisting that he or she has been unfairly hospitalized for the purpose of "mind control," not treatment—a discharge or leave of absence is unlikely to be considered appropriate. At the least, discharge or leave requires appealing to the staff in terms that indicate alignment with the staff's frame of reference.

Case 1 concludes with the patient being granted a leave of absence.

Case 1

DR. HAND: The next one is [patient's name].

DR. STONE: Oh, she'll be here. She's a live one, "hellzapoppin" with her.

> *Dr. Hand reads briefly from a patient's folder, indicating age, sex, race, date of admission, diagnosis, previous hospitalizations, previous leaves, current treatment program. The progress note written by the ward attendant especially for staff is also read. This note usually indicates patient's relationships with others in the ward, and her general cooperativeness or non-cooperativeness with ward staff. Dr. Stone recommends a leave of absence.*

DR. HAND: Will you call her in, Dr. Craig, and question her? I have to step out for a minute.

> *The patient enters and sits down.*

DR. CRAIG [*questioning the patient*]:

Q. How long have you been here?

A. About two years.

Q. Have you got a family?

A. No.

Q. You sure you won't have any kids now if you leave?

A. No, I had one of those operations.

Q. Are you going to be an out-patient here?

A. I don't know.

> *Dr. Hand returns at this point, and Dr. Craig turns patient over to him.*

DR. HAND [*questioning the patient*]:

Q. Have you ever been on an open ward?

A. No.

Q. You taking any medicine now?

A. Yes.

Q. What are your official plans?

A. I want to go home to my husband.

Q. Are you anxious to go home?

A. Yes.

Q. Does anything bother you?

A. No.

Q. Do you think you need to be here?

A. That's for the doctors to decide.

Q. What happens when you have your nervous breakdowns?

A. I just get all upset, and sometimes I hear voices.

Q. How's the world treating you?

A. Okay.

DR. HAND: Do you want to ask questions, Dr. Miller?

DR. MILLER [*questioning the patient*]:

Q. Is your husband working?

A. No, he gets social security checks.

Q. How much does he get?

A. I don't know.

> *Dr. Miller indicates he is done.*

DR. KIRK [staff psychologist]:

Q. You say you heard voices—tell us about them.

A. Oh, most of the time they're not too clear.

DR. HAND: When did you hear them last?

PATIENT: Couple of months ago.

DR. KIRK [*questioning the patient*]:

Q. Do the voices make you angry?

A. No.

Q. Are there any other signs of mental illness that you have?

A. Sometimes I think my periods may be some of it. I bleed an awful lot, and just feel terrible that time.

Q. Do people talk about you?

A. No.

DR. HAND: Dr. Stone, you want to ask anything?

DR.STONE: No, that's all right.

DR. HAND: Okay, you can leave now, Mrs———. Thank you for coming.

> *The patient leaves.*

DR. HAND: She takes Thorazine now, 150.

DR. STONE: She just cooled down. She was high as a kite before.

DR. KIRK: Do you think there's anything significant about her comments on menstrual flow and her illness? Freud said something about it . . .

DR. STONE [*cutting off Dr. Kirk*]: Sure he did. I'll give you a lecture on Freud; he was as crazy as a bedbug.

DR. HAND: What shall we do?

DR. STONE: Can't we get Social Service to check on the home before giving her an L.A.? They want her, but I didn't think the home situation was so good.

DR. CRAIG: Let her go home before she gets sicker. She's all right now.

DR. HAND: Let's put her on three months' L.A. instead of six months. That all right with everyone?

> *Everyone supports the director's suggestion.* (Perrucci 1974:140–42)

In this case, the patient clearly acknowledges problems and improvement, using the staff's framework to depict her experience. She presents herself in a way that allows the staff to typify her as releasable because progress can be described in terms that fit with the staff's general expectations for a person of her type. Note the difference in structuring in Case 2, in which release is denied. The patient frames her hospitalization as "mind control," an approach that, to staff, is not characteristic of someone who is responding to treatment. To the contrary, it is obviously typical of a "really" sick individual, someone who sees the hospital's efforts nontherapeutically.

Case 2

DR. HAND: The next one is [patient's name], a discharge request. She says she can get a lab job in Benton Hospital. Would you tell us something about her, Mrs. Rand [the patient's ward nurse]?

MRS. RAND: Well, [the patient] has been after a discharge for a while now. I asked Dr. Powell if we shouldn't try, and he said maybe we should. I think it's a shame to keep her here. She's a very bright girl, and she's really learned her lab work. Lately, she has refused to take her medicine. She says it doesn't help her; and besides, she says she doesn't need us to take her medicine.

DR. HAND: I have a note here from her work supervisor indicating that she works well in the lab and has picked up a great deal.

DR. MILLER: Shouldn't we wait for Dr. Powell before we handle her case?

DR. HAND: No, he won't be able to make it today, so we'll have to go on without him. Will you show her in, Dr. Craig?

The patient enters.

DR.HAND [*questioning the patient*]:

Q. I see where you want to get a job at Benton Hospital.

A. Yes, I talked with their lab director last time I was in Benton and he was interested.

Q. Do you think you would like lab work as a permanent job?

A. Oh, yes, I enjoy my work here very much.

Q. It's really not easy work running all those tests. Are you bothered by the blood tests?

A. No, I don't mind them.

Q. Do you know who the governor of [state] is?

A. [Appropriately answered.]

Q. Do you remember when you first came to Riverview?

A. [Appropriately answered.]

DR. CRAIG [*questioning the patient*]:

Q. How do you know you'll get a job at Benton if you're discharged?

A. I told you I talked to the lab director, and he was interested.

Q. Suppose he's not as interested as he appeared to you? Where will you work if you can't get in at Benton Hospital?

A. I think I know my lab work well enough to get a lab technician job somewhere.

Q. Well, let's see how much lab work you really know.

Dr. Craig asks the patient more questions pertaining to various procedures and lab tests. After the last response, Dr. Craig indicates that the patient does know her lab work.

DR. HAND [*questioning the patient*]:

Q. How do you get along with the other patients?

A. Not very well. I have a few close friends, but I don't socialize with the other patients.

Q. What bothers you about the other patients?

A. Oh, I don't know. I just don't like living in the hospital.

Q. Do you think we've helped you while you've been here?

A. No, I don't.

Q. What kind of treatment have you had here?

A. Lobotomy and shock.

Q. Do you think it's helped you or tortured you?

A. I think it's tortured me.

> *This response brings a stir from others present at the staffing.*

Q. You mean that we did these things just to torture you?

A. Oh, no, I'm sure that when they give shock they mean to help. I don't think they have.

Dr. Stone [*questioning the patient*]:

Q. Besides not liking it here, why do you want to go to work?

A. For one thing, I want to start earning my own money, and making my own way.

Q. If you want to make money, we can probably find plenty of opportunities for you to make money right here.

A. You mean like washing cars. I'm already doing that.

Q. [*in an annoyed tone*]: No, I don't mean washing cars. You could probably work full-time in the lab right here on a work placement.

A. I already asked Dr. Galt about an opening in histology, and he said there wasn't any. Anyway, I'd do much better if the hospital would free me.

Dr. Hand [*questioning the patient*]:

Q. What do you mean, "free you"?

A. Well, it would be just like the other work placements I've had. You're never really free.

> *It was at this point in the staffing session that the observer noted the beginnings of the change in the staff behavior. The patient's response about "never really being free" was followed by the exchange of glances among the physicians. These glances indicated that they had, so to speak, "picked up the scent." Staff participation at this point no longer followed the orderly procedure of the staff director asking individual members if they had any questions. The physicians spoke whenever they wished, sometimes cutting in on each other, and sometimes several speaking at the same time. The normal speaking tone vanished as pronouncements and accusations were directed at the patient.*

DR. CRAIG [*cutting in to question the patient*]:

    Q. Do you mean we control your mind here?

    A. You may not control my mind, but I really don't have mind of my own.

    Q. How about if we gave you a work placement in [job]; would you be free then? That's far away from here.

    A. Any place I went it would be the same setup as it is here. You're never really free; you're still a patient, and everyone you work with knows it. It's tough to get away from the hospital's control.

DR. STONE [*cutting in*]: That's the most paranoid statement I ever heard.

MRS. RAND: How can you say that, [patient's first name]? That doesn't make any sense. [Nurse is standing at this point.] It's just plain crazy to say we can control your mind. [Nurse Rand turns to Dr. Stone, who is looking at her.]

MRS. RAND [*still standing*]: I had no idea she was that sick. She sure had me fooled. [Turning to patient again.] You're just not well enough for a discharge, [first name], and you had better realize that.

DR. STONE: She's obviously paranoid.

    Immediately following Dr. Stone's remark, Dr. Craig stood up, followed by social worker Homes. Dr. Stone himself then stood up to join the others, including Nurse Rand, who had been standing for some time. It should be noted that this took place without any indication from Dr. Hand, the staff director, that the interview was completed. He then turned to the patient and dismissed her. After the patient left, the standing staff members engaged themselves in highly animated discussion. Nurse Rand was involved in making general apologies for having indicated support of the patient's discharge request at the beginning of the staff meeting. Drs. Stone and Craig were engaged in monologues interpreting and reinterpreting the patient's statements. Amid the confusion, Dr. Hand managed to comment, "I guess there's no need to vote on her; it's quite clear." (Perrucci 1974:155–58)

BEING "ON TIME" OR "OFF TIME"

Notions of a typical life course also serve as an interpretive resource for discerning normality in relation to chronological age. The image of being "on time" or "off time" often leads to attributions of normality or accusations of deviance, abnormality, or deficiency. Vernacular assessments of abnormality—such as "she's acting like a big baby" or "he's old before his time"—are virtual articulations of lives or actions out of synchrony with age.

Consider an example from an involuntary commitment hearing where the continued hospitalization of twenty-eight-year-old Sarah Cook was under consideration. During the court proceedings, a psychiatrist testified that Cook should be hospitalized for an extended stay because she was "out of touch with reality." He argued that she experienced several episodes over the past few years where she totally neglected her own basic needs—refusing to eat, bathe, or even go out of the house—as well as those of her three children (aged seven, eight, and ten). The judge, however, decided that her brief hospitalization and a medication program had stabilized her psychiatric condition, and she was now ready to go home. He offered the following explanation:

> I'm (releasing her) because I think we're seeing some progress here. I know your history of hospitalizations, Sarah, but each time you've managed to stay out a little bit longer. I think we're seeing a pattern here. At least I hope so. Sometimes it's just a matter of growing up a little. What I hope I'm seeing is a little girl who's finally becoming an adult. You've got a family that needs you, and from what you've said, it seems like you're finally realizing what they really mean to you. Sometimes people get into things, get married before they're ready. They're just kids and they aren't emotionally ready for the responsibility. I'm sure that didn't help your mental problems, Sarah. But what are you now, twenty-seven? I think it's time you took control of yourself, control your emotions and accept your responsibilities. Don't you agree? (Holstein 1990:123)

Note how the judge assimilated Cook's history of psychiatric disturbances to a model of age-specific maturation. While not discounting her mental problems, he aligned them with a view of her life course that was pointed toward emotional growth. Typifying the normal life course, he implied, that everyone "grows up" as they get older, and as they become more "adult," they develop greater emotional stability and a sense of responsibility. The judge's account integrated Cook's history of troubles with a model of maturation in such a way as reasonably to predict, for the practical purposes at hand, that Sarah would be able to stay out of the hospital, especially now that she was twenty-seven years old. If she stayed on course, she would leave behind those immature and irresponsible traits of her past and gain some control over her mental problems.

Professional assessments of social or psychiatric troubles may be quite similar in their age linkages. When psychiatrists, for example, offer professional diagnoses, they frequently refer to age expectations to establish the sense in which particular behaviors can be seen as normal or abnormal. Age or life course location can provide the basis for interpreting a person's behavior as seriously "inappropriate" and hence psychologically unhealthy, as in the following instance from an involuntary mental hospitalization hearing. In this case, a psychiatrist, Dr. Haas, uses age to assess the mental status of Jake Donner, a person under consideration for commitment.

Jake [Donner] has the, shall we say, the enthusiasm of a much younger man. His landlord says he's out every night, and sometimes doesn't come back until the next morning. When I examined Mr. Donner he made no secret of his, let's say, passion for members of the opposite sex. He was extremely distraught about being hospitalized because he said he was dating several women and they would all be upset if he stopped coming round to visit them. He said some pretty outrageous things for a man his age. He claimed that he needed to have sex at least once a day or he would, as he put it, lose his manhood. And he said these women were anxious to oblige him. Now, here's a man in his fifties — what is he,

fifty five, sixty—saying the kind of things you'd expect
from some teenager bragging to his buddies, but I'd
have to say they were clearly inappropriate from him.
(Holstein 1990:116–17)

Dr. Haas elucidates Mr. Donner's symptomatology with reference to age, using age points on a typified life line as marks of
contrast. The typical life course is a standard for appropriateness.
Portraying Donner as being way "off time" establishes his mental
illness. Donner's sexual talk and behavior are not considered intrin-
sically outrageous; they are inappropriate only in relation to Donner's
location on a life line, in relation to his age. Being "off time," in this
case acting and talking like a teenager, is a sign of pathology for a
fifty-five-year-old man.

Psychiatrists appearing in involuntary commitment hearings
regularly portray candidate patients as "off time" to substantiate
diagnoses. In another court case, Dr. Peters diagnosed William
Frederic, who was forty-nine years old, as schizophrenic, citing,
among other reasons, her belief that Frederic was "acting progressively more immature" and "not acting his age" (Holstein 1990).
According to the psychiatrist, Mr. Frederic caused a public disturbance by "childishly" refusing to ride as a passenger in his own car
while his daughter was driving. He refused to sit quietly in the
passenger's seat and tried to wrest the steering wheel away from the
daughter as she drove the car out the driveway. Frederic clung to the
steering wheel, which sounded the car's horn, and would not budge
when the car came to a halt in the middle of the street. His outburst
became so vociferous that traffic backed up, a crowd gathered, and
someone called the police.

During the commitment hearing, Dr. Peters argued that while
Frederic's insistence on driving himself might be understandable,
Frederic's agitated, animated outburst and his refusal to abandon the
steering wheel violated standards of decorum and judgment expected from "someone his age." The doctor might have characterized Frederic's behavior as disturbed in its own right, but chose
instead to underscore its inappropriateness by reference to age-
related expectations. Dr. Peters's comments suggested that as people
grow older, they develop "mature" responses to frustration that do
not involve uncontrollable public outbursts. Mr. Frederic, she im-

plied, was becoming progressively more "immature," a clear sign of mental disorder.

Age expectations are similarly cited by the police (Sanders 1976), juvenile court personnel (Emerson 1969), educators and social workers dealing with "troubled" and "troublesome" children (Buckholdt and Gubrium 1985; Leiter 1974) and other human-service professionals as the basis for discerning normality and deviance. In such cases, across the various settings, the idea of being on or off time typifies the normality or abnormality of behavior.

Define what is "supposed-to-be"

4 **PREDICTING FUTURES**

Typifications of life change are both retrospective and prospective. Immediate statuses, events, and circumstances are seen in light of what has transpired and what is forthcoming; the interpretation of "what is going on" is affected by beliefs about what has already occurred and what is likely to happen. For example, a wife's response to what she believes to be her husband's "cheating" will depend on her understanding of his past relations with her and with other women, as well as expectations about his future behavior. A father's interpretation of his son's dismissal from college will include the consideration of the son's past academic record and his future chances for educational achievement. In this chapter, we emphasize the prospective orientation to life change, focusing primarily on school settings, where predicting future growth is an important concern.

While predictions of the future rely on diverse formal methodologies, from intelligence testing to placement assessments, they are also constructed. As a practical matter, prediction relies on occasioned and ostensibly reasonable estimates of future alternatives that are seen as more or less probable. It is also conditional, routinely containing an implicit "if" clause; expectations are contingent on things staying the same, but can be altered on the basis of new circumstances. Envisaging the future, then, involves a great deal of ordinary interpretive work that implicates images of the life course.

Life change is dynamic and complex, more circumstantial than most conventional approaches would suggest. Certainly, in some sense, we are rational beings, weighing alternative routes to desired ends and making reasonable choices from possible means. And actions are influenced by early childhood experiences, role models, and class background. What the conventional depictions are most likely to ignore, however, is that people are continually interpreting and reinterpreting experience in their own right, recognizing their past, defining their present, and looking ahead to the future. And they do so in concrete settings, in relation to the settings' existing and developing interpretive resources, constraints, and political agendas.

As with other interpretations, predicting the future may be complicated by points of view, implicating both the past and the present. Staff members of a treatment facility for emotionally disturbed children, for example, routinely predict the likelihood of successful treatment in their assessments of the children's current behavior and circumstances. A child's actions and demeanor may lead his treatment team to believe that the boy is stable, harmless, and a good prospect for rehabilitation—the prediction of a positive future. Accordingly, staff may take special care and interest in the boy. Simultaneously, however, the boy is establishing his image, or what he typically is and can be expected to be, with the other children and adolescents in treatment. The cues that convince staff of his good prognosis may not be viewed as positively by these others, who orient to the virtues of not cooperating with the staff (see Buckholdt and Gubrium 1985). Holding an orientation similar to that of adult inmates in the correctional system (see Sykes 1958; Wieder 1988), they may see "no future at all" for a boy who gets too friendly with staff members. Staff members' positive responses to the boy merely compound his peers negative assessments. The interpretations of the future are thus intertwined with views of the present, for both the boys and the staff members.

THE SCHOOL AS A FUTURE-ORIENTED SETTING

Some social or institutional settings give the future special attention, with certain participants having a formal responsibility for directing the lives of those in their charge. Many of these settings are places where socialization takes place, where the normative order of a society is presumably passed from one generation or group to the next. Families, schools, churches, and youth organizations, for example, claim to provide children and adolescents with skills, rules, morals, and values. Adults are taught these in the armed services, colleges and universities, personnel and training divisions of business organizations, therapy sessions, and rehabilitation programs. In these future-oriented settings, the past and present take on special meaning in terms of what they might indicate about forthcoming behavior.

As formal organizations, schools possess the essential elements of legal-rational bureaucracy, at least in its ideal form (Weber 1958). Abstract rules govern and guide behavior in the coordinated pursuit of rational ends. Rules of behavior as well as goals are presumed to be clear and unambiguous. Duties and authority are located in a set of hierarchically arranged offices or positions sanctioned by administrative regulations. Policy decisions, administrative acts, and routine business are recorded in writing and maintained in filing systems.

This picture of organizational rationality, however, misses much of the dynamic internal life that exists in such settings. According to Gouldner (1959a), complex organizations also can be viewed from the "natural system" model. This view stresses the importance of spontaneous, unplanned activity within the formal structure of the organization. The words "spontaneous" and "unplanned" refer to actions that cannot be understood from the perspective of a rational-legal model. For example, there are "latent social identities," such as the classroom clown, that are not rationalized in the official demands of the organization. There are very personal problems, concerns, and ambitions. Jealousies, career anxieties, sexual desires, headaches, and angry feelings exist side by side with formal organizational goals. Routines are not so standardized as to exclude personal interpretation based on biography, the occasion, and previous events. Rules and expectations are sufficiently ambiguous to leave room for spontaneous, creative behavior.

The two models provide rather different images of complex organizations. One depicts rational participants who know the ends to be achieved and the accepted means for achieving them. Participants are able to identify alternative courses of action and to estimate probable, desirable, or undesirable outcomes in terms of well-defined organizational objectives. The second model underscores the limits of rational behavior, where goals may be unclear in specific circumstances. Situations can present opportunities for conflicting goals, the range of viable alternatives may not be known, and the probable consequences of alternative means may be difficult or impossible to estimate.

Gouldner argues that both models are needed to explain the complexities of life in organizations. As far as schools are concerned, on some occasions behavior appears to be unplanned and spontaneous, not formally articulated with educational goals. At other times, official calculation and consideration of alternative actions appear to dominate. Yet, neither model provides a basis for linkage. Behavior that appears to be spontaneous may in fact be thoughtfully constructed and responsive to past interaction and future expectations. Behavior that appears rational may not originally have been oriented to official methods or goals, but on a later occasion may be interpreted to fit legitimate categories of organizational rationality. Neither model provides a view of how participants in school life in particular, and organizational life in general, use both rationality and spontaneity to accomplish everyday organizational business and, in the process, construct predictions of growth.

Classroom Life

Many commentators on classroom life look for ways to improve its rational organization, following what Gouldner calls the legal-rational model. Behaviorists study the stimuli and reinforcers provided by the teacher and curriculum materials in relation to students' responses. Their goal is to understand the learning process and to make it more efficient in the service of school objectives. Educational technologists have a similar objective, although they may not adhere to the behaviorist perspective. Educational psychologists develop tests, study teacher and student characteristics, and conduct research in the areas of learning and motivation, again with the aim of enhancing the learning process.

Proponents of open classrooms, free schools, and alternative learning programs have been somewhat more concerned with improving the quality of life of the child. The formal educational goals of the organization take a back seat to individual creativity, mental health, and happiness. It is generally assumed that these alternate goals are fostered when the child is free of the constraints and pressures generated in traditional classrooms.

Most conventional studies of schooling emphasize the end products of the educational process, paying less attention to the daily activities in schools that produce the outcomes (Mehan 1992). Schools are seen as places for socialization, for preparing students for later life. Students arrive at school with widely varying backgrounds and potentials. The school personnel then, relying on a blend of technology and art, attempt to convey certain positive cognitive skills, "real" motivational characteristics, and normative preferences. Schools are revealed to be more or less successful with pupils, depending on the children's background and intelligence and the technology or instructional resources available to the school. If the children are from poor backgrounds, the school is not likely to have as much success with them as with children from middle-class families. Indeed, schools are likely to reproduce the status distinctions characteristic of the populations they serve. Likewise, if the child lacks intelligence or motivation, performance in school will suffer. The school is then said to be constrained by the type of student it educates (Coleman et al. 1966; Jencks et al. 1972). Presumably if a lower-class school suddenly received a deluge of middle-class or upper-middle-class children, its services would be used much more effectively, and its results would improve.

Of course, the career of a student is not tied just to background or ability characteristics. Decisions about placement and progress are made throughout the child's school career, and these decisions affect the future options available to the child in the school as well as in the occupational world. The daily experiences of school personnel with the child provide additional information, which is used to evaluate and place students. For example, some children are said to be "underachievers"; their performance does not match their capacity. Others are "overachievers"; they do much better than test results suggest that they should. This sort of information contributes to the more or less rational process of deciding what is both best and possible for a particular child.

In this view, students are said to possess characteristics that can be developed in the school to varying degrees, given the current state of instructional technology. Unfortunately, this technology is not considered powerful enough to make up for social, cultural, and personal disadvantages of background, race, and intelligence. Thus, the more advantaged have the resources to make more of their time in school and subsequently reap the rewards of a better education in the occupational and professional world. It is claimed that public education could provide a powerful force for more equality of opportunity if only students had more equal resources with which to pursue their opportunities.

In the search for more rational, humane, or successful schools, however, the day-to-day, routine aspects of classroom life have been largely ignored. As Hugh Mehan (1992) puts it, the "scientific arithmetic" of status-attainment research and the debate over the relative influence of family background versus schooling on student achievement has so dominated educational sociology that the every-day dynamics of school life are all but forgotten. There has been a tendency to neglect how teachers and students practically organize their daily lives, the ordinary problems they speak of, and how they concretely convince themselves and others of solutions. So much serious and earnest attention has been given over to theorizing about how structural problems can be solved, how to make schools more efficient and productive, or how to make school life more satisfying for the child that research on everyday life has generally been overlooked.

Despite this neglect, an important set of observational studies of the school environment has given us a more intimate look at day-to-day life in classrooms (Jackson 1968; Smith and Geoffrey 1968; Rist 1973; Mehan 1979). In addition, studies of "constitutive action" (Mehan 1992) in educational settings have described everyday life in school settings, and how institutional practices determine whether students' behavior counts as instances of certain educational catego-ries (Buckholdt and Gubrium 1985; Cicourel and Kitsuse 1963; Cicourel et al. 1974; Marlaire and Maynard 1990; Mehan 1979; Mehan et al. 1985). Jackson (1968), for example, describes the world of a teacher and twenty-five to thirty students as a reality constrained by the significance of the trivial. Life goes on, day after day, in a standardized environment marked by repetition, redun-dancy, and ritual. The children are the same, as are the curriculum, the class periods, and the organizational rules and procedures. It is a crowded environment that requires management of supplies, time, space, attention, and distractions. Evaluations are constantly being made of children based on test scores, daily performances, judg-ments of motivations, and character traits. These judgments are difficult to make because performance may be different in several contexts and children may feign interest or motivation.

Still, the immediacy of classroom events constantly intrudes on the best-conceived plans. Moment-to-moment events cannot be anticipated; teachers do not know what weight to attach to alternative actions or even what the range of possible alternatives is. Yet they manage to use fleeting behavioral cues to interpret and manage circumstances as they emerge. In practice, they come to know "what's happening" because they have observed similar behavior before and, using these typifications, they extend the various alternative possibilities into the future. However, their solutions are never permanent; they are open to new interpretations as matters develop.

In a complementary analysis, Smith and Geoffrey (1968) frame classroom life as an ever-changing reality. They describe the teacher as subjectively rational, as orienting means to desirable ends in a situation in which decision making is constantly adjusting to changing assignments, situational perspectives, and multiple, often conflicting, goals. The job of teaching involves much more than processing rewards and punishments. Events from the past are interpreted in light of current behaviors, predictions are made about future behavior, and preparations are made for alternate future contingencies. The teacher may invoke the notion of continuity from the past into the present in order to establish the meaning of present events and to predict their likely future course, creating an interpretive trajectory of a student's life.

Awareness is constantly demanded if the teacher is to stay on top of the multiple and simultaneous events in the classroom. The shaping of future events and a smooth transition from the present into the future depend upon accurate information about a number of realities in the present. The teacher sizes up the situation from moment to moment, projects current behavior into the future, and makes tentative decisions on how to maintain current development or institute changes. In practice, the teacher draws upon the logic of the conventional approaches presented in chapter 1 in order to construct students' life courses.

Mehan (1979) concentrates on an alternate aspect of the construction of classroom realities, focusing on the conversational organization of teacher-student interaction during classroom instruction. He describes these situations as sequentially and hierarchically organized events assembled through the "structuring" work of teachers *in interaction* with students. Teaching and learning, he emphasizes, are grounded in the locally managed conversation that produces the meaningful, orderly reality of just what school activities come to be, which bear on predicting growth.

A number of related studies concur that the flow of classroom questions and answers that constitutes much of daily life in the classroom unfolds dynamically as teachers formulate questions, solicit responses, judge the correctness and appropriateness of answers, and continue on. Teachers then accumulate the assessments to form the empirical bases for placing students into ability groups (Cole and Griffin 1987; Collins 1986; Eder 1981; Wilcox 1982). Similar practices are used to assess student behavior for placement in different educational tracks (Cicourel and Kitsuse 1963; Cicourel et al. 1974; Mehan et al. 1985; Oakes 1985).

Together, the studies of everyday life in schools provide us with much-needed intimate detail about schooling. Their descriptions rise above pure advocacy or mere concerns for efficiency to focus on the critical problems of how teachers and students manage the complexity of their relations and how they handle day-to-day contingencies in the classroom. As Mehan (1992) suggests, they reveal schooling as a reality constituting activity.

Schoolchildren's Futures

Depending on whether personal or cultural characteristics are emphasized, conventional theories about human development and education lead to propositions about deficient intelligence or disadvantaged environments. Both sorts of theories have serious shortcomings. In particular, they unwittingly fail to make explicit the connections between personal or cultural characteristics and concrete events in the school setting. Observers of the day-to-day intimate life that occurs in every school have clearly told us that schools process and differentiate students (Holt 1964; Kozol 1967; Kohl 1968). They do not simply present opportunity. Schools reproduce social inequalities by implementing a curriculum that rewards the "cultural capital" of the dominant classes and systematically devalues that of the lower classes (Bourdieu 1977). Teachers, administrators, and other school personnel judge, evaluate, reward, and punish. They make decisions about which group a child should belong to, how much attention he or she should receive, what instructional materials he or she should have, how fast or slowly he or she can work, and so on. Decisions are made against a complex and fluid background of personal beliefs, test results, daily behavior, and organizational expectations and constraints. These decisions are seen as routine jobs in the line of teaching and educational administration, decisions based on the strengths, weaknesses, or problems presented by a child or a group of children. They are routine or mundane because they are hardly thought about or reflected on by those who make them. The decisions have major consequences, however, for they are the very stuff of children's future growth.

One way to view schoolchildren's futures is as a product of ordinary interaction and interpretation involving school personnel and the children. Background characteristics, test scores, and personal encounters are not simply neutral or self-evident facts; they are subject to definition. Definitions stem from typifications and both lay and professional theorizing about people and what can be expected from them. From this perspective, the critical problem is to understand how classroom reality and related predictions of growth are constructed in the school. The approach argues that students do not present problems or opportunities that are independent of the concrete meaning assigned to them by school personnel. We need to know how events and behavior displays are given meaning and shared among school personnel, how they come to be seen as important, and how various criteria are developed and used for making judgments about children and their qualities.

PREDICTING GROWTH IN THE EARLY DAYS

Several years ago, one of the authors (Buckholdt) did intensive observation of a first-grade class in an inner-city school of a major midwestern city (Hamblin et al. 1971). The teacher and all the children were African American. Within ten days after the beginning of school, the teacher had arranged the children into three ability groups. When asked about her reasons for assigning children to one group or another, the teacher explained that she used several criteria. The kindergarten teachers had given her reports on reading readiness, ability to listen and work on assignments, behavior problems, and attendance. A group intelligence test had also been administered near the end of the kindergarten year, and the results were given to the first-grade teacher. The teacher claimed that she used this information from kindergarten as well as her own observations and evaluations during the first two weeks.

When the observer (O) asked the teacher (T) about how she placed particular children, the following discussion ensued regarding Terry, one of the children:

O: Okay, I'd like to find out about some particular children. Why did you put Terry in the lowest group for example?

T: Ha! That's an easy one. Look at what Jones [kindergarten teacher] said about him. He should have stayed in kindergarten if there weren't so many new kids this year. And his IQ, 57. He probably won't be with us long.

O: What do you mean?

T: I know his parents, both winos and poor. His brother was here two years ago but we had to send him to "special." Terry's a sure candidate, too.

O: Were there any other reasons why you put him in the bottom group?

T: Well, you've seen how he acts. He just sits there and stares into space. At least he doesn't bother anybody. You know, I haven't heard him say one intelligible word since school started.

The teacher claimed to have used several indicators for the decision that Terry should be in the lowest group. His parents were alcoholic and poor. The home environment was bad, causing problems for both Terry and his brother. Terry had not acquired the necessary readiness skills in kindergarten and his IQ was extremely low. She also claimed that she could see from his behavior in first grade that he was prepared and capable only of being in the lowest group.

Terry remained "sullen" and "unresponsive," according to the teacher, for the first six months of first grade. He rarely answered questions from the teacher or completed more than a small portion of his work. He rarely interacted with other children, and when he did, he usually got into verbal or physical encounters. By February, the teacher was planning to have Terry placed in a "special" class for the following year. She invited the principal and several other teachers into her classroom to observe him, to confirm her judgment as well as to advise her about Terry's placement.

At the end of February, a series of events caused the teacher to reconsider briefly her evaluation of Terry. All the children in the "low" group were making little progress in the first grade. They did not appear to recognize the letters of the alphabet or, more importantly, the phonetic associations for the letters. At that time, Buckholdt was interested in finding out if young children could teach one another. He asked the teacher to allow him to pair children from the "advanced" group with the "slow" children for about twenty minutes each day. The pairs of children were taken from the room and allowed to work together in the privacy of a small office. The observer either remained in the office with the children or listened to their conversation from outside the room. After twenty minutes of work, the observer tested the children to see how many new letters and sounds they had learned. In most instances, the more advanced children were able to teach letter names and their associated sounds to the other children.

One day shortly after this experiment began, the observer, who was listening outside the room, could not recognize the voice of the child who was serving as instructor. When he entered the room, he found Terry helping the supposedly more advanced child with letter recognition. Terry continued to switch between the tutor and the learner roles with his partner for several days, until they both knew all the letter names and sounds. At first, the teacher did not believe the reports about Terry. Finally, she came to see for herself and found that it was true. She asked Terry and his partner to give a demonstration to the other children in the class and invited the principal and several other teachers to observe his performance.

Terry made many other unexpected advances during the remainder of the semester. He became a leader in spelling, reading, and arithmetic. He was tested again at the end of the year and received a score of 131 on a group-administered intelligence test. Yet, ironically, the teacher kept him in the slow group. When she was asked why she had not allowed him to move to another group, she responded, "It takes more than a couple of weeks of work to get out of that group."

The observer followed this same group of children into the second grade. Unfortunately, Terry had moved from the area and was no longer enrolled in this school. Several teachers reported that his aunt had taken him to live with her after his parents had beaten him; others claimed that his parents had been evicted from their home and had moved from the neighborhood. Near the end of the school year, however, Terry returned to the school and entered the second grade with his old classmates. Once again, he appeared sullen and unresponsive to the teacher. He did not read, nor would he identify letter names or sounds. His official record now showed that his intelligence was "untestable"; it was too low to assign a score from the norming chart. For the following year, he was assigned to a "special" class for learning and emotional problems.

The second-grade teacher was aware of Terry's progress during the last part of his first-grade year. Still, she dismissed this as unimportant because, as she claimed, he had received so much personal attention. "He won't make it in the regular classroom," she asserted. "We can't give special attention with so many kids. With his home and IQ, he won't cut it." So a boy who had temporarily risen to the top of his class was now assigned to a terminal-track class for children judged by school personnel to have deficient backgrounds or talents for succeeding in the regular classroom.

Terry's case is interesting for several reasons. First, it shows the practical work of teachers in locating and understanding the "problems" of children. One could construct several alternate explanations for Terry's behavior, but the teacher's tacit model led her to locate the source of his difficulty in the family situation. According to her, problems in the home accounted for his low IQ and inadequate cognitive and interaction skills. The teacher's typification of Terry as a classic "deprived child" allowed her to interpret the meaning and source of his behavior. The teacher's theory thus mirrored the more professional theories that explain many educational problems in terms of cultural disadvantage or family troubles.

Second, Terry's case illustrates the reality-sustaining logic of the typification process. While both the first- and second-grade teachers admitted that Terry had shown remarkable improvement during the latter part of first grade, they dismissed this evidence as irrelevant to his standing. The first-grade teacher argued that a few weeks of outstanding performance provided insufficient evidence for expecting continued growth and for removing Terry from the group of children that she saw as essentially ineducable. The second-grade teacher similarly dismissed any attempt to reconsider Terry by attributing his apparent gains to the individual attention he received, attention that could not be provided in her classroom. The dominant interpretive framework remained basically intact. Because of this, Terry's tested IQ of 131 could not be his "real" IQ. The teacher's theory of intelligence apparently demanded that IQ be evident in large, noisy classrooms where children receive little individual instruction from the teacher. In this case, intelligence, as measured by the test, had little relevance for her unless it could really operate in the context of the classroom as it was currently structured.

The teachers' typification of Terry had profound predictive implications. The teachers not only located the sources of his problems and understood their meaning in terms of Terry's background, but they also envisioned his future school career as being determined by those circumstances. The first-grade teacher saw his assignment to a special track as "inevitable." The second-grade teacher made a similar prediction: "With his home and IQ, he won't cut it."

Terry's case, of course, is unusual in that few teachers are confronted with information that is apparently so discrepant with a public typification. The problem for the teachers could have been especially severe in that the information arose from officially recognized sources — intelligence and performance tests — not simply from parents' and students' pleas that a child is more able than he or she appears. The presumed atypicality of this case, however, serves to highlight teachers' reality-making and reality-sustaining procedures. Moreover, it shows how Terry's intelligence was "realized" through the related, ongoing work of the classroom and the assessment process. Typifications allowed the teachers to manage apparently contradictory information about Terry, assimilating it to prior understandings and projecting the pattern into the future.

Constructing Tracks

Ray Rist (1973) has reported similar processes of student differentiation and tracking in the kindergarten of an all-black, urban elementary school. In this case, the teacher possessed four pieces of information about each child as he or she entered school for the first time: a form showing preschool experience and medical history; a questionnaire in which parents reported on behaviors of their children, such as bedwetting, lying, and disobedience; a list of children from families who were receiving public funds (e.g., welfare payments); and reports and gossip from other teachers about the parents and older siblings of the kindergarten children. The teacher had no information about language skills, intelligence, special talents, or problems. By the eighth day of school, however, the teacher was able to assign each child to one of three ability groups.

Rist observes that the three groups could be distinguished on the basis of clothing and other aspects of physical appearance, body odor, interactional behavior among themselves and with the teacher, and the use of standard American English. According to Rist, the teacher had begun to evaluate student behavior and appearance from the very first day. When this information was combined with what she already knew about family and social-class background, she was able to group children into supposedly homogeneous ability tracks. Certain criteria were used to predict future success, while others were seen as indicative of failure.

Tracking or assignment to ability groups is common in many schools. While school personnel justify student differentiation as a rational process that implements deliberately conceived plans of action, formal rules of assignment are inevitably vague, and assignment practices involve great discretion. Teachers rely massively on working understandings to identify signs of competence, motivation, and the like to make assignments in particular cases. In this instance, physical appearance, body odor, and the use of standard English apparently "told" the teacher something about academic potential.

These early judgments had serious consequences for the quality and amount of instruction and attention that the three groups received for the remainder of the year. Rist reports that the leading group received two to three times as much of the teacher's time as the members of the other two groups. Members of the first group were more likely to be assigned positions of responsibility and authority in the classroom, to sit closer to the teacher during large-group instruction, and to receive praise from the teacher. Members of the other two groups were much more likely to be the targets of control statements, threats, and ridicule. They also more often did "busy work" while the teacher presented new concepts or instructional material to the first group.

Once the groups were formed, there was no movement across the castelike categories. Further evaluation apparently convinced the teacher that her initial judgments were correct. "Facts" tacitly constructed out of practical reasoning were corroborated on the same grounds. Near the end of the year, when Rist asked the teacher about the performance of the children in the various groups, she replied as follows:

> Those children at table one gave consistently the most responses throughout the year and seemed most interested in what was going on in the classroom. The children at table two and most all of them at table three, at times, seemed to have no idea of what was going on in the class and were in another world often by themselves. It just appears that some can do it and some cannot. I don't think it is the teaching that affects those who cannot do it, but some are just basically—I hate to say it—low achievers. . . .I guess it is that parents do not pay any attention to the children and take no pride in the work that the children bring home from school. The children just do not get encouraged. Did you notice at the play yesterday how so many of the children came so nicely dressed and clean and their hair was combed? And did you see how Lilly came? She was dressed in a dirty dress, dirty socks, and her hair wasn't even combed. It must be that some parents just have a different set of values. The child can be no better than his association with his parents. Maybe some of the children will change when they get older, but most of them will be in a rut for their whole life. (Rist 1973:176–77)

It is noteworthy that the teacher not only assessed the children's current status in light of theories of background causation but also predicted their future growth potential—projecting an expected life course in the process.

Rist followed these children into the first grade. The group assignments were almost identical to those first made in kindergarten. Now, however, the differentiation was made on putatively more "objective" grounds. In addition to observed behavioral and attitudinal characteristics and records of progress in kindergarten, scores on intelligence tests and reports from the kindergarten teacher were available for the evaluation of each student.

The separate groups continued into the second grade. Now the groups even had names to designate their status: the Tigers (presumably referring to the Detroit Tigers baseball team that had recently won the World Series), the Cardinals (the other team in the Series), and the Clowns. When Rist asked the second-grade teacher about the children in the three groups, the teacher had well-developed notions of why each child had been placed. In response to a question of whether the term "cultural deprivation" applied to her second grade children, she said:

> Yes, definitely. . . . I think most of these children get their cultural experiences through school. They really wouldn't have any cultural education if it was not for the school because most of these children are in families that don't have the time, money, or interest in their children. . . . They come to school and they are absolutely filthy. I can never remember so many ragged kids as now. Some of these kids even come to school without underwear. (Rist 1973:216)

In response to questions about the futures of the children in the three ability groups, the teacher explained:

[Tigers]: . . . Well, they are my fastest group. They are very smart. . . . They all feel an education is important and most of them have goals in life as to what they want to be. They mostly want to go to college. (Rist 1973:217)

[Cardinals]: . . . They are slow to finish their work . . . but they do get finished. You know, a lot of them, though, don't care to come to school too much. . . . But I guess most of the Cardinals want to go on and finish and go to college. A lot of them have ambitions when they grow up. It's mostly the parents' fault they are not at school more often. (pp. 217–18)

[Clowns]: . . . Well, they are really slow. You know, most of them are still doing first-grade work. . . . They are playful. They like to talk a lot. They are not very neat. . . . They are always so restless. . . . I don't think education means much to them at this stage....For example, take Nick. He is not going to do anything. . . . Curt won't amount to very much and neither will Orlando. Amy tries, but she hasn't got it. Lilly is the type that will drop out and go to work. (pp. 218–19)

These accounts come from urban schools that serve poor, mostly African American children. The teaching processes that begin in the very first days of school, however, occur in all schools. As Jackson (1968) has noted, there are few social contexts in which behavior is subject to such continuous and multidimensional evaluation. Students are continually tested, sorted, and classified. The result is a stratification of students within schools, a within-school variation, which is larger than variation between schools (Jencks et al. 1972). Thus, schools "create" differences between students on the various dimensions that they choose to measure. The differences between the top and bottom students in both rich and poor schools are substantial, larger than the average overall differences between rich and poor schools. Conventional analyses generally locate the source of between- and within-school variations in the children's intelligence or family or other background characteristics. The child is viewed as the important unit of analysis, since it is believed that individual characteristics determine his or her life course.

These approaches gloss over the practical differentiating or sorting processes that allocate children to relative positions of superiority or inferiority. From a constructionist perspective, children's characteristics are not self-revealing; nor are they objectively evident in behavior, performance, or test scores. Teachers and other school personnel interpret behavior based on ideas about ability and potential; they develop expectations about what to anticipate from particular types of children. Everyday theories of development and competence—like some of those discussed in chapter 1—filter the variety of information that is available for assessing each child. Thus, dirty hair, tattered clothes, family on welfare, and poor language skills are viewed as relevant predictors for children who are seen as having these characteristics. They indicate what type of child this is, enabling teachers reasonably to predict what the child will become. The fact that children may appear as highly verbal in other contexts, or may display what could be interpreted as imagination and curiosity on occasions outside the classroom, is generally ignored, or at least not looked for, since, obviously, "that's different." The teachers' theories not only identify important characteristics for predicting growth but also tacitly specify the taken-for-granted contexts in which they can be discovered.

From the very first days, then, children are "constructed," their pasts typified and their futures tracked. Background characteristics and personal qualities may indeed correlate with measures of schooling outcomes, but these relationships can only be understood in light of the situated processing that mediates their formal documentation. Students do not simply take more or less advantage of school. Teachers and other school personnel categorize students and project their futures in the organization with regard to the working interpretive contingencies of schooling. As Dorothy Smith (1989) has shown in her studies of mothers in relation to their children's schooling, important definitional practices are at the very center of the educational process, insinuating both formal and informal activities.

ASSESSING POTENTIAL

When children first arrive at school, teachers have little information about them except what they know about background characteristics. As time passes, teachers come to know more about individual children, their strengths and weaknesses. This information is not easily articulated with formal theories of child development, language acquisition, or instructional technology. Daily events are too complex and occasioned to interpret or evaluate simply in terms of competencies or deficiencies.

An organization that claims to teach and change lives by means of a rational process of instruction, however, cannot afford to justify its behavior or plan its activities on fleeting impressions or vague evaluations. Parents and other community members want to know more than "Jesse is doing poorly in math" or "Dana doesn't seem to be motivated." The significant audiences of the school, as well as its own internal planning and evaluation personnel, demand more precise, informative, and objective reports on what is going on.

Schools provide this information in a variety of ways, standardized tests being among the most prominent.

Standardized tests yield a single total score, or a set of subscores, which provide an evaluation of a child in relation to other children (the children on whom the test was standardized) either on the dimension of general intelligence or on several dimensions of learning. Test scores are generally considered to provide a clear and accurate interpretation of a child's capacity or intellectual progress. They are seen as more reliable and valid than the inconsistent, subjective evaluations made by teachers.

Several tacit assumptions are made when school personnel interpret test results (Mehan 1973). First, test questions are assumed to be unambiguous stimuli that elicit responses that are indicative of the respondent's knowledge. The meaning of the stimulus-response event is shared by the person who constructed the test, the person giving the test, and the person taking the test. Given this presumed continuity of meaning, there can be only one correct answer to a question. Correct answers result from adequate knowledge and satisfactory search procedures, while incorrect answers can be traced to faulty reasoning and/or insufficient knowledge, ability, or understanding. Second, the relationship between the stimulus and response is assumed to be context free. Factors such as frequent interruptions, time of day, or experience with this kind of test are ideally not relevant to the final score; factors other than underlying abilities and acquired information and skills are considered extraneous. In other words, one testing situation is, in principle, the same as another. Third, the tester is assumed to record each response from the child passively and objectively and assign it the status of a correct or incorrect answer.

These assumptions, and therefore the notion that tests directly measure an objective, underlying ability, have been questioned on several grounds. The motivational conditions surrounding the test, including the reasons given for taking a test and the incentives or reinforcement offered, can influence scores (Zigler 1970; Ayllon and Kelly 1972). The race and sex of the teacher-tester may affect expectations and the performance of students (Entwisle and Webster 1974). Also, the language of the teacher-tester and the linguistic structure of instruction and testing may artificially limit student performance, particularly if the student normally uses nonstandard English or is bilingual (Baratz and Baratz 1970).

Objections to the adequacy of test scores as indicators of cognitive processes, learning potential, or acquired skills generally stress problems of motivation, cultural bias, and setting. The assumption is that test scores will be more valid and reliable if tests are administered by the right people, in appropriate contexts, and in relevant cultural settings. While these objections are probably valid, they do not address several interpretive issues relating to meaning.

When we speak of meaning, we are referring to an ongoing, emergent process. The meaning assigned to a social act or object is located in actors' occasioned interpretations. Therefore, the meaning of a test item or answer is never merely apparent, but is situationally mediated. Partners in interaction work out a sense of meaningfulness as they signal, through talk and interaction, what they are intending or how they are "defining the situation" (McHugh 1968). Of course, persons who engage one another regularly, or who share the same culture, develop expectancies that guide and articulate this process. Yet norms or expectations are not fully adequate guides for working through specific interactions or event.

Measurement of cognitive process, growth, or potential typically relies upon assessment situations in which answers are solicited for ostensibly standardized questions. Despite standardizing procedures, however, what someone is doing or asking in any situation is not self-evident, since occasions inevitably shape and alter meaning. Often, when questions are asked and answered, further information is needed before meaning gains some practical, momentary stability. Likewise, the appropriateness or acceptability of answers to questions is not self-evident; the correctness, incorrectness, completeness, or inadequacy of a response is always an interpretive matter. As we illustrate, meaningful indicators of growth potential emerge from the routine interpretive practices of "hard data" production (Gubrium and Buckholdt 1979) that virtually construct the facts upon which predictions about the future courses of lives are based.

Producing Appropriate Answers

As part of classroom routines, teachers often present children with problems or questions that are similar in form and content to items found on a standardized test. The assumption is that the teacher asks what appears to be an obvious question that should elicit a correct answer from children who understand the concept or have learned the skill. In any case, the behavior of the child should provide a correct or incorrect response to the question or direction. The child's evaluative process, however, which appears on the surface to be so straightforward and objective, is a practical undertaking involving considerable interpretive work. The question must be viewed in a context of constantly changing features that cannot be entirely anticipated. The way the question is asked, the behavior of other children, previous lessons, gestures and facial expressions of the teacher, and other highly variable conditions can affect the meaning inferred by the child.

In answering test questions, a child's response will often indicate that the initial question was incomplete or that unstated assumptions need to be made explicit. So, additional information or feedback is provided and children are asked for further answers. Once again, children interpret the request in light of previous experiences, present contexts, and anticipated events. Their response is interpreted in turn by the teacher as an indication of the need for more information, additional examples, correct answers, and so on. The point is that the children and the teacher continually interact to produce the meaning of questions and answers as a test or lesson unfolds. Answers are accomplished within an environment that is not nearly as straightforward or certain as test procedures assume.

Consider the following lesson segment observed by one of the authors (Buckholdt). A teacher and eight first-grade children are sitting in a circle. The teacher is holding a box that contains plastic forms of various sizes, shapes, and colors. In previous lessons, the children have learned to identify several characteristics of the forms. The teacher begins the lesson:

TEACHER: Today we will select shapes that have several things alike. Watch me now. I have the small blue triangles. [Holds up the objects for the children to see.] Now I have big red squares. Now I have small green rectangles. Now you try it. Johnny, can you come over here and select the small green squares?

Johnny approaches the teacher and points to some objects in the box.

TEACHER: Good, Johnny, those are small green squares. Show them to the children.

Johnny picks up two small green squares and holds them in his hand.

TEACHER: Are there any more in the box? I want you to find all of them.

Johnny looks in the box and points to several objects.

TEACHER: Are those small green squares?

JOHNNY: Yes.

TEACHER: Will you show them to the children?

Johnny puts down the other two objects. He picks out three small green squares from the box and holds them in the air.

TEACHER: I want you to show all of the green squares. What happened to the other two?

Johnny now picks up the other two and holds all five of them.

TEACHER: Good, now tell us what you have.

JOHNNY: Green squares.

TEACHER: Are they small or big?

JOHNNY: Small.

TEACHER: How many do you have?

JOHNNY: Five.

TEACHER: So tell us, "I have five small green squares."

JOHNNY: I have five small green squares.

TEACHER: Good.

The teacher's evaluative criteria for this lesson become evident only as the interaction with Johnny proceeds. She wants the children to select all the items of a particular shape, color, and size, hold them up for the other children to see, and finally construct a complete sentence of a particular form describing what they were holding. These several criteria are not clear in the initial instructions.

The lesson continues:

TEACHER: Rose, will you find the big red triangles.

Rose comes over to the box and points to several objects in the box.

TEACHER: Children, when I say "find" some objects, I want you to pick them up and show them to us. Now Rose, find the big red triangle.

Rose selects and shows four big red triangles and one small one.

TEACHER: Is that a big red triangle? [Pointing to the small one.]

ROSE: No.

TEACHER: Well, see if you can find another big red triangle.

> *Rose searches for and finds another big red triangle and continues to hold the four other big triangles as well as the small one.*

TEACHER: Rose, put the small triangle back in the box. [Rose complies.]

TEACHER: Now, tell us what you have.

ROSE: Big red triangles.

TEACHER: Say "I have five big red triangles."

ROSE: I have five big red triangles.

TEACHER: Fred, find the big yellow circles.

> *Fred gets up from his chair but instead of approaching the teacher, he heads toward the back of the room.*

TEACHER: Fred, where are you going?

FRED: To get the big yellow circles.

> *There are several cardboard circles on the desk at the back of the room that are much larger than the plastic circles in the teacher's box.*

TEACHER: Come back here, Fred. We are only interested in the shapes in this box. Now show us the five big yellow circles. [Note that the teacher now says "show us" and tells Fred how many to show.]

> *Fred picks up and shows five big yellow circles.*

TEACHER: Now tell us what you have.

FRED: Five yellow circles.

TEACHER: Say, "I have five big yellow circles."

FRED: I have five big yellow circles.

TEACHER: Fred has five big yellow circles. You say it, David.

DAVID: Fred has five big yellow circles.

When she began the lesson, the teacher assumed that she had a definite plan for what the children should do and how they should demonstrate their knowledge of size, shape, and color. She felt that her initial explanation was clear. As the lesson unfolds, however, it is evident that some elaboration is needed, that what she might have initially described as her plan is not adequate to the specific task at hand. The children are not only to select the appropriate shapes following her directions but they must also show them to the other children. The shapes selected are to be taken only from the box that the teacher holds. The demonstration is to be accompanied by a complete sentence using the pronoun "I" plus numerical, size, color, and shape descriptions.

The material presented here shows how expectations gradually become clear as children respond to questions posed by the teacher and as the teacher redefines and adjusts her expectations and criteria in relation to the children's responses. The teacher's directions do not provide the children with sufficient guidelines to accomplish what the teacher desires. The needed information emerges only during the interplay between the teacher and the children. The appropriate form of the correct responses and the criteria for judging the responses emerged as the lesson proceeded, with the children tacitly informing the teacher how to proceed as they interacted with her. They are as much a part of the instruction as the teacher is.

"Practically" Adequate Solutions

Hugh Mehan (1974) and Aaron Cicourel (1974) argue that most questions or directions presented by a teacher in classroom or testing situations can be interpreted in a variety of ways. For example, the question, "Where is the triangle, Joey?" might be answered with any of the following responses: "On the paper," "in the room," "right here," "right above the square," and so on. The question presents the child with more than the problem of simply providing *the* correct response. He or she must find the one answer among several alternatives that matches the teacher's unstated assumptions concerning what the right answer is and how to determine its correctness. Mehan (1974) summarizes the problem of emergent reality in the following way:

> Because the teacher's instructions are indexical expressions [sensitive to occasion], their meaning changes for the child as the lesson unfolds. This emergent sense of meaning defies a static description which presumes that the meaning of instructions is clear at the outset of an exchange and remains constant throughout; it requires a description which openly includes retrospective and

prospective assignment, indefiniteness, and indeterminacy as features of meaning. (p. 126)

When a child takes a standardized test, it is assumed that a stimulus in the form of a picture or a set of directions should lead the child to the single correct answer if he or she has developed the skills to perform the task. If the child indicates the correct answer, it is assumed that he or she possesses the skill. Likewise, if the answer is incorrect, the child supposedly does not have the required skill. While it has an appealingly simple logic, this model is inadequate for capturing the complexities of test taking in practice.

Mehan (1973), for example, observed educational testing situations, then asked children *why* they had selected particular items on a basic language and concepts test. The answers revealed considerable linguistic and interpretive ability that was hidden by the simple test rating of a "right" or "wrong" answer. For instance, one test item showed pictures of children with their heads obscured. The task was to indicate the tallest child. The "correct" response was not to make a selection because relative heights could not be determined. Several children, however, selected one of the pictures. They justified their decision on the perceived fact that "his feet are bigger." The children thus understood the intent of the question, to discriminate and compare, but they did not use the same criterion of comparability — visible height — as the test developer. Although their answer was marked wrong, their response was as much an indication of a different scheme of interpretation as a lack of skill.

On another item, children were asked to mark the "animal that can fly." The test displayed pictures of a bird, an elephant, and a dog. Many first-grade children selected the elephant — an ostensibly incorrect response. When later asked about their selection, they reported that the elephant was Dumbo, Walt Disney's famous flying elephant. Again, although these children were "wrong," they used logical and interpretive skills in arriving at an answer that, given the meaning they provided, was reasonable. After all, they were not told that the worlds of fantasy and cartoons were to be excluded from testing consideration.

In still another item, the test presented a picture of a medieval fortress, with moat, drawbridge, and parapets, evidently a castle. The child was to select the initial consonant in the word that described the picture. The alternatives were D, C, and G. Many children chose D (rather than C for castle) because, they explained, the picture showed a scene from Disneyland.

MacKay (1973) reports a similar analysis of the inherent ambiguity in test items and the practical ability of children to "fill in" meaning. In a test designed to measure reading ability by marking the picture that illustrates the situation described in a preceding phrase, sentence, or paragraph, one item shows a boy apparently swimming, a boy presumably walking, and a car. The stimulus phrase reads, "I went for a ride." The car is to be marked, supposedly because it obviously provides the best illustration of the phrase. But, this one correct association is not so obvious if a child recognizes the past tense of the phrase and the current action shown in the picture. Certainly the interpretation "I went for a ride, but now I am walking" might lead a child to select the second picture. The reading would be accurate and considerable interpretive skill would be used, but the response would be marked as incorrect.

A second example taken from MacKay's research demonstrates how a correct answer can result from an interpretive process that is creative, but considerably different from what the test developer intended. The stimulus phrase reads, "The bird built his own house." The phrase is followed by three pictures that respectively show tree branches, a man-made birdhouse with a small entrance, and a bird's nest containing several eggs. The child selected the third picture, the correct alternative. When an interviewer asked the child to reread the stimulus phrase and explain his reasons for choosing the third picture, the child mistakenly read "owl" rather than "own." He then explained that the hole in the birdhouse portrayed in the second picture was too small for an *owl*, so he picked the picture of the nest. This was an imaginative and reasonable answer for the child, one that he constructed in response to his interpretation of the question — even though he had *misunderstood* the question. The child displayed inferential abilities in arriving at his answer, but the correctness of the answer was not obtained by means of the reading and inferential process intended by the test developer.

GLOSSING OVER INTERPRETIVE PRACTICE

We could provide many more examples, but the theme, we hope, is clear. Meaning is an emergent, occasioned property of everyday life, including life in the classroom. Through talk, gesture, and other symbolic activity, persons signal what is intended, relevant, and expected in a particular context. While general, presumably context-free rules may orient persons to patterns of interaction, these rules are never sufficient guides for behavior. Persons must interpret messages as they arrive at definitions of the situations in which they are members. The job of interpretation requires considerable cognitive, representational, and interactional skill from all participants.

Teachers see instruction, in principle, as explicitly unambiguous. Children gradually acquire knowledge as they listen to directions and practice skills. Yet, in their interaction with children, teachers must deal with the ambiguity of rules, instructions, and assignments. Teachers and students continually engage one another through questions, requests for further information, requests for feedback, and evaluative comments in search of additional information. Teachers and students are continually orienting and reorienting themselves to one another, based on past experience, the interpreted meaning of the present context, and anticipated future events.

This process through which meaning is constituted is glossed over in appraisals of intelligence test results. Test developers construct items that are presumably clear to them and that are thought to tap underlying language, cognitive, and other skills. Correct answers are taken to indicate the presence of these skills, while incorrect answers indicate deficiencies. The number of correct items is tabulated and used as an index of development and learning. But reliance on a test score as an indicator of ability obscures the social practices through which the score was created.

Testing is a social occasion, one with emergent properties that are created and managed by participants. Testers provide a rationale for the occasion and a more or less controlled set of stimuli or directions. Yet, these "standard" conditions are often altered by teacher-testers (Mehan 1973; Friedman 1968), as well as by the test takers. Teachers provide their own versions of the standard directions, permit more or less time than the directions allow, and provide subtle clues to the children on some items. They may also permit children to practice with similar tests and provide "rules of thumb" for guessing, reading directions, and figuring out what the test developer intends for them to do. In other words, teachers tacitly know of the difficulties that children have in searching for meaning in test situations where knowledge and interaction are restricted.

They try to provide more clarity, but testing occasions and test items nevertheless remain highly ambiguous and subject to a wide variety of individual interpretations.

Test scores are taken as valid indicators of ability and skill development and are used to predict intellectual growth. The fact that a child may have utilized rather complex conceptual and analytic skills to arrive at a reasonable but "wrong" answer, given his or her interpretation of the item, is ignored in principle. Likewise, the possibility that a child may have arrived at a "correct" answer by a way of an unanticipated reasoning process is not given general consideration. The score provides an image of the child based on the oversimplified model used to construct and administer the test. The model ignores the situational and contextual intricacies of testing events as social occasions and forces a standard interpretation of results. Prediction, based on these results, is similarly structured by models of "ability" built into the evaluation instrument. Projections of growth and potential development are constructed in terms of that model, with little or no recognition of how past, present, and future are being interpretively assembled.

NEGOTIATING PLACEMENT

Schooling is not just about teaching, learning, and evaluation. It is also full of practical decisions that shape learning paths through the school years. Decisions on how and where children should be placed in schools both reflect the view of a child's anticipated future and provide the context in which that future will be worked out. Consider how negotiated meanings of development and potential are implicated in determining the educational programs into which students should be placed.

One of the authors (Buckholdt) attended a series of conferences between a principal, several teachers, and a social worker. The participants were deciding which eighth-grade students were to advance to an academic high school and which to a terminal program. The discussion revolved around students who, the participants believed, could possibly be assigned to the terminal program. The principal had asked the teachers and the social worker to submit a list of students who would be considered. The students' records were available for the meeting, and they included academic histories, scores on intelligence and achievement tests, family information, and reports from teachers and other school personnel.

The principal asked the group first to select the children about whom there was "no doubt." One teacher suggested that the principal should provide them with the criteria to be used, so they would not be making judgments on different grounds. The principal replied, "Two things are important. If the IQ isn't 80 or above, they have to go to terminal. And if their achievement scores are bad, they should be terminal."

The teachers decided to organize their job by first separating all the children with IQ scores of 80 or lower. They then began inspecting the records of the children with "acceptable" test scores. "How bad do they have to be?" one teacher asked. "Well, that depends," the principal replied. "Generally, if they're below fifth-grade level, they won't make it. But you know these kids. You tell me."

As the teachers started to make decisions, the teacher who at present had a child in her class usually took the lead in making the decision. The others generally concurred, but occasionally there was debate, as the following exchanges show.

TEACHER 3: Michael Phillips. He can do it if he'll come to school. Let's send him on.

PRINCIPAL: He wants out. He told me he wants a full-time job.

TEACHER 3: I know, but he's a bright kid. He just doesn't apply himself. Give him the chance anyway.

PRINCIPAL: Okay.

TEACHER 1: Lonnie Briggs is a tough one. His scores are low, but he's had problems. Those boys he runs with—well, if only he had other friends. I think he can do the work.

TEACHER 2: I don't. I had him last year. He's hopeless. We've had the same smartass behavior from him for four years now.

PRINCIPAL: Yeah, he won't change. We can't just pass our problems on.

TEACHER 1: Okay. You're right.

The meeting continued until a decision had been made about each of the children. Before concluding the meeting, the principal directed their attention to two children who were originally placed in the terminal category because of low intelligence scores:

PRINCIPAL: Let's look at Earl James and Brenda Washington again. They're in the low IQ pile. I don't think their tests were any good. They both do fairly well in school and I know their families. They have big hopes for the kids. I want them tested again and I will give them some extra help.

TEACHER 3: Okay with me. Why not test Morris Wright again, too?

TEACHER 2: Yeah, and Sylvia, too.

PRINCIPAL: Okay, the tester from the board will be around in three weeks. Get your kids ready.

Seven children were retested and six of the seven scored above 80 on the second trial.

What is most noteworthy in these decisions and accounts is the way teachers' past experiences, practical theories, and typifications differentiated the potential of ostensibly similar cases. In the allegedly problematic cases involving Earl James, Brenda Washington, Morris Wright, and Sylvia, for example, it is evident that anticipations of family cooperation and concern in the future were used to construct interpretations that rendered the children's current test scores uncertain. Background knowledge about the children's family lives offered an alternate way of understanding, and responding to, the "hard data" provided by the IQ tests. Practical theories provided some latitude and direction for discovering alternative senses of potential.

Leiter (1974) reports similar examples of occasions on which typifications of both students and teachers are used as the basis for placement decisions. In one instance, two kindergarten teachers and their principal met to decide how to distribute the kindergarten children across three first-grade sections for the following year. The principal had a picture of each child from each of the two kindergarten classes. The teachers were to write two or three descriptors of each child on the back of the picture, then place the child's picture under the name of the first-grade teacher who was most appropriate for the particular child. The conversation proceeded as follows:

PRINCIPAL: Now what I want you to do is take each one of these and on the back with a felt pen or something write two or three descriptors. [Picks up a picture.] What's outstanding about this child, Pa (— — —): sunny, cheerful, aggressive, retiring?

TEACHER 2: Would you please write a long list that we could choose from, those are great. [Laughs.]

TEACHER 1: Now, she's outgoing, an' strong academically strong.

PRINCIPAL: Okay then that goes on the back here. Now recognizing that . . . [First-Grade Teacher A] is a different kind of person, what would be good for this child? Now does this child need somebody strongly oriented academically? Does she need that kind of strong hand? Here's a warm mother [tapping First-Grade Teacher B's card]. . . . Now we're going to have some kids in here who are going to need a Momma-type. All right, here's your Momma. . . . Here's a gal we want to protect [pointing to first-grade teacher C's card which is actually going to be the new teacher's class]. We don't want to give her really tough ones. I will not have her picking up all the kids that are difficult. (Leiter 1974:34–36)

The teachers then proceeded to divide the children into three groups, the strong, the average, and the weak. The strong students were given to the teacher typified as "strongly oriented academically," while the average went to the new teacher and the weak to the "warm mother."

Not all school placements involve regular classrooms. Troublesome students, for example, may be designated for special education. The future for such students is predicated on the ideas that continued growth requires remediation, something in addition to standard regimens of teaching, learning, and assessment. Yet the implicit model for making such decisions parallels the model underlying evaluation in general. The idea, in principle, is that the student's abilities or deficits can be assessed by applying standardized criteria to performance on tests, or to related information.

When school personnel decide that a student's ability cannot be accommodated within the framework of a regular classroom or that the student's behavior or personality falls outside the range of what is acceptable, they may seek special placement for the student. Two of the authors (Buckholdt and Gubrium 1985) conducted participant observation in a residential treatment center for emotionally disturbed children, where students judged to be unteachable in regular school classrooms because of the inability to control emotions were placed for treatment. The decision to seek outside treatment was ostensibly made on the grounds of educational and behavioral deficit. Special placement required certification in writing by a professional multidisciplinary team composed of a community school psychologist, a clinical educator, and other school personnel. Observing a multidisciplinary team's deliberations, it was evident that the meaning of educational or behavior deficit was not straightforwardly drawn from cognitive or behavioral characteristics. The team's certification assessments revealed the same kinds of interpretive dynamics that we have illustrated from other educational settings.

In student Teddy Green's team staffing, for example, we encounter commonplace interpretive practices such as a typification process that selects information from Teddy's case file and assembles it in a coherent pattern that documents his ostensible disturbance and projects future clinical needs. In the following excerpt from the staffing, note how Dee Lerner and Dave Bachman, a clinical educator and school psychologist respectively, attempt to fill in what is lacking in Teddy's file in order to produce a consistent portrait of Teddy's problem that justifies their prognosis and recommendation for further treatment. At one point Lerner and Bachman, together with Floyd Crittenden, the center's principal, focus on Teddy's home neighborhood and the family's residential origins as the relevant interpretive framework for understanding his problems. They use this to make further inferences about the nature of Teddy's disturbance. As in all such decisions, it is important to keep in mind that decision making rests on the unspoken assumptions by the staff that emotional disturbance exists in principle as an educational and behavioral deficit and that students placed at the center are obviously emotionally disturbed, part of what is mundanely taken for granted in order to accomplish the activity at hand (Pollner 1987).

CRITTENDEN: [*opening the staffing*]: We have new psychs [complete psychological reports] on Green and Jones.
BACHMAN: Good. Green first then.
    Staffers try to locate Green's home address because it is not clear in the file where his parents reside.
LERNER: When I don't know the home address, I put the local foster home down. I guess it doesn't matter as long as I'm consistent. Everyone does these [multidisciplinary team reports] differently. [*Turning to Bachman.*] You know that, don't you? I'll put that down anyway. He's ten years old. So he's three years below grade level. Right?
BACHMAN: Uh-huh.

There is a five minute pause for writing.

BACHMAN: He's from Mayville.

CRITTENDEN: They moved into Morley [the local metropolitan area] on Logan Street. Have you ever seen Logan Street? It's like an alley. It's narrower than an alley.

BACHMAN [*laughing as he reads Teddy's file*] When he's in the classroom it says here that the teacher had to put him in his seat at least twice [on the average] in ten minutes of the school day.

CRITTENDEN [*sarcastically*]: Active.

BACHMAN: That was two years ago.

LERNER: It says here that he's two years below grade level. But I think he's three years below. So I'll put that down.

There is another pause for writing.

CRITTENDEN: His gross motion is good.

LERNER: No special hearing or medical [difficulty] either?

CRITTENDEN: No. There's some hearing loss.

BACHMAN: Let's see. He's been here almost two years then?

CRITTENDEN: Teddy? Yes.

LERNER: Does he wear a hearing aid?

CRITTENDEN: No. No. It's a mild loss.

LERNER: Which doesn't affect ...uh...?

CRITTENDEN: No.

BACHMAN [*laughing as he reads the file*]: It says you've decreased his running [being away from the center without permission]. He only runs to the A&P now.

CRITTENDEN: Yeah. You should have seen him go before.

Teddy's running behavior is discussed and elaborated. There is much amused commentary and sarcasm over the image of Teddy's running. Staffers then return to their report writing.

BACHMAN: Millikin [one of the center's consulting psychologists] questioned the language dysfunction here. [*Bachman reads from Teddy's file.*] Two or three years below average. Do you think we should put that in?

CRITTENDEN: He doesn't have a speech problem, really.

LERNER: I think it's cultural deprivation. They seem like hill people. They live in an alley on the south side.

CRITTENDEN: They're from the South, and you might say that they're hill people. He doesn't have any deficiency in swearing though.

You should see his home. What a mess!

LERNER: It's funny about emotionally disturbed children. They really know how to swear. I became an adult after I started to work with these kids.

As the staffing continues, Crittenden describes what he calls the "funny" variability in emotional disturbance, whereupon Lerner offers an explanation for the anomaly, making the variability reasonable.

CRITTENDEN: Yeah. It's funny all right. They're all so different. Like Randy Jones. She [a part-time psychologist] has him as having poor eye-hand coordination. But if you see his handwriting, it's beautiful. He draws carefully. You should see it.

LERNER: It's probably that he wasn't up to par that day.

CRITTENDEN: The mother used to drive me crazy. She was always telling me when Teddy ran. He'd run from anxiety, frustration, and all that.

BACHMAN: Is the mother divorced?

CRITTENDEN: No. But whenever the mother disciplines the kids, it's always, "I'll club you."

Crittenden's pager buzzes and he leaves. Bachman and Lerner take a ten-minute break, then resume their report writing.

LERNER [*talking as she reads Teddy's file*]: This is a classic, isn't it? The typical emotionally disturbed kid, nothing exceptional, just problems of one sort or another.

BACHMAN: Are you saying that academic achievement is around two or three years?

LERNER: He's not a solid third-grade worker. See, he tested a little over three for the psychologist. But the teacher says that he's not quite up to three. But I think its the daily performance that should be counted. Don't you?

BACHMAN: Sure. Yeah.

They pause for writing. Crittenden returns.

LERNER: Now, let's see if I can remember our classic statement for the [center's] goals. I feel like I'm plagiarizing every time I copy it down. [*Laughing as she writes and repeats*.] "Continued placement in a residential treatment center with complete therapeutic remediation with includes family and individual therapy and where a structured social experience can take place." Gee! This is a good statement! We really put our heads together on that one. We should have typed copies of this, Dave [Bachman]. *They write in silence.*

The typification process we see in the assembly of the coherent pattern of Teddy Green's problem provided the basis for both projecting a troubled future and trying to do something about it. The constructionist perspective sensitizes us to the situationally bound practical reasoning that shapes the process through which school personnel assemble and interpret information about their students. This image of organizational processing differs from the commonsensical view that children either possess or do not possess abilities or deficits, or possess them to varying degrees, and that school personnel simply observe, measure, and record them. Teachers and others are directly involved both in making things happen in and out of the classroom, and in deciding or interpreting what is happening. They are, in practice, part of the child's intelligence or deficits. Inasmuch as their participation is articulated through local cultural understandings, such as beliefs about the causal effects of particular regions or neighborhoods on children's achievements or deficits, local culture becomes an integral feature of predicting future growth (Gubrium 1991a).

As a practical setting envisaging the future, moreover, the school and its alternatives are not simply either rational bureaucratic entities or natural systems. Instead, they are constellations of concrete constructive occasions. Both rationality and spontaneity are elements of practical reasoning. This occasioned process constructs and manages growth and change as interpreted entities in their own right, separate and distinct from the rational-bureaucratic and the spontaneous.

Chapter 5 CONSTRUCTING COMPETENCE

"Maturity" and "competence" are popular terms for describing standards of human growth and development. As we noted in chapter 1, many life course theorists—Freud, Erikson, Piaget, and Kohlberg, among others—have used physical growth as a model for the development of psychosexual, cognitive, affective, and moral aspects of the person. In these conventional approaches, the individual grows from relative simplicity to greater complexity of structure and differentiation of function. The physical and social environments may stimulate or retard development, but the sequence or hierarchy of stages follows biogenetic characteristics. Maturity and competence reflect the gradual emergence of innate capacities.

Of course, some individuals seem to mature more quickly or develop greater competencies than others. While acknowledging the developmental course of of human growth, some psychologists have been more interested in the correlates of variation, leading them to investigate both the personality characteristics of the mature or competent individual (e.g., Heath 1965; Elkind 1967; Rogers 1964; Carlson 1965; McKinney 1968) and the environmental conditions that stimulate maturation (e.g., Havinghurst 1951; Hunt 1961). Their findings lead to the conclusion that development is not an inevitable unfolding process, but depends on the proper combination of human potential and environmental contingencies.

Sociologists have also been interested in maturity and competence, but have generally worked with the concept of socialization rather than human development. The concept references both what is to be learned and its functions. The former includes a wide variety of norms, values, skills, and expectations required for the social integration of the person and the stability of society. Socialization is considered to be functional for both the person and the social order if it provides for individual and social integration. Infants are considered incomplete, incompetent, and asocial; they are not yet

118

human inasmuch as they have not been socialized. They cannot yet participate in the integrative work of society, that is, perform in its network of interdependent roles and positions. Through experience gained within a variety of formal and informal settings and institutions, they gradually acquire the cultural resources and interpersonal understandings by which they both recognize themselves and are recognized by others as competent members of the social order.

Maturity and competence, then, are typically construed as individual qualities that people acquire or develop with age and experience. Despite their many differences, psychological theories of human development and sociological ideas about socialization share a strikingly similar view in this regard. The fully socialized or mature adult provides the standard by which we judge competence. Change is developmental—moving in the direction of more complete socialization—if it results in greater maturity, rationality, or responsibility. Lack of change or movement "off course" is seen as faulty socialization, inadequate development, personality defect, immaturity, and the like. The child is naturally deficient vis-a-vis the adult. Although children may have their own sets of interpretive skills, the skills are valuable only if they contribute to further development. If there is perceived continuity between a child's current behavior and desirable future states, we say that growth is evident. Perceived discontinuity between the present and the desired future signals problems. The warning is signaled by labels such as "immature," "irrational," "incompetent," and "unenculturated," depending on whether the interpreter is, say, an ordinary citizen, teacher, psychologist, sociologist, or anthropologist (MacKay 1973).

Conventional theories of aging share the commonsense perspective that development or socialization brings about real changes in individual capability. Change is considered an objective feature of human behavior. It can be differentially evaluated for whether it appears to be moving in the proper direction, toward greater maturity, personal and social integration, and cognitive differentiation and elaboration. Competence is something real, an objective thing that can be studied with scientific precision to reveal process and effect.

Following the theme that life change is socially constituted, this chapter suggests a different perspective. Instead of being a set of traits, we analyze maturity, competence, and related terms as labels people use to assign evaluative meaning to individual capability. In this context, traits are interpretively and interactionally assigned. Orienting primarily to present-time matters, we examine how maturity and competence are circumstantially accomplished.

SITUATED ASSIGNMENT

Developmental psychologists traditionally focus their attention on the particular skills, general abilities, and personality characteristics that individuals acquire at sequential life stages, while sociologists usually consider the structures and processes by which persons internalize the norms, values, and attitudes of their society. Both approaches tend to cast the person as a passive participant in these processes. More significantly, from our standpoint, they fail to examine how various competencies are actually recognized and displayed, how people interpret behavioral displays as indices of competence.

Conventional theories are not sufficient for understanding how personal and social structures are produced and maintained in daily interaction. Developing biogenetic capabilities have no inherent or self-evident meaning. They are assigned meaning by those who witness behavior and interpret it in specific situations, based on tacit and shared understandings of human growth and development. The interpretive practices through which persons identify, label, and judge relative competence show that maturity, wisdom, ability, realism, competence, and related terms are a constitutive vocabulary for assigning developmental meaning to the individual's present capability. Equally important, the vocabulary takes its specific content and relevance from concrete settings and situations.

Competence is a concern in all walks of life. Leiter (1974), for example, describes how typifications of capability are used by teachers to differentiate students. It is evident that the teachers, as others do in different circumstances, invoke their practical agendas and use relevant aspects of their background knowledge of everyday classroom relations to formulate their constructions. One familiar type of student they recognize is the "immature child." This child is easily distracted, cannot sit still during a lesson, and has a short attention span. Boys are less capable than girls in this regard, as are children who are physically smaller than others their own age. A second type is the "bright child." This child learns quickly, without demanding much time or effort from the teacher. His or her social skills may be poor but if he or she learns quickly and his or her verbal skills are good, the child is considered to be bright. A third type of child is the "behavior problem." This child is usually a boy, often of large build, who fights with other children for "no reason at all." A fourth type is the "independent child." He or she can work with very little supervision and finishes assigned tasks before beginning other activities. In other settings, these same children might be typified somewhat differently, such as a child being "basically a good boy" at home or "irreverent" at church, again reflecting the practical issues and local cultures of the context (Gubrium 1989).

The teachers described by Leiter were able to assign children to a "mature" and an "immature" class in one case and to specific teacher types (mamma types, strongly academically oriented, weak academically) in another. They accomplished their classifications without apparent embarrassment or sensitivity to the ad hoc, situated nature of the process. It was routine business for them, undertaken as part of their educational activities. Teachers did not question one another's actions, in principle, nor did they argue about the appropriateness of the categories. The apparent ease with which the teachers applied the typology shows that a system of normative usage was referenced, allowing teachers to sense they were "talking the same language" and pursuing the same objectives in an orderly and rational way.

The teachers possessed the interpretive skills to see and describe behavioral displays as examples of general types, as well as the accounting skills to explain their classifications to an interviewer. Life course imagery filtered in throughout their discussions. Consider the following exchange between a teacher (T) and an interviewer (I) (Leiter 1974:44–45):

T: Now this is Pa, . . . a very interesting child because he's one of the ones who's extremely bright but he is a behavior problem in school. And umm one of the reasons he's a behavior problem is because he — well, I guess I really shouldn't say he's a behavior problem but he's immature. Because he's young and we probably expect too much of him. He's an October birthday which would make him one of the youngest in the class. . . .

I: What are some of the things that give you the impression that he was bright?

T: Oh, he has a fantastic memory. In the group I can read a story and he can be looking out the window or talking to his neighbor and I can ask him the question and he knows the answer like that, you know. At first I would, he would be talking so after I read something or if we'd been discussing something I would say "Pa, what have we been talking about?" And I was doing it because I figured he wouldn't know—and he did.

I: Um humm.

T: And so it was in the total group that he's catching a lot of what they're hearing and if he's a child who can talk to his neighbor and still know the answer you know you've got a bright child on your hands. . . .

Specific behaviors may likewise be assessed for competence. Turning to later life, consider how a so-called activity of daily living—the ability to control one's bowels—was interpretively constituted at Murray Manor, a nursing home for the aged (Gubrium and Buckholdt 1979). A highly touted bowel-training program had been instituted to help residents become more self-sufficient. The program required staff nurses to monitor effectiveness in terms of participants' ability to control their bowel movements. While this would seem to be rather straightforward, in practice it was mediated by locally contingent understanding. On one occasion, for example, an aide entered a resident's room to find that the resident had fully soiled her bed and clothing with feces. One of the nurses on the floor noticed the aide cleaning up and remarked, "I guess Helen's at it again, huh? The program is not helping her too much, is it?" (p. 121). The aide, who was none too pleased at having to tend to the mess, blurted:

> Oh, she knows damn well what she's doing. She just shit everywhere because I was busy helping Stella [another resident] down the hall and you know how she hates Stella. Well, . . . she [Helen] just had to wait a little longer until I could finish. She didn't like that, of course. So she got mad and just BMed all over the place. (p. 121)

Later, when it was time to record Helen's progress in the training program, the aide did *not* count the episode as an instance of incontinence, explaining, "That was different. Helen knew what she was doing and was just trying to get back at me" (p. 122).

The next day, the same aide entered Helen's room to find Helen "red-faced and squirming." She quickly took her to the bathroom where Helen promptly moved her bowels. Helping Helen off the toilet, the aide complimented her on her control. Later, the aide informed a nurse that Helen was "clean" all day, adding, "I think she's really coming around, you know what I mean? I think she's gonna come out one of the best on the floor" (p. 122). While Helen's attributed intentions had been used earlier to discount a soiling episode as incontinence, here intention is glossed over to produce the day's "fact" of total control.

IMPUTING READINESS

For developmental psychologists, the idea of readiness refers to the successful mastery of the characteristic skills of a stage of growth as a prelude to moving on the next. Recall that Piaget, for example, argued that the child cannot begin to perform concrete operations until he or she can extract concepts from experience and make intuitive use of them. Although such skills are not strictly defined by age, they are thought to conform generally to certain age periods.

Notions of developmental readiness are not the exclusive concern of human scientists, however. They are given serious attention and used by laypersons in the commonsense management of their everyday affairs. Assumptions about relationships between age, training, experience, and background and a person's competence to perform adequately in real-life settings guide much of our everyday thinking. Some schoolteachers, for example, believe that children are not "ready to read" until they are six and a half years old (see Hamblin et al. 1971). The teachers locate the reason for this in the children's developmental readiness and not in the historical development or organizational structure of the school. There also is the commonsense theory concerning the relationship between age and the ability to be an "informed" voter. For decades, a person had to be twenty-one years old to vote. Now, apparently because our younger citizens are developing more quickly and have more education, we, as a society, have decided that eighteen-year-olds are capable of participating rationally in the election process. And take the example of a friend of the authors who once applied for the position of chair of the sociology department at a major university. His teaching and publication record were apparently fine enough to place him among the finalists for the job. When he visited the campus, however, department members became quietly concerned about how "young" he was (thirty-one at the time) and how young he looked. Presumably a desirable chairman was more mature, or at least looked more mature. The candidate was not offered the job. Off the record, several department members implicitly linked age and experience with competence as they informally accounted for the decision.

Individual characteristics such as physical size and chronological age are used for imputing readiness in schools in much the same way as educational credentials are used in employment decisions. Take the following rationales teachers provided for placement decisions (Leiter 1974). In this case, teachers were deciding who would go on to first grade and what kind of first grade class would be best for each child.

> . . . Then we have had one other little boy who is very, very immature and he was a November birthday. Just a little, little boy. (p. 43)

> . . . Maybe I ought to put her five plus because she does have a May birthday. (p. 33)

> . . . Because he's young and we probably expect too much of him. He's an October birthday which would make him one of the youngest in the class. (p. 44)

> . . . She's a large child. Now, here's a case where even though she would not be ready for first grade—she's ready for a low first grade—but even if she were not ready in other ways, I still would pass her on to a first grade because that girl...another year in kindergarten?

Look how big she'd be before she went into the first
grade. (p. 63)

Shared understandings linking age and size to behavior help teachers "make sense" of both their observations of children and their
assessments of the children's competence and readiness. Age and
size criteria were invoked both to make the decision and to justify
and explain it.

Age, of course, is only one criterion by which to assess competence. Training or, more important, the certification of training, is
also relevant. Persons are not presumed to be ready or qualified for
most important work unless they have the proper credentials, such
as a college or graduate degree, professional license, or certificate of
apprenticeship. The process of training itself represents a life course
preparation that is understood and invoked to signal readiness.
Commonsense reasoning tells us that education, for example, has a
strong positive, and desirable, relationship with both personal well-
being and economic productivity. The idea is supported by the so-
called human-capital economists who inform us that improvements
in the quality of human resources are a major source of economic
growth (Schultz 1962).

Ivar Berg (1971) questions the validity of arguments that imply
a simple, direct relationship between education and job performance. He reports that interviews with personnel directors, managers, and foremen reveal adamant claims that better-educated workers are better employees. They presumably are more promotable and
possess more "stick-to-it-tiveness." Yet respondents also indicate
that the actual content of the training is not as important as the fact
that employees have completed a program and thus supposedly
demonstrate desirable personal qualities. Berg thus reinterprets the
meaning of education and training, contending that training is a
putative indicator of an ability to adapt and persevere as much as it
represents acquired competence.

Few of the firms Berg studied had ever tested their assumptions,
so Berg attempted to do a systematic study of the relation between
education and job performance. His conclusion was that there was
little, if any, evidence for believing that more highly educated
persons performed better on the job. To produce these findings,
however, Berg had to create measures of job performance, such as

absenteeism, turnover, and job satisfaction. Concern over the relative worth of training hinged on interpretive matters relating to just what it was that education was supposed to affect.

Berg also argues that the sorts of decisions involved in many jobs that require advanced educational credentials do not need the kinds of skills that education and training are supposed to provide. He illustrates his point by quoting a report produced by three Brookings Institution economists in which they describe pricing decisions in "a representative sample of large enterprises," decisions that officially require a good deal of training and technical skill. Berg notes (1971:73) that complex decisions were indeed made, but he characterizes them as being of the "it seemed like a good idea" variety, rather than decisions based on the application of general rules or formulas. He then goes on to argue that the kinds of skills that are ostensibly acquired from education or training are not really the ones needed on the job.

Our interest in Berg's analysis is not to join in the debate about the relevance of educational credentials. Instead, we wish to show how the relevance of education and training is interpretively assembled and *used* to typify persons, to elaborate the notion of readiness, and to make accountable, organizationally relevant decisions. A wide spectrum of opinions coexist and compete. Human-capital theorists hold that training is a necessary investment; they believe competence is a prerequisite for productivity. Some administrators say educational attainment is used to assess a person's "readiness" to be a competent, trustworthy employee. Educated persons are said to be better gambles for the company. Other managers and personnel directors say that important skills are learned on the job; from this point of view, competence is an outgrowth of performance. And while the reasoned and reasonable explanations compete, nearly half of the "well-trained" college recruits leave their companies within the first five years on the job. The point is not that one explanation is better than another but that a variety of accounts centering on competence and training — professional, scientific, and commonsense — are available and are used to make sense of organizational behavior and outcomes.

The various typifications are self-sustaining. For example, when "well trained" recruits fail to work out, the belief in the positive relation between training and job performance is not abandoned.

Instead, descriptions of existing capabilities are reformulated. Organizational personnel argue that those who leave "think they are better than they are." They are called "kids who want too much" or "who haven't yet learned the facts of life, that you have to bide your time." In other words, despite their education, they "really" are not yet competent or mature.

COLLABORATIVE ACCOMPLISHMENT

Clearly, the interpretive activity that constitutes life change and human development is concretely social. Indeed, interaction is so deeply implicated in the production of traits and behaviors that our commonsense belief that these are features of particular individuals must be questioned. In this regard, recall our illustrations of school lessons and testing in chapter 4. The competence, maturity, or developmental readiness established by tallying correct and incorrect answers is typically attributed to the testtaker. A child, for example, takes an IQ test on which he or she responds to questions correctly or incorrectly. The test results are then treated as an indicator of the child's intelligence. But if test answers—putative documents of competence, intelligence, readiness, and so on—are joint productions, attributing test scores to the testtaker alone obscures the interactional process involved, the complex interactional skills of both tester and testtaker. Let us now consider in greater detail how intellectual competence is interactionally produced.

Educational or developmental testing are prototypic instances of the construction and documentation of individual characteristics. Standardized procedures are employed to elicit responses to predetermined questions. The test-taker's responses to the questions are believed to represent the test-taker's competence or development on the dimension being evaluated. Close examination of the testing process reveals cooperative interactional practices that are central to the production of test results. Yet these practices are invisible in reports of performance.

Courtney Marlaire and Douglas Maynard (1990) have studied testing procedures in a developmental disabilities clinic. The clinic attempts to diagnose and correct children's problems that might be the result of mental retardation, learning disability, attention deficit disorder, autism, or other developmental disorders. Clinicians use a variety of tests to assess intelligence, aptitudes, achievement, and general development. Marlaire and Maynard note that these tests rely upon vast unacknowledged interactional processes and skills to produce test scores for the children. While the scores are treated as documents of the children's competence, Marlaire and Maynard argue that they are better understood as the "collaborative productions" of the children and their testers.

Consider, for example, a test that requires the child to provide a synonym for the stimulus word. The testing takes place within verbal exchanges between a child (*CH*) and a clinician (*CL*) like the following sequence: [1]

1. CL: Tell me another word that means angry.
2. CH: S—[.5-second silence while child gazes at the clinician,
3.   who is looking at the test instrument.] Angry, mad.
4. CL: Good. Tell me another word that means the same as lawn.
5. CH: Onk.
6. CL [*points with pencil*]: Lawn.
7. CH: Long—longer?
8. CL: Okay. Tell me another word that means small.
9. CH: Smaller?
10. CL: Another word that means the same.
11. CH: Kay. Small.
12. CL: Yeah, what's another word that means small?
13. CH: Little.
14. CL: Good. You're thinking good now. (Marlaire and Maynard 1990:94)

Superficially, the procedure seems to be a straightforward pattern of stimulus and response, but Marlaire and Maynard point out a necessary interactional component to the child's replies. The child is tentative in proceeding through this test. At line 2 she starts a reply, then hesitates. At line 5 she offers a sound mimicking the clinician's prompt (*onk*) that is not clearly a response to the question. In response to the first hesitation, the clinician strongly and positively responds to the child's eventual answer, confirming its correctness, then moves to another question. The child is credited with a correct response (line 4). In the second instance, however, the clinician repeats the prompt (line 6). This signals the unacceptability of *onk* and provides the child with another opportunity to answer correctly. The exchange thus elaborates the stimulus and provides the child with an additional chance to give the "right" answer. When the correct answer fails to emerge in the child's next utterance, the clinician accepts the answer as given ("okay,"—line 8) and moves on to another prompt. This effectively completes the test item sequence and results in an incorrect response for that item.

Later in the test (lines 8–14), a similar exchange takes place. The clinician asks for another word meaning "small," and the child replies with a version of the prompt ("Smaller?"). This utterance is ambiguous; it is not clear if it is the child's answer or an attempt to clarify or repair the clinician's question. The clinician takes it as the latter and offers an alternate version of the the prompt, soliciting "another word that means the same" but omitting the original stimulus item—"small" (line 10). The child responds by repeating the omitted word (line 11), leading the clinician to repeat the entire prompt (line 12). Thus, instead of responding to the child's utterances as candidate (and incorrect) replies, the clinician treats them as bids for further information or clarification. The clinician's *elaborations* lead to the child's correct answer at line 13.

From this, and similar exchanges, it is clear that the emergence of right and wrong answers depends on the tester as well as the test taker; producing test scores is a collaborative venture. Note, in the next example, how an answer requires both a reply from the test taker and the clinician's acceptance of the child's reply as an answer. Until the answer is mutually established, the testing sequence remains open-ended, with the child's competence unresolved. In the test sequence, the child is asked to specify the appropriate behavior for the situation that the clinician describes. The child has responded to several such prompts before this excerpt begins.

1. CL: What do you do if you cut your finger?
2.   [1 second silence]
3.   What would you do if you cut your finger?
4. CH: Put a Band-aid on it.
5. CL: That's right. What do you do when you're sick?
6. CH: Go to the doctuw.
7. CL: That's right.
8.   [1 second silence]
9.   What do you do when you see your hands are dirty?

10. CH: Go wash em.

11. CL: That's right. [.75 second silence] What do you do if you
12.   go into a room and it's all dark in the room?

13.   [1 second silence]

14. CH: Sweep.

15. CL: Okay. C—is there anything else you can do?

16. CH: Yeah.

17. CL: Let's say you wanna play in the room and you walk in the
18.   room.

19. CH: You wanna pway in the room, you walk in the woom, you
20.   know I have a wight switch on mine, to tuwn the lights
21.   on and off.

22. CL: Yah, so you can turn the lights on and off, can't you.

23. CH: Y.

24. CL: So if it's dark and you wanna play, you turn the lights on.

25. CH: Yup.

26. CL: Yup. Good fer you. (Marlaire 1990:255–56)

As Marlaire (1990) shows, the sequence from line 11 through line 26 clearly results in a co-produced answer. The clinician refuses the child's first answer ("Sweep,"—by which the child may mean "sleep") and asks for another one (line 15). The ensuing exchange finds the clinician elaborating the scenario (line 17) and the child further developing the clinician's input (lines 19–21). At line 22, the clinician elaborates on the child's description, suggesting the behavioral possibility that follows from the presence of a light switch that can be turned on and off. By line 24, the clinician has essentially provided the correct answer for the test prompt, with which the child agrees.

While the score that resulted from this test was treated as a document of the child's competence and maturity, it was the interactional exchange that allowed for its production. Shorn of its interactional particulars, it became an accountable test score, that is, one that will be taken as a reliable, valid, and objective indicator of the child's developmental stage or level. As Marlaire and Maynard (1990) suggest, the practices and skills of both participants in the test are overlooked when assessments are made. Yet they are the invisible interactional scaffolding upon which such tests depend. The more general point relates to where we typically locate competence. While we commonsensically understand it to be an individual characteristic—a matter of an individual capability—we can see that competence is occasioned and interactionally constructed.

Competence is an issue for persons of all ages. Negotiating the routine transactions of everyday life without incident or disruption generates a tacit sense of competence, yet interactional breakdowns may occasion doubt, if not outright questions. But, as Michael Lynch (1983:161) suggests, passing for competent or normal in everyday life does not simply reveal mastery of social conventions; it is a constant project involving others.

Lynch presents a number of common ways by which persons manage others' ostensibly problematic behaviors so as to sustain routine interaction and the others' appearance of competence or normalcy. He notes, for example, how we frequently *humor* others, maintaining a veneer of agreement and geniality even as potential interactional troubles simmer. Instances are commonplace. One manages interactions with an "eccentric" aunt by not discussing specific topics and persons that "set her off." An aging grandmother is mollified—"kept on an even keel"—by agreeing with everything she says and otherwise keeping quiet. She *is screened* off from anything that might "agitate" her. A circle of friends and relations manage the household and do all the driving for a "distracted" acquaintance, *taking over* his responsibilities so he cannot display his inability to discharge them. Or when things go wrong, others provide *accounts* and *excuses*, or *cover up*, for the offending person. The upshot of such practices is to insulate the person being interactionally managed from circumstances that might evoke untoward behavior. Failing this, such behavior can be interpretively monitored and recast. In the process, normalcy is sustained and competence is preserved.

Competence can be managed even when it is the explicit object of attention. Consider, for example, some exchanges from involuntary mental hospitalization hearings where one of the practical issues being considered is the candidate patient's interactional competence or the candidate patient's ability to manage consequential situations without "talking crazy," a colloquial sign of incompetence (Holstein 1988a, 1993). In defending the candidate patient, counsel attempts to prevent "crazy talk." The following extract is from the direct examination of a candidate patient, Katie Maxwell (KM), by the Public Defender (PD) who was handling her case.[2]

1. PD: If they let you go today, Katie, do you have a place to live?
2. KM: Uh huh my mother's (place).
3. PD: Where is your mother's place?
4. KM: In Bellwood.
5. PD: What's the address?
6. KM: One twenty Acton street. I can come // and go as I please.
7. PD [breaking in]: That's fine Katie.
8.   Does your mother say you can live with her?
9. KM: Yeah it's okay with her.
10. PD: Can you eat your meals there?
11. KM: Yeah there's no one there // always watching me.
12. PD [breaking in]: You can just answer yes or no. Okay?
13. KM: Okay.
14. PD: Do you have clothes at your mother's house?
15. KM: Yes.
16. PD: Can you dress yourself?
17. KM: Of course I can.
18. PD: Do you get an (SSI) check in the mail?
19. KM: Yes.
20. PD: Will you give it to your mother?
21. KM: Yes.
22. PD: And will you let her give you your medication?
23. KM: Yeah, whenever I // need it.
24. PD [*breaking in*]: That's good Katie. (Holstein 1988a:462–
       63)

This exchange reveals a set of conversational practices that promote forms of talk that help display a sense of the candidate patient's interactional competence. Note, for example, how the PD's questions were formulated to elicit brief, direct answers. All but one question (line 5) were answerable in a single word. The PD established the adequacy of such answers both explicitly, by instructing the witness simply to answer yes or no (line 12) and tacitly, by accepting brief answers as complete and moving directly to the next question without hesitation. Speaker transition was immediate as the PD claimed her preallocated turn. When Maxwell attempted to elaborate on her answers, however, the PD broke into her response. In three instances (lines 6, 11, and 23), Maxwell tried to embellish or qualify her minimal answer to the PD's question and, each time the embellishments met with intrusions of simultaneous speech. The content of each overlapping utterance indicated that the patient's answer was adequately completed (e.g., line 7: "That's fine Katie."), and, just as significantly, the intrusions into the patient's turns discouraged continuation. The PD thus managed the patient's talk to accomplish the appearance of concise, direct testimony. The PD organized her questions to constrain Maxwell's answers at the first possible turn-completion point (see Sacks et al. 1974), trying to keep testimony directly responsive to the questions asked.

A continuing worry in these hearings, from the PD's point of view, is that candidate patients may begin to "talk crazy." For example, when Maxwell began to elaborate answers at lines 6, 11, and 23, the PD immediately broke in, competing for speakership perhaps as a precaution against Maxwell's iteration of inappropriate answers. On other occasions when talk that might be heard as "crazy" or inappropriate begins to emerge, PDs move quickly to terminate it, as in the following instance involving candidate patient Fred Smitz (FS).

1. PD: Where would you live?
2. FS: I think I'd go to a new board and care home not populated
3.   by rapists // and Iranian agents
4. PD [*breaking in*]: Fine, Mr. Smitz now would you take your
5.   medication?
6. FS: I would if it didn't pass // through the hands of too many
7.   Russians.
8. PD [*breaking in*]: Do you get an SSI check, Mr. Smitz? (Holstein 1988a:463–64)

Here, the candidate patient initially offered an apparently appropriate answer in line 2, but then began to introduce referents that could be heard as delusional. The PD broke in, using the patient's name to refocus his attention, then moved immediately to a new question about medication. In line 6, the patient answered and again began a qualification that culminated in a hearably delusional reference. The PD simultaneously produced another new question. The effect of these intrusions was to override, if not obliterate, the seemingly inappropriate talk that was emerging. Development of topics introduced by "crazy" utterances was aggressively curtailed for the sake of the clients' competence. While the management of witnesses' responses is a feature of all courtroom proceedings, PDs have a special substantive interest in candidate patients' responses in commitment hearings.

While PDs question candidate patients in ways that manage their competence, soliciting brief answers and discouraging elaborations, District Attorneys (DAs), who argue for commitment, encourage more expansive testimony, hoping to elicit instances of incompetence or "crazy" talk. The practice is illustrated in the following excerpt. After asking candidate patient Lisa Sellers (LS) fourteen consecutive questions in a relatively straightforward manner, the DA began a new approach.

1. DA: How do you like summer out here, Lisa?
2. LS: It's okay.
3. DA: How long have you lived here?
4. LS: Since I moved from Houston
5.   [Silence 1 second]
6. LS: About three years ago.
7. DA: Tell me about why you came here.
8. LS: I just came.
9.   [Silence 1 second]
10. LS: You know, I wanted to see the stars, Hollywood.
11.   [Silence 1 second]
12. DA: Uh huh
13. LS: I didn't have no money.
14.   [Silence 1 second]
15. LS: I'd like to get a good place to live.
16.   [Silence 5 seconds]
17. DA: Go on. [spoken simultaneously with next utterance]
18. LS: There was some nice things I brought.
19.   [Silence 1 second]
20. DA: Uh huh
21. LS: Brought them from the rocketship.
22. DA: Oh really?
23. LS: They was just some things I had.
24. DA: From the rocketship?
25. LS: Right.
26. DA: Were you on it?
27. LS: Yeah.
28. DA: Tell me about this rocketship, Lisa. (Holstein 1988a:467)

While the sequence culminates in Ms. Sellers's hearably delusional references to a rocketship, the DA was instrumental in cultivating its display. Throughout the exchange, he encouraged Sellers to take extended and unfocused turns at talk by removing interactional constraints on her speaking turns. He asked very general questions or open-ended requests for information (lines 1, 3, 7, and 17) so that it was never clear precisely when Sellers might have finished her answer. He repeatedly refused to take up his turn at the possible completion of her turns, allowing silence to develop and thus inviting her to fill it. In the face of these repeated silences, Sellers continued to speak and eventually made reference to the rocketship. At this point, the DA responded immediately with "Oh really? (line 22), encouraging confirmation.

Now, this type of response marks a significant noticing that might have accomplished several things. First, it could focus attention on the prior utterance so as to invite further talk on the subject. Such noticings might also call attention to a "faulted" quality of an utterance, suggesting the need for repair. Here, the DA highlighted Ms. Sellers's statement about the "rocketship." His use of "Oh really?" could be heard as an expression of surprise or disbelief, a call for elaboration that invited Ms. Sellers to dispel implied doubts by altering, repairing, retracting, or reframing the problematic utterance. That she declined to retract or explain the claim might be interpreted as further evidence that she was incapable of recognizing and correcting conversational "gaffes" that any competent interactant would probably not make, and certainly would repair, if given the opportunity.

Clearly, this "incompetent" talk is an interactional achievement. The DA requested testimony from the candidate patient, but repeatedly withheld acknowledgment of the testimony's adequacy, promoting more unfocused talk in the process. He further encouraged Sellers to speak, using "Uh huh" to indicate an understanding that an extended unit of talk was in progress and was not yet complete (Schegloff 1982), and by declining possible turns at talk altogether. He resumed an active role in the dialogue only after hearably "crazy talk" emerged, at which point he attempted to focus the discussion on the "crazy" topic and encourage Sellers to elaborate. For her part, Sellers sustained the ongoing conversation by terminating silences that had begun to emerge at failed speaker-transition points. She repeatedly elaborated responses and eventually produced the "crazy" talk cited as evidence of her interactional incompetence. But, ironically, it was her ability to cooperate with the DA in extending the conversation—her *conversational* competence—that allowed for the emergence of that very talk.

While involuntary commitment proceedings are not typical everyday interactions, we find similar displays in more common-place settings. Since interactants' practical interest in everyday encounters is generally to conduct the exchange so that everything goes smoothly (Garfinkel 1967), we are much more likely to collaborate in the production of competence than to promote the sorts of interactional disruptions that make incompetence visible and interaction difficult. In either case, however, it is clear that much of what we commonsensically attribute to individuals as internal or individual traits and abilities can be construed as social construc-tions.

Interactional monitoring and management may lead one to actually speak and act for others in the interest of sustaining the public impression of competence, a form of interlocutorship. Con-sider the following encounter that took place in a neighborhood market. An elderly couple, Henry and Millie, met a female acquain-tance named Marge. After exchanging greetings with Millie, Marge turned to Henry and initiated the following "conversation":

MARGE: So how have you been feeling Henry?
MILLIE: Oh, he's been perkin' right along.
MARGE: Think winter's about through huh Hank?
MILLIE: He sure does. He's really happy to be able to get out.

Without a word from Henry, Henry's thoughts and feelings are conveyed by his wife. This "conversation" takes place in the sequential environment of questions and answers that, in most important respects, resembles normal conversation (see Sacks et al. 1974). Typically, speakers transfer speakership by explicitly or tacitly designating the next speaker. While Millie has apparently violated what might be seen as Marge's right to select the next person to talk, Marge does not treat it as such. Instead she asks another question, indicating that, for all practical purposes, the original question has been adequately understood and answered, thus confirming the trajectory of the conversation. Marge and Millie do the talking in this sequence, while Henry's silence makes him an accomplice in sustaining the impression of "his" participation as competent.

Nowhere is this sort of practice more poignant, perhaps, than in the case of victims of Alzheimer's disease (Gubrium 1986a, 1986b). Alzheimer's disease, or senile dementia, is widely assumed to "rob" persons of their minds. Victims experience confusion, forgetfulness, depression, disorientation, and agitation. Severe dementia virtually disables the victim so that one no longer recognizes once-familiar persons or objects and is unable to manage routine activities such as eating, voiding, and grooming. Yet, while the victim's outward appearance and gestures may provide little or no indication of an underlying competence, dedicated caregivers may persist in sustaining the last glimmers of a once-vital, competent person.

Caregivers, for example, often express the sentiment that "it is up to us" to look and listen carefully for what the Alzheimer's victim is trying to communicate. A familiar claim is that those who truly love the person can make the difference between the continued realization of the victim's personhood as opposed to his or her becoming the "mere shell" of a former self. In the words of a member of an Alzheimer's disease caregiver support group:

> We all have gone through it. I know the feeling . . . , like you just know in your heart of hearts that he's [the Alzheimer's victim] in there and that if you let go, that's it. So you keep on trying and trying and trying. You've got to keep the faith, that it's him and just work at him, 'cause if you don't . . . well, I'm afraid we've lost them. (Gubrium 1986b:41)

Caregivers may persist in "articulating" the victim's mind long after he or she has lost any capacity for self-expression. Contrary to Mead's (1934) view that the individual expresses him or herself to others, the Alzheimer's experience finds others literally speaking and "doing" the mind of the victim as a way of preserving it. Mind thus becomes a social entity, something interactionally assigned and sustained, both by and for whomever assumes it to exist.

Whether it is dealing with victims of senile dementia, developing children, an "embarrassing" husband, or an "eccentric" aunt, characteristics like mind, maturity, and competence are pervasively dialogic — interactionally constructed, sustained, and preserved (Coulter 1979, 1989; Pollner 1975; Gergen and Davis 1985). The sheer ubiquity of competence-sustaining practices thus requires an analytic reassessment of just what competence is in everyday life. As we notice the extent to which the meaning of traits and behaviors is socially constructed, we must reconsider the entire issue of the human agency involved, as well as its attendant structures — mind, self, personality, intelligence, and the like. Persons across the life span are constitutively assisted in displaying their competence. Examples are commonplace in everyday interaction. The competence of children (Marlaire 1990; Marlaire and Maynard 1990; Mehan 1973, 1974; Pollner and McDonald-Wikler 1985), college students (Holstein 1983; Lynch 1983), young and midlife adults (Holstein 1988a; Sampson et al. 1962; Yarrow et al. 1955), and old people (Gubrium 1986a, 1986b) have all been documented as social accomplishments.

ACCOUNTING FOR INCOMPETENCE

Whereas competence-producing practices may be practically invisible, ascriptions of incompetence are often accompanied by behavioral explanations. Everyday reasoning can invoke accounts (Scott and Lyman 1968) for deviance or incompetence that sound remarkably sociological or criminological, or even gerontological, as Gubrium and Wallace (1990) and Holstein (1990) show for everyday reasoning about the causes and consequences of age-related experiences.

Consider the practice of accounting for delinquency in this regard. Juvenile delinquents are believed to be incompetent in terms of various criteria that are especially tuned into age or life course location. Psychologists locate problems of youth in emotional conflicts of one sort or another. Sociologists investigate factors such as the family, adult community, peer influences, and/or the structural inconsistencies that lead to delinquency. The fact that delinquency exists — as indicated by police, court, school, and other records — is more or less taken for granted. Yet the social process of recognizing delinquents and reaching some decision about their official classification is by no means a straightforward application of legal statutes to behavioral displays.

Irving Piliavin and Scott Briar (1964) report, for example, that police exercise considerable discretion in encounters with juveniles. Five alternative dispositions are available: outright release, release and submission on an interrogation report, official reprimand and release to parent, citation to juvenile court, and arrest and confinement. Police discretion is supported by an unofficial belief among police officers that correctional or rehabilitation alternatives do not help most young people, as well as by the official training manual, which states that "age, attitude, and prior criminal record" should be considered in all but the most serious offenses. The character of the juvenile, in most cases, rather than the specific offense, is officially used to determine disposition. The process closely resembles the decision-making process that Robert Emerson (1969) describes in juvenile courts.

Piliavin and Briar note that in the field, officers have little or no information on the past offenses, school performance, personal adjustment, or family situation of individual juveniles. Decisions are based on cues that emerge from the immediate encounter and that are used to assess character. These cues include age, race, grooming, dress, and especially demeanor. Those who act their age — appearing neither overly immature nor worldly beyond their years — are generally not seen as serious problems. Juveniles who are contrite, show fear of sanctions, and are respectful are judged to be "salvageable" and are released with only a reprimand. Those who display nonchalance, rebelliousness, or impenitence are seen as "would-be tough guys" or "punks." Black males are judged to be particularly problematic and are most likely to be stopped and interrogated, and they receive more serious sanctions.

Police discretion, then, is considerable, even in very serious cases. Take the following two situations involving alleged sex offenses observed and recorded by Piliavin and Briar (1964) in this regard.

Case 1

The interrogation of "A" (an eighteen-year-old lower-class white male accused of statutory rape) was assigned to a police sergeant with long experience on the force. As I sat in his office while we waited for the youth to arrive for questioning, the sergeant expressed his uncertainty as to what he should do with this young man. On the one hand, he could not ignore the fact that an offense had been committed; he had been informed, in fact, that the youth was prepared to confess to the offense. Nor could he overlook the continued pressure from the girl's father (an important political figure) for the police to take severe action against the youth. On the other hand, the sergeant had formed a low opinion of the girl's moral character, and he considered it unfair to charge "A" with statutory rape when the girl was a willing partner to the offense and might even have been the instigator of it. However, his sense of injustice concerning "A" was tempered by his image of the youth as a "punk," based, he explained, on information he had received that the youth belonged to a certain gang, the members of which were well known to, and disliked by, the police. Nevertheless, as we prepared to leave his office to interview "A," the sergeant was still in doubt as to what he should do with him.

As we walked down the corridor to the interrogation room, the sergeant was stopped by a reporter from the local newspaper. In an excited tone of voice, the reporter explained that his editor was pressing him to get further information about this case. The newspaper had printed some of the facts about the girl's disappearance, and as a consequence the girl's father was threatening suit against the paper for defamation of the girl's character. It would strengthen the newspaper's position, the reporter explained, if the police had information indicating that the girl's associates, particularly the youth the sergeant was about to interrogate, were persons of disreputable character. This stimulus seemed to resolve the sergeant's uncertainty. He told the reporter, "unofficially," that the youth was known to be an undesirable person, citing as evidence his membership in the delinquent gang. Furthermore, the sergeant added that he had evidence that this youth had been intimate with the girl over a period of many months. When the reporter asked if the police were planning to do anything to the youth, the sergeant answered that he intended to charge the youth with statutory rape.

In the interrogation, however, three points quickly emerged which profoundly affected the sergeant's judgment of the youth. First, the youth was polite and cooperative; he consistently addressed the officer as "sir," answered all questions quietly, and signed a statement implicating himself in numerous counts of statutory rape. Second, the youth's intentions toward the girl appeared to have been honorable; for example, he said that he wanted to marry her eventually. Third, the youth was not in fact a member of the gang in question. The sergeant's attitude became increasingly sympathetic, and after we left the interrogation room he announced his intention to "get 'A' off the hook," meaning that he wanted to have the charges against "A" reduced or, if possible, dropped.

Case 2

Officers "X" and "Y" brought into the police station a seventeen-year-old white boy who, along with two older companions, had been found in a home having sex relations with a fifteen-year-old girl. The boy responded to police officers' queries slowly and with obvious disregard. It was apparent that his lack of deference toward the officers and his failure to evidence concern about his situation were irritating his questioners. Finally, one of the officers turned to me and, obviously angry, commented that in his view the boy was simply a "stud" interested only in sex, eating, and sleeping. The policemen conjectured that the boy "probably already had knocked up half a dozen girls." The boy ignored these remarks, except for an occasional stare at the patrolmen. Turning to the boy, the officer remarked,

> "What the hell am I going to do with you?" And again
> the boy simply returned the officer's gaze. The latter
> than said, "Well, I guess we'll just have to put you away
> for a while." An arrest report was then made out and the
> boy was taken to Juvenile Hall. (Piliavin and Briar
> 1964:211)

The presumed character of the person is not the only consideration that influences police discretion in particular cases. Researchers have reported, for example, that situational factors such as the presence of an audience or a complaining witness, or a satisfactory place other than jail to deposit the person, may influence the decision to arrest or release (Sudnow 1965; Bittner 1967a, 1967b). From the constructionist perspective, it is important to note how mundane theories of criminality are used to interpret "what really happened" and what sort of person was involved. One cannot predict the disposition of cases merely from a knowledge of the law. Theory-like accounts of people's actions, including hypotheses about why different kinds of people behave as they do and what they can be trusted to do in the future, articulate behavioral displays with the penal code. In an important sense, the law is used to justify whatever practical decisions or character imputations criminal justice personnel have made.[3] If the person is judged to be a "good risk," a way can be found to avoid formal booking and detention. Likewise, the law can be used to legitimize more punitive treatment for "bad risk" cases. The work of law-enforcement personnel in interpreting the meaning of behavioral displays and in articulating behavior with the law is an important instance of what Robert Emerson and Sheldon Messinger (1977) call the "micropolitics" of trouble, interactional negotiations through which persons are judged to be incompetent, immature, and such, and through which practical decisions are made.

Aaron Cicourel's *The Social Organizational of Juvenile Justice* (1968) provides further illustration of the accounting process among probation officers who decide the meaning of the particular actions of young persons on probation. Cicourel argues that the probation officer and youthful offender implicitly develop a sense of trust between themselves that includes expressed feelings of regret about previous behavior, admission that it was wrong, and promises to try to do better. Future behavior is interpreted in light of this implicit trust. The probation officer, for example, may reevaluate past behavior and conclude that there actually was no basis for the trust or that the present incident really does not require any basic reinterpretation of the trusting relationship but only a reminder of its existence.

Consider the following dialogue between a female probation officer (PO) and Audrey (A), a fifteen-year-old female juvenile who had been reported to the police by school officials for fighting. Audrey was already on probation at the time of the incident. The following segment of the conversation comes after Audrey has admitted that it is wrong to fight and has promised that in the future she will simply "walk away" from situations where a fight may be brewing.

PO: Well, Audrey, you've overcome a lot of your problems, you really have. But now that we see maybe another problem is going to start getting you in trouble, this is the time to start handling that problem. [*Pause*.] Right? Not wait until it becomes so serious that it is difficult to tell other people that you're going to stop doing it. Now they'll still believe you, like Mr. James. If you're not going to fight any more or not get mixed up in this stuff any more, he'll believe you. But if you went on doing it for a couple of months, you know, he'll find it difficult to believe you, wouldn't he?

A: Yes.

PO: So you stick by what you've told him [*pause*], that you're not going to get in any more trouble, all right? [cut off as "all right" is uttered]

A: You know, I could have went to juvie again, but Mr. James say uh . . . [cut off by probation officer].

PO: I know it. He helped you.

A: I know, 'cause he said I hadn't been in no trouble since I had been in.

PO: See [*pause*], so that good time helped you. If you had gotten in trouble right away he wouldn't have known if you could behave yourself. And he probably would have, you know, let you go to Juvenile Hall, but since you had all this — how many months? — six or seven months?

A: I figured eleven months.

PO: Eleven months.

A: At the home.

PO: Eleven months with no real difficulties either at home or at school, right?

A: Yeah.

PO: So that's why he knew if you said you won't get in more trouble he knows you can if you stick by that.

A: You see I gotta . . . [cut off by probation officer].

PO: He trusts you, Audrey, so it is up to you to keep his trust. . . . [The conversation continues.] I, I would have to figure out what would be best for you, Audrey. I don't know what would be best, but if you don't stop having these problems that you just started having, I'd have to think up something.

A: Oh, I can stop having problems.

PO: Well, then you'd better. You show me that you can and then I won't have to make any decisions. Right? I'm coming out here today mainly just to warn you about what can happen if you do any more of this. Do you understand that?

A: Uh, hmm.

PO: You have anything you want to talk about? If you want to stay there, well, this is fine with me. I go along with that. I think it's a real good idea. I'm not saying forever. I can't promise you forever either. Right?

A: Yeah. (Cicourel 1968:153–57)

Cicourel notes that the probation officer has not chosen to see this incident as a violation of probation. Yet the officer makes it clear that further troubles may force her to a different conclusion. The juvenile apparently displayed a "cooperative" or "right" attitude on this occasion, but there is a warning that future problems may cause the officer to reevaluate her interpretation of "what is best" for the juvenile.

The probation officer must now articulate her interpretation of the meaning of Audrey's recent behavior and her decision about what should be done about it with general policies or rules of the criminal justice system. The articulation is accomplished by producing a report (a portion of which is presented here) which manages the impression or interpretation that the probation officer wishes to give:

A couple of minor incidents since — yesterday she and some other girls jumped on a laundry truck at school and Audrey didn't obey bus driver on bus. However, Mr. J. reports that Audrey's attitude was good — admitted everything and promised she wouldn't any more. (Cicourel 1968:163)

The description of the situation as "minor" and of Audrey's attitude as "good — admitted everything and promised she wouldn't any more" justified the decision to treat this incident as insignificant and not to reevaluate the current disposition. Audrey had earlier been placed in a foster home after she had been accused of several thefts. The probation officer discovered what she called "a lack of adult and parental supervision and control. Both parents are employed and either unable or uninterested in having Audrey properly supervised." To the probation officer it was "obvious that Audrey has quite a problem with thievery and should have some type of professional help."

Hospital authorities agreed: "She has an...extremely low self-esteem which she compensates by stealing" (Cicourel 1968:131). Audrey was thus typified as a clinical type, a girl with "deep underlying problems" that caused her to break the law. The probation officer interpreted her current behavior as one more unfortunate example of Audrey's difficult, but potentially winnable battle with emotional problems, rather than an additional episode in a developing career of a hopeless "criminal" type. Thus, Audrey's troubled life course was given a psychological, rather than criminal, cast.

The production of a delinquent career does not simply grow out of the juvenile's experience. Probation officers, police, school authorities, and parents participate in the work of deciding what has really happened to a troubled youngster, what the behavior means in terms of the kind of person this is, and what can be expected from him or her in the future. The youth may behave in ways that can be taken as signs of good character, cooperation, rebelliousness, defiance, being in or out of line with age, and myriad similar typifications. The talk of the parents, their personal appearance and the condition of their home, and their expressed (or lack of) concern for their child is used by police and probation officers to reveal positive resources for change or continuing contributions to delinquency (see Gubrium and Holstein 1990, chap. 5).

The police apply commonsense theories of criminality to view some juveniles as "kids with normal problems" and others as "future criminals" who need to be dealt with now. The probation officers, armed with vernacular psychological explanations of juvenile problems and rehabilitation, see deep, emotional problems rooted primarily in the family and cultural environment and secondarily in schools and peer relationships. Juvenile courts routinely respond in similar ways to what they consider typical troubled lives (Emerson 1969). All told, the full range of ordinary reasoning has many conceptually affinities with the spectrum of conventional approaches to life change presented in chapter 1, showing native facsimiles of scientific usage.

Cicourel (1968) describes the production of delinquent careers in detailed case studies. We draw on his study for the following illustration of the ways that police and probation officers use practical theories to decide what to do with a troublesome youth — a boy named Smithfield. Smithfield, an African American, was accused of burglary, petty theft, and defiance of school authority on at least eight occasions over a period of three years. The following reports on the boy's behavior were prepared by school personnel:

> Smithfield is mentally retarded, or at least appears that way. He would profit from placement in a special class. Smithfield responds well to praise and recognition, and these methods should probably be used in teaching self-control and acceptable social behavior [sixth grade]. (Cicourel 1968:204)

> During the time that Smithfield has been in the room, his adjustment has been very ineffective. His social values seem to be functioning at a different level than the rest of the class. He appears to have no personal goals and does not appear to recognize significant problems which face him. The antagonistic attitude with which he meets both students and teachers aggravates all of his social situations [seventh grade]. (p. 207)

Would rather tell a lie than tell the truth. A typical
sentence: "I didn't do it. Besides you did not catch me."
Has a hard time keeping his hands off other people's
property. I have changed his seat in class several times,
hoping he would improve, to no avail. . . . What
suggestions can one make for a boy who is dishonest, a
chronic liar, a very poor student, and constant troublemaker [eighth grade]. (p. 217)

The accounts provided by the school give a graphic picture of
Smithfield and his troubles. His academic progress is poor and he is
considered disruptive, a chronic troublemaker, and a liar.

There also were reports from juvenile authorities. According to
one report:

Smithfield appears to be an emotionally disturbed boy
who has considerable difficulty relating to peers. He is
loud and aggressive, and has a tendency to pick fights
with the smaller and less physically adept group members. He refuses to accept authority of any nature. When
counselled, concerning his negative conduct and attitude, he becomes emotionally upset using crying tactics
as a means of getting sympathy instead of admonish-
ment. (pp. 218–19)

Apparently the police and school officials agree that something
is wrong with Smithfield. They describe him as a poor student,
mentally retarded, emotionally disturbed, aggressive, and disre-
spectful of authority. The "underlying problems," however, are not
consistently revealed. They are left to the diagnostic skill or interpretive ability of the probation officer who determines not only what is
wrong but what should be done, implicating the family in the process
(see Gubrium 1992). The probation officer reports the following:

Mrs. Elston [Smithfield's mother] is handicapped in
coping with her son's problems, primarily because of
her inability to be firm. She does realize, after firm
counselling, that it is her responsibility as a parent to
work with agencies that are attempting to assist her. It

is encouraging to note the mother figure has taken a
firmer attitude in the matter of her delinquent son and
will attempt to be more realistic in the future. (Cicourel
1968:211)

Cicourel notes that there is little the probation officer can add to
the above remarks. At this point it appears to the officer that a change
of environment as well as schools possibly will assist those concerned in rehabilitating this child. Cicourel continues his description
of the case:

It appeared to this writer that Mrs. Elston was able to
control Smithfield's activities and companions for a
long period of time but that during the current year
Smithfield acquired undesirable companions without
the knowledge of his mother. Consequently, his general
attitude regressed. The school personnel have acknowledged that they are willing to continue working with
Smithfield and the minor's mother has acknowledged a
desire to continue working with him and further acknowledges that she will contact the Probation Officer
if the minor does not conform. Therefore, the Probation
Officer is recommending that Smithfield be continued
on probation and allowed to remain in the custody of his
mother, but it is further recommended that the court
instruct the minor and his mother regarding their responsibilities and inform them that if they are not able
to meet them, the Court will find it necessary to remove
the minor from his home and place him elsewhere. (p.
221)

These official reports do not reveal the complete range of
practical information used by the police, school officials, and
probation officers to interpret Smithfield's behavior as exemplary of
a type of person. For example, while it was not evident in the
foregoing extracts, Smithfield's racial and social-class background
was cited by the police to account for their claim that he would be
a source of trouble and a likely suspect whenever there is a crime.
The police assumed that he would lie about his involvement and
would attempt to conceal evidence. An unhappy marriage that ended

in the separation of the boy's parents and the supervision of "trouble-prone" children by an overburdened mother was also useful information for the probation officer. Such knowledge apparently allowed the officer to "understand" how such behavior and attitudes could develop and to suggest remedial intervention.

The reports do not provide sufficient detail to allow us to know what Smithfield actually did or said on particular occasions. But even if we had more descriptive information, the reports would still require interpretation. Individuals do not simply possess immature, incompetent, delinquent, or similar characteristics that are self-evident in their behavior, even while they may be recounted as such. Smithfield's case was made understandable through the application of commonsense theories about "boys like Smithfield." Race, family problems, cultural deprivation, bad peer influences, and other undesirable effects were believed to be evident or easily "read" from his behavior. Police, school, and probation personnel took this for granted.

In order for a person to be salvageable, the origin of his problem must be found in some set of correctable conditions. Home, school, or peer groups can figure in a process of intervention, both as putative causes and as justifications for proposed solutions (Darrough 1990). In Smithfield's case, the typification of a juvenile as an "emotional problem" provided the probation officer with a ready-made account for a variety of problematic behaviors as well as a general strategy for change. The probation officer was reluctant to recommend severe punishment because he believed he had identified the reasons for the problems and felt sure that remedial action could be helpful. Knowing that the police believed that probation officers were too "soft" on delinquents and that punishment was called for in more cases, the probation officer's official reports to the court downplayed the significance of the delinquent activity as such. He argued instead for a clinical interpretation of "deep problems," which might be corrected with the appropriate treatment. For the probation officer, Smithfield was salvageable, while for the police he was on the course of an inevitable delinquent career, reflecting the respective officers' organizational standpoints.

INTERPRETIVE VARIABILITY

Patterns revealing competence are actively assembled, reflecting practical circumstances and orientations. The job is never finally completed, as persons' characteristics and competence, and the meaningful course of their development, are not interpretively fixed. As concrete as they may seem to us in everyday life, traits, identities, and competencies are reformulated in light of changing information, orientations, and the practical demands of circumstance.

Consider, for example, Houston Wood's analysis of the fluid character of traits, problems, and incapacities attributed to patients on an inpatient psychiatric ward (reported in Mehan and Wood 1975). The ward staff used a variety of categories to characterize the patients in their charge. They saw the ward as populated by "babies," "good patients," "niggers," "sociopaths," "depressives," and "lost souls," among others. While some terms were borrowed from professional vocabularies, they all were used as vernacular categorizations that reflected the attendants' practical concerns about, and appraisals of, those being labeled.

One patient, Jimmy Lee Jackson, was originally typified as a "nigger" by the ward attendants. For them, Jackson was "lazy, and . . . without morals or scruples." The attendants said that Jackson was "cunning" and would attempt to ingratiate himself with staff in order to get attention and special treatment (Mehan and Wood 1975:21). To the extent Jackson's past or future was noted, it referenced the purported life course of the typical "nigger."

One evening, Jackson suffered from a toothache. Unable to get the staff to do anything about it, he rammed his arm through a window pane in one of the ward's locked doors, inflicting severe lacerations that required many stitches. Out of the bloody scene emerged an account of the incident as a suicide attempt. A new typification of Jackson accompanied the account. Virtually overnight, Jackson was interpretively transformed from being a "nigger" into being a "depressive." His past behavior on the ward — behavior that had made it "clear" that he was a "nigger" — was reinterpreted in light of his suicide attempt and what it now implied about the kind of patient Jackson actually was. Particulars were reconstructed to fit with the new categorization. Prior "laziness" was now a manifestation of depression. Behaviors previously seen as disingenuous were regarded as sincere. Ward personnel now listened to Jackson with sympathy. They gave him whatever he requested and no longer pressured him to do more work on the ward. The attendants came to believe that Jackson had *always* been a depressive and that they had always seen him as such.

The staff treated Jackson as a depressive for quite some time. Wood reports, however, that new events and circumstances later led staff members to alter the characterization. They reinterpreted the window-breaking incident, reformulating the "suicide" attempt as a "fake," an attempt to "con" the staff. Jackson became known as a "sociopath" and behavior toward him aligned with the new view.

As Jimmy Lee Jackson's problems and characteristics were transformed, the ongoing process of interpretation reorganized the course of his problematic behaviors on the ward. His history of troubles did not build progressively and incrementally from incident to event toward a final outcome in a cumulative fashion. Instead, his problem and its history were reformulated through interpretive leaps, from one understanding of what had happened to another— a process Foucault (1965) might have described as a practical archaeology of madness at the level of social interaction. The process of interpretation made visible concrete life patterns, which could evaporate in an instant with the application of a new framework.

ORGANIZATIONAL EMBEDDEDNESS

As fluid as the interpretation process is, it is not without substantive organization. Particular, local categories combine with more general vocabularies to give a situated cast to competence. In a manner of speaking, one interpretive domain's assigned sense of competence for a person is not necessarily the same as another's. Local interpretive cultures and practical goals and orientations influence the assignment of meaning; context delimits the diversity of interpretation. Despite the variability of interpretations of Jimmy Lee Jackson, for example, the categories applied all reflected the psychological orientation and custodial concerns of the psychiatric ward, with its staff's decided bent toward psychological vocabularies. In general terms, the process that yields patterns of competence, development, and change is situationally sensitive, indeed organizationally embedded (Gubrium 1988a).

The situated character of interpretive practice is vividly illustrated in a case one of the authors (Holstein) observed at a child guidance clinic. The clinic had several departments and programs providing a variety of outpatient therapies and services for children reporting emotional and related troubles. One client, twelve-year-old Charles Grady, was originally referred to the clinic by the police department as a "diversionary alternative" to the juvenile justice system. He had a history of disruptive behavior in school and a growing record of informal encounters with the police. After being apprehended for loitering at a fast-food restaurant with a "rowdy" group of boys and refusing to leave, a police juvenile officer told Charles and his parents that Charles would either have to enroll in the clinic's Delinquency Prevention Program or face charges in juvenile court.

One of the central principles that guided the program was the belief that juveniles engaged in deviant and disruptive activities in response to peer-group pressure, a vernacular version of conventional theorizing about the identification of selves in relation to others. One of the clinic's goals was to provide positive alternatives to so-called gang pressures. Charles was assigned to a peer group led by a counselor named Mr. Burke. Under Burke's guidance, Charles was integrated into adult-supervised, peer-oriented activities that took him away from his normal after-school routines. Burke explained that the problem with boys like Charles was they were extremely susceptible to the bad influences of friends and others of their own age group whom they looked up to or admired. Charles, and others like him, would gravitate toward gang membership because "preadolescence is a time when kids are looking for acceptance, approval, anything to prove that they belong." According to Burke, Charles's misbehavior in school, his brushes with the law, and his tendency to get into fights and skirmishes was proof that Charles was trying to impress a crowd of "undesirables," to become one of them. Charles's inability to integrate into normal activities and settings was considered to be a manifestation of his need to belong to another group.

Three weeks into the program, Charles was again apprehended by the police, this time for minor vandalism on school property. Returned to the clinic, Charles's case was evaluated by the Youth Programs supervisor and one of the staff therapists, a Mr. Miller. In the course of the discussion, Miller commented on the results of the cognitive and emotional development tests Charles had been administered at intake. Miller suggested that perhaps he should "take a look at Charles," and, following a two hour interview, he offered an alternate perspective on Charles' problem. Writing in Charles's case file, Miller indicated that Charles's "antisocial outbursts" were due to "misdirected frustration and energy." Shifting the characterizing discourse from the social to the psychosexual, Miller noted that Charles was "going through a difficult adolescence. He has difficulty adjusting to newly developed sexuality and physical maturity. He vents his feeling and frustrations in aggressive outbursts and senseless acts of hostility and destruction." Miller recommended that Charles begin weekly therapy sessions, explaining to the supervisor that "Charles' psychosocial development and social skills haven't caught up with his hormones," which was now understandable in the context of Charles's referral to the clinic's youth program, which was psychologically oriented.

Charles' participation in clinic activities continued, apparently without major incident, for another month. Reports from the school and file entries by both Burke and Miller, however, indicated that Charles was still prone to disruptions and fighting. By sheer coincidence, Charles's parents arranged for Charles to have a general physical examination by a physician, Dr. Cook, in anticipation of enrolling Charles in a summer camp. During the examination, Charles's mother apparently mentioned some of Charles's recent troubles. She later told the supervisor at the clinic that Dr. Cook had suggested the possibility that her son was hyperactive. Cook apparently had done some tests and written a prescription for Ritalin, the local pharmacological treatment of choice at the time. Mrs. Grady reported that the doctor said, "Charles acts so immature because he probably has some sort of medical disorder."

As the case moved from one setting to another, its interpretive jurisdiction changed. Charles's traits and behaviors fell into three contrasting organizational contexts, each with its own behavioral understandings. Burke brought a distinctly social outlook to the interpretive enterprise, while Miller's focus was oriented to Charles's psychosexual makeup. As might be expected, the MD's interpretation was physiological. Their views were not idiosyncratic, however, as each oriented to professional and organizational ways of dealing with the problem under consideration. Burke worked within a "socialization" program, Miller within a psychotherapeutic setting, and Cook in a medical office with its arsenal of psychopharmaceutic resources at his disposal.

The emergent interpretations of Charles and his problem reflect practical objectives and local interpretive groundings. Charles's life course is embedded in related organizational and professional outlooks and concerns. Burke, for example, characterized Charles as a "preadolescent" in the throes of a battle with peer pressure. For Miller, the psychotherapist, the problem was Charles's adolescence with its untamed hormonal advances outstripping Charles's ability to cope with, and properly channel, them. Dr. Cook portrayed Charles's disruptive behavior as "immature," the product of hyperkinetic disorder. The life course was prominent in each of these descriptions, but each located the boy differently. While organizational embeddedness does not determine how its participants categorize things and occurrences, it does provide locally "customary and usual" means of doing so. And, in the process, the locally-grounded discourses "deprivatize" persons' characteristics and problems, making ostensibly private, personal traits into matters of public interpretation.

NOTES

1. These transcripts have been slightly simplified from the original published versions.
2. In the following excerpts, double slashes (//) indicate the onset of simultaneous speech.
3. Ironically, criminals reference their own rules or code to make sense of "deviant" behavior. See, for example, Wieder's (1988) account of telling the "convict code."

Chapter 6   BIOGRAPHICAL WORK

In chapters 4 and 5, we explored several issues associated with the future and the present as time orientations to life change. We now turn to the personal past and consider its social construction, using the term "biography" to refer to a description or account of events in someone's past. We continue to focus on ordinary usage and how biographers of everyday life construct and reconstruct personal histories and life stories. Everyday biographies take diverse forms, from a casual reminiscence about growing up, to a newspaper account of a "shady" past that is consistent with a disturbingly shocking present, or the professional interpretation of documents in a medical patient's file in relation to the patient's current problems. In each case, biographical work produces historical sense in the life under consideration.

BIOGRAPHY AS WORK

Let us begin by distinguishing two important senses of biography. In one respect, the term refers to the depiction of a life history; a biography is the objective record of a personal past. Emphasis is on subject matter, either written or described. The process of writing or describing is almost incidental, merely a technical matter. In another respect, biography may be thought of as the activity or constructive work of writing or conveying a life, the shape and substance of the personal past being integrally linked with the process. Emphasis is on how a life account or story is assembled, rather than on the final story.

Much of the work of assembling a life story is the management of consistency and continuity, assuring that the past reasonably leads up to the present to form a lifeline. Erving Goffman (1963) suggests that people assume that each individual has a single biography:

> Anything and everything an individual has done and can actually do is understood to be containable within his biography, as the Jekyll-Hyde theme illustrates, even if we have to hire a biography specialist, a private detective, to fill in the missing facts and connect the discovered ones for us. No matter how big a scoundrel a man is, no matter how false, secretive, or disjointed his existence, or how governed by fits, starts, and reversals, the true facts of his activity cannot be contradictory or unconnected with each other. (pp. 62–63)

Yet, how is it possible to assume the obviousness of single, individual biographies while occasionally encountering the seeming multiplicity of individual lives? For example, what sense does a young woman make of her boyfriend, whose devotion has always been obvious to her and whom she unfailingly described as "very masculine," when she learns of his long history of discreet homosexual encounters?

People work to make their knowledge of others consistent with their assumption of the unity of biography. They refer to, and account for, apparent biographical inconsistencies in terms such as "passing," "covering," and "going incognito." For our young woman, the heterosexual devotion of her boyfriend might be reinterpreted as having "actually" been his way of "passing as a real man." The consistency assumption suggests that other characteristics be integrated into the new schema. The young woman, for example, now refers to the boyfriend's athletic interests and prowess as indications of what should have been obvious all along.

Biographical work is the ongoing effort to integrate accounts of a person's life. In this context, biography is continually subject to reinterpretation because it is always the *biography-at-hand*. In some place, at some time, an individual's past is under consideration for some purpose. Specific contexts provide guidelines for what is relevant to incorporate into a biography. For example, where elementary school staff assign students to teachers and classrooms for the coming school year, the pasts of individual students come into focus in terms of who should be assigned to which class. For immediate purposes, the child's complete biography is school centered. Kai Erikson (1962) implies that the pasts of "deviants" are similarly attended:

> When a community acts to control the behavior of one of its members, it is engaged in a very intricate process of selection. Even a determined miscreant conforms in most of his daily behavior—using the correct spoon at mealtime, taking good care of his mother, or otherwise observing the mores of his society—and if the community elects to bring sanctions against him for the occasions when he does act offensively, it is responding to a few deviant details set within a vast context of proper conduct. Thus a person may be jailed or hospitalized for a few scattered moments of misbehavior, defined as a full-time deviant despite the fact that he had supplied the community with countless other indications that he was a decent, moral citizen. (p. 308)

Biographical work serves to frame and organize one's character and actions, selecting and highlighting the defining aspects of one's past. Extending this theme, Gustav Ichheiser (1970) cites an example of the reasoned integration of certain facts of a man's life into a single biography of criminality:

> A man is under suspicion of murder. During the investigation certain definite abnormalities of his sexual behavior come to light, even though there is no evidence that they are related in any way to the committed murder. Again, the frequent reactions in many people, if verbalized, would read something like this: "This man whose sexual life deviates so strangely from the norm can also be expected to deviate from other social norms in any other respect." However, here again the overestimation of personality unity has probably misled their interpretative reaction. (pp. 50–51)

Consider local media accounts of the biographical pasts of mass murderers in this regard. Most biographical work is relatively private. The contents of organizational files, records, and reports, for example, are not widely distributed. Media biography, in contrast, is broadly public. Here, audiences are not restricted, whereas, by definition, organizational files, charts, and other biographies of record are restricted to institutional settings. The process of generating such public biographies is subject to moment-by-moment review. Media of various kinds, especially daily newspapers, exemplify the construction process.

The media are not simply vehicles. They contribute substantively to the content of news by the way they report it (see Altheide 1985; McLuhan and Fiore 1967). John Lofland (1969) describes the role that biographical reconstruction plays in what he calls "escalating" someone to a deviant identity. His examples are taken from newspaper (*Detroit Free Press*) accounts of the personalities and personal histories of two mass murderers, Richard Speck and Charles Whitman. Lofland argues that biographies are subject to the ongoing practical biographical work of those who generate them. Not only do biographers make the past lives of individuals meaningful by placing the facts of those lives into some kind of interpretive framework, but they also use a variety of explanations to make or dismiss facts as really or not really factual. "Reliable sources," for example, are cited as the basis of facts, while "misreports" account for the nonfactual.

Lofland argues that it is imperative for reasonable persons to be consistent in description and explanation. This, of course, applies to the relation between personal pasts, presents, and futures. Lofland (1969) describes how a deviant biography is produced in retrospect:

> Whatever may have been the preexisting selection of facts from the Actor's life line that supported a view by Others of him as a pivotal normal, there now begins a reexamination of that life line to discover if these selected biographical events are consistent with the prospective reclassification. Efforts are made to render the known facts consistent, either through discounting (or redefining the significance of) what is known or through undertaking to discover additional facts that support the new *imputation*. (pp. 149–50)

Newspapers strive for consistency as they generate public biographies, in part by manipulating the visibility of facts about someone's past. For example, when a public figure has committed some highly commendable or gravely repugnant act, speaking of it necessitates "making" sense of it, putting it into historical perspective, and integrating it with what is already known about the person. Lofland argues that one technique of managing the visibility of inconsistent facts is to place such facts on back pages of the newspaper, literally consigning them to the background. When a public figure is highly newsworthy and facts are consistent with what the figure has typically and publicly come to be, *the* facts become part of front page news.

Now consider the case of Richard Speck. In July 1966, he was charged with the murder of eight student nurses in Chicago. As Lofland (1969) puts it, "wire services and local newspapers went into a frenzy of research to find out about Richard Speck" (p. 150). At first, the results of interviews with people who knew Speck found him to be "an intelligent, gentle and sensitive young man." Lofland found this buried in the back pages of the *Detroit Free Press*. These "facts" about Speck's behavior seemed inconsistent with the "fact" that Speck stood accused of murdering eight women in cold blood.

A few days after Speck's apprehension, however, "facts" seemingly consistent with the murder became more visible, placed more prominently in the newspaper. As Lofland continues:

> Under the headline "Richard Speck's Twisted Path," the rite of consistency could begin:
>> Charged with the brutal slaying of eight student nurses, Richard Speck was trapped by the tattoo that bore his credo: Born to Raise Hell. Here is a special report on the man accused of mass murder, a report on the twisted path that led to tragedy. (*Detroit Free Press*, July 24, 1966).
>
> And, of course, the facts were consistent. He was a "murder suspect" in another case who "had been hating for a long time," and "had been arrested 36 times." In his youth he was already "a reckless tough . . . with the leather jacket crowd" who "would drink anything." "A high school dropout" who was "divorced," he had

> served three years for burglary and was "woman crazy."
> (Lofland 1969:150–51)

Compare this to the newspaper account of Charles Whitman's shooting of fourteen people from atop a tower at the University of Texas about a month after the Speck murders. Lofland describes the consistency effort as "more strenuous" in this case, since the facts on Whitman's biography "were less amenable to reconstruction than were Speck's." Whitman had been an Eagle Scout in his youth, had a record of exceptional service in the Marines, and had excelled academically in college. The "All-American" image did not square, in the public mind, with the fact of mass murder.

According to Lofland, it took a whole week to generate a biography even partially consistent with the image of a mass murderer. As Lofland reports:

> Buried in the third section of the *Detroit Free Press*, a *New York Times* story headlined: "Friends and the Record Dispute Sniper's All-American Image."
>
> Charles J. Whitman . . . has been described as an All-American boy. But according to his friends, he has gambled with criminals, poached deer, written bad checks, kept illegal guns and tried to sell pornography (Detroit Free Press, August 19, 1966).
>
> Interestingly enough, the concrete acts that are then spelled out in the story seem less malevolent than the abstract characterization of them given above. This is perhaps why the *Detroit Free Press* felt the story merited only page three of section three for that day. (Lofland 1969:151)

The difficulties of building even these allegedly consistent facts into the "reasonable" biography of a mass murderer might explain the later popular acceptance of a brain tumor as the explanation for Whitman's acts, according to Lofland. The seeming lack of a properly factual social or psychological account for Whitman's shootings led the search for a reasonable biography to Whitman's physiology.

More recently, media coverage of Jeffrey Dahmer, an admitted mass murderer whose long string of ghastly killings was discovered in 1991, shows evidence of the principle of biographical consistency at work. In the course of his arrest and trial, myriad accounts and explanations for his behavior were offered by psychiatric experts, lawyers, law-enforcement personnel, sociologists, people "on the street," and reporters. Commentators eventually made sense of Dahmer's past in terms of his troubled relationship with his parents; some said this was a certain antecedent to, if not a cause of, Dahmer's killings. *In retrospect*, his relational past was made to fit with the current descriptions and diagnoses of a deranged killer.

Instances of animal mutilation in Dahmer's childhood were also worked into accounts of a "long-standing" disregard for life and a fascination with death and dismemberment. These facts of his early years provided basis for seeing a progressive pattern of development, with Dahmer moving from lesser to greater offenses. The course of his life and tragic behavior, then, made sense in light of this constructed trajectory.

Noticeably absent from media accounts were any references to warm or loving relationships, friendships, acts of kindness, indeed any accounts of behavior that might have made Dahmer appear to be anything other than the deranged murderer he was portrayed to be. Potentially "normal" activities of everyday life were ignored or reinterpreted to fit better with what was known. For example, a former resident of Dahmer's apartment building where several murders and dismemberments had occurred, gave the following description of his encounters with Dahmer:

> He was always real quiet. I'd see him and he'd just smile. He never said much, never did nothing you could notice. Never had nobody going in and out. It was real strange. You could just see he was a strange kinda guy. (WISN-TV: 2/29/92)

What could otherwise be understood as "nondescript," ordinary behavior was interpretively transformed into now-visible documents of Dahmer's strangeness, the pattern of Dahmer's murderous character informing the meaning of his everyday behavior.

BIOGRAPHICAL WORK SETTINGS

Like work in general, everyday biographical work takes place in identifiable settings. From the media to treatment organizations and less formal situations, socially organized circumstances provide the relevant criteria for assembling the personal past. Especially important in this regard are settings whose participants specifically attend to pasts, whose jobs explicitly involve assembling biographical information, such as psychiatric assessments in treatment facilities or medical records in hospitals. As the ordinary meaning of lives becomes increasingly embedded in organizations and their interpretive domains, such work settings provide distinctive circumstances and orientations for constructing lives. At the same time, despite their differences, organizations engage in a ubiquitous process of constructing pasts that are consistent with the present.

Consider how local interpretive contingencies affect the way everyday biographers do their work. Some contingencies are material, others interactional and ideological, yet they all have rhetorical bearing on the interpretive process and its outcome. One contingency is the believed or claimed prestige, status, or power of the subject. The past life of a young man who repeatedly makes wild remarks about his "psychic powers" may be variously interpreted depending on whether he, say, can directly or indirectly influence the lives of those interpreting the claims. If, for example, the young man's father sits on the board of directors of an organization where the young man's past and, now, his present conduct has come under scrutiny, interpretation may take a different course than if the man were a mere employee with no familial connections.

A second contingency is the professional or expert standing of the biographers themselves. Biographical workers who present themselves as expert or professional at the reading of the past of particular persons—such as the forensic psychologists who offer public personality profiles of serial killers or psychological autopsies of suicide victims—may be more persuasive than those who merely claim to have once been acquainted with such persons.

A third contingency is the presence or absence of files or dossiers. This material contingency requires the rhetoric of biographical work to attend to the persuasion of "documented" particulars of a person's past. In an increasingly legalistic society, documented information is very influential, considered to be more relevant than mere hearsay. This contingency bears more generally on the claims for, and accepted quality of, biographical data.

A fourth contingency is the time frame available for doing biographical work. One organization may condense the time frame to as little as ten to fifteen minutes per subject, within which the pertinent facts of the subject's immediate or distant past must be collated into meaningful relation to his or her current status or condition. With the increasing pressure for public accountability, highly formularized, standard renditions of pasts may be constructed, such as well-known short- and long-term goals set for "individual" patient care in nursing homes.

A fifth contingency is the audience that biographical workers take into account in considering the possible impact of interpretive decisions. After the Los Angeles riots of May 1992, which erupted when jurors found four white police officers not guilty in what was seen by many on videotape to be a clear case of brutality against motorist Rodney King, judges in pending cases of police brutality were said to wonder publicly if the particulars of such cases could be presented without rendering automatic guilty readings, lest the public be outraged or further rioting break out. In a broader, international historical context, the biographical particulars of venerable heroes of the Soviet Union—Lenin, for example—became interpretive victims of new, less sympathetic audiences when the Soviet Union's former republics became independent.

A sixth contingency, especially salient in biographical work settings formally committed to particular intervention philosophies, is the locally available or accepted theory of life change used to frame biographical data. We realize the extent to which the interpretation of the past lives of troubled family members is organizationally embedded, for example, when we find that certain organizations are formally committed to the positive effects of clear household authority hierarchies, while other organizations promote domestic democracy, equality, and open communication (Gubrium 1992). A troubled father with a past record of taking a "strong but judicious hand" with his children, having been of the opinion that children should be seen but not heard, would be approached differently in the two organizations. The intervention philosophy stressing the positive effect of clear domestic authority relations would yield a positive reading of the father's past, while the intervention philosophy based on democratic communication would view it negatively.

Select contingencies of setting can combine with the rhythms of organizational processing of biographical material to highlight the constructive character of biographical work. In this regard, let us concentrate on an important type of biographical work, namely assembling and interpreting personnel and clientele files or records. Our discussion makes use of ideas presented in Stanton Wheeler's (1969) edited collection of essays on files and dossiers in American life.

When someone is hired by, or becomes a client of, an organization, a record is born. The record establishes administrative grounds for one's organizational existence. Biographical material soon becomes available for interpretation, which means that biographical work can be concurrently done by anyone who consults the record. File contents may initially include such documents as academic transcripts, letters of reference, vitae, resumes, and samples of written work. Memos related to the subject's work performance, statements about the subject that have come to someone's attention and now need to be archived, and formal or informal notes of praise or complaint may be added later. This, of course, does not exhaust the contents of personnel files. With the increased mechanization and proliferation of information storage and retrieval systems, files may contain such unwritten material as videotapes and personal information stored on computer disks.

Now distinguish two relatively separate organizational rhythms: the process of building up a file and the process of file consultation. Compared with the interpretation involved in file consultation, the process of building up a file is relatively casual. Filers (persons who place something in a file) do not usually plan what the overall content of someone's file will be. We say "usually" because a filer may indeed conspire to plant a document in someone's file in the hope that, upon consultation, those who consult files will take the document into account in their interpretation of the file's contents. Still, there is no guarantee that consultants will interpret the content of a file in a particular way since various combinations of the preceding interpretive contingencies may rhetorically come into play at the time of consultation. The process of building up a file also includes sorting materials that might be filed and expunging documents from a file.

That the process of generating a file is usually casual tells us a number of things about filers. First, filers typically have no comprehensive biographical reason for placing documents on file, save the fact that documents presumably relate to the file's subject. What is on file at any point is a product of the more or less unconnected occasions when filing occurs. Second, there is no overall patterning to the times when documents are placed in someone's file, although particular documents may be filed at regular times. Indeed, there may be no reason for adding to a file at some point in time other than that there is information at hand relating to the subject that requires administrative disposal. Third, in general, the persons allowed to contribute to a file are seldom formally specified. This contrasts with the usual rather explicit category of persons who may consult files, such as members of a promotion review committee.

Consultation has greater formality than the process of building up a file. The latter is mainly a response to the occasioned need to deposit and store personnel information, while consultation takes place at formally designated times for explicit purposes such as quarterly personnel reviews, annual promotion or dismissal hearings, and recruitment conferences.

Consultants aim to make overall sense of the meaning of documents on file in light of the purposes of their consultation. There are two ways this can be meaningfully understood: as conventional interpretation or as social construction. Conventionally, consultants treat file contents as documentary evidence of organizationally relevant events in the subject's life. A natural or mundane attitude centers on discerning, as accurately as possible, what a file's contents may mean about its subjects in matters under consideration. In principle, in this mundane attitude, consultants do not see themselves as creating biography, only discovering pattern in what is already there. From a constructionist perspective, consultants' biographical work, particularly its underlying natural attitude, itself produces biography as much as the record in its own right. For example, when a file is consulted for purposes of possible termination, consultants meaningfully assemble contents in terms of the task at hand. They reasonably orient to the subject as someone under consideration for termination, setting the stage, as it were, for interpreting file contents in that framework, regardless of the ultimate decision. The language of termination underpins communication. For example, letters of reference originally filed to support a decision to hire an individual may now be perused for possible "hints" of undesirable things to come. In turn, newly discovered hints may inform—from the very start, it might be said—a now evident pattern of the employee's incompetence. The framework orienting consultants to file contents and the language of termination works, in its own right, to construct file contents in a particular way, casting the subject's biography accordingly.

In general, occasions of consultation such as the termination review of an employee's file provide an organizational rhythm with much more decided potential for biographical patterning than routine file-building activity. As a constructive process, the occasion itself virtually demands that a biography be assembled to address the question of termination, collecting material data with no particular defining linkage into a meaningful whole. What is more, the ostensible weight of documented biographical particulars adds to the persuasiveness of the matter at hand, concretizing the practical reasoning of the occasion.

The occasioned quality of biographical work is widely visible, from interpretations of the so-called normal to the abnormal, in their respective settings. As with personnel files, patient charts or records in treatment facilities are consulted when business necessitates obtaining biographies of treatment, recovery, care, and custody. Consider a brief example of biographical work on patient charts presented in Charles Suchar's (1975) study of institutional staffing in a state mental health clinic for emotionally disturbed children. Although Suchar considers his topic to be "deviant labeling practices," the processes he describes may also be construed as biographical work. Suchar analyzes an in-service training program for social workers involved in child psychotherapy. The program is directed by a psychiatric social worker and a small staff of coordinators. Analysis focuses on the in-service training seminars supervised by a consulting child therapist, a Mr. K.

Like other institutional clients, the children who are patients at this mental health facility have clinical records. The records are built as staff members make diagnostic assessments and add to the records. Periodically, these records are consulted by the same staff as they check on the reliability of their diagnoses. Suchar describes this process as rather curious, since the staff who check the reliability of their assessments with facts on record have previously established the facts to justify their diagnoses. What is said to be a way of checking on the reliability of assessments becomes a process of making current biographical data (diagnostic assessments) consistent with existing "facts" in the child's record. In practice, staff work to construct a consistent biography of the child from beginning to end. Take the following statement by Mr. K.:

> It is important to be informed about diagnostic information about [the] child before we interact with him; we must develop a picture in our mind before we go into the session. As soon as things click, you realize that what is happening related to previous information about the child, you're on the right track. (Suchar 1975:14)

The pattern read into the record supplies the interpretive framework for understanding the child and its history. The understanding, in turn, confirms what has been written into the record, thus interpretively blurring the line between the process of building up and consulting a record. Suchar (1975) puts it this way:

> . . . the influence of the recording system and the norms that develop concerning it, upon the biographical conceptions that the clinical staff have of these cases, is quite significant. The early typifications or characterizations of the case help to structure the accounts that are made later in the career of the patients . . . . In this way, the call for consistency essentially becomes a call for the fulfillment of the diagnostic prophecies made in the pre-patient phase of the institutional career. (p. 15)

As such, Mr. K., members of the staff, and the social work trainees together construct pertinent pasts for the children as they periodically create and concretely sustain organizationally relevant biographies.

THE USE OF EXPERTISE

Settings for biographical work vary in the extent to which experts are involved. This contingent feature of setting is an increasingly significant measure of the value of interpretation in our society. The benefits of expertise are widely celebrated. With professionalization, expertise takes on a respect and legitimacy stemming from an aura of selflessness and collective responsibility.

The value of expertise and respect for professionalism provide a persuasive vocabulary, a way of making claims for related work (see Larson 1977; Collins 1979). As forms of rhetoric, expertise and professionalism may be used to convince those who formally or informally adhere to the same language that work done by a claimed expert or professional is more credible than that done by others (Miller 1991). This extends to biographical work. What we have gained with the professionalization of biographical work is a new body of accounts, better known as personality theories, developmental schemas, role expectancies, and the like — indeed, the full range of conventional theories of life change described in chapter 1. Acknowledged masters of such accounts include psychologists, psychiatrists, counselors, therapists, sociologists, social workers, and the clinical clergy.

The use of expertise is graphically illustrated by a psychiatrist in the mental health clinic for emotionally disturbed children that Suchar studied. The following are extracts from conversations between a child psychiatrist, Dr. J., and staff counselor trainees during psychiatric staffings, where the cases of several children would be reviewed and evaluated by the child psychiatrist. In the first extract, the psychiatrist and the child's counselor, a Mrs. Star, are discussing the progress of a nine-year-old boy diagnosed as having "childhood psychosis of a chronic nature." The child has been in the program for about one year and the staff members are evaluating his progress. The psychiatrist sounds hopeful, while the counselor seems to be pessimistic about the child's track record and future prospects.

DR. J.: I see something in him. I can smell it, something hopeful. Since he's rejected all avenues of pleasure, I don't think you should give him tasks to do. I think you're [counselor] doing all right with him. . . . [To the program director:] I suggest we also

begin seeing this mother and child together for a few visits for
diagnosis.

MRS. STAR: The father's a jerk—he's too rigid. I don't know if he'd
like that. Anyways, I don't know, he's [child] still twiddling
[major symptom of child]. It's so sad. . . . There's this kid in
my neighborhood who's 20 and still does that. I don't know if
[child] will ever change. It's so sad. . . .

DR. J.: He [child] may do that at 20 also. He should have physical
contact with someone. Mrs. Star, you're too pessimistic. . . .
The hopeful thing with this type of kid is their opposition, I
know. It takes experience with these kids to understand this.
Once they give in and "yes" you all the time—they're cooked.
Why don't you talk to him about his not talking. In time, he'll
begin responding in a variety of ways, you'll see.

MRS. STAR: He is a great listener. I guess you're right. He knows what
I'm saying. You can tell he knows. (Suchar 1975:19–20)

In deciding what to do, Dr. J. and Mrs. Star seem to be momentarily at odds. Mrs. Star suggests avoiding a family session with the
child and his parents. Then, on the basis of what Mrs. Star knows of
the biography of someone in her neighborhood who is similar to the
child but older, she expresses her pessimism about the child's future.
In opposition to this, DR. J. speaks of the typical biography of "this
type of kid," who "in time" will begin to respond if her suggestions
are followed. Dr. J. suggests that her biography has greater merit
than Mrs. Star's because, as Dr. J. claims, "I know" and "it takes
experience" to understand such matters, clearly implying Dr. J.'s
superior interpretive skill in such matters.

In another staffing, Dr. J. and a counselor, Mr. E., discuss a
twelve-year-old boy diagnosed as borderline schizophrenic. As in
the preceding case, the boy has been in the program for about one
year. Again, invoking the typical biography of "such cases," Dr. J.
claims expertise, this time in the latter part of her final utterance. Her
rhetoric apparently brings the conversation, but not the disagreement, to an end.

DR. J.: I'll tell you what he is, he's pervasively anxious, he's
absolutely driven by his anxiety. [Addressing the boy's counselor, Mr. E:] If you really want to know what a hyperactive
child looks like, you've got him . . . .Yeah, okay, he's begun
to build controls for himself, but it was all built around his

anxiety; all his activity is frenzy . . . . I think with him there is a vast split between what he says and what he feels. Most of what he says is garbage.

MR. E. [*visibly angered by the psychiatrist's last statement*]: But sometimes he does mean what he says!

DR. J.: But look, even from your material [progress notes written on a daily basis by counselors and submitted to the psychiatrist before the staffing] I get the feeling that what he verbalizes means nothing.

MR. E.: But one time, for example, he told me "I miss you" and he meant it.

DR.J.: But that's different. Some things like that may touch him, but I'm still very dubious that words mean anything to him. I do not think words reach him at all. [The psychiatrist's tone of voice becomes more insistent and the counselor is still angered by the evaluation.] Look . . . Mr. E., I know what I'm talking about. I've seen cases like this before. It takes time to understand this. You must not kid yourself that what he says means anything. There's a lack of integration between his feelings and his words. (pp. 20–21)

Suchar notes that after the final statement the counselor did not again verbally respond to the evaluation made by the psychiatrist but remained visibly angered for the remainder of the meeting (pp. 20–21).

Suchar goes on to describe how Mr. E. expressed himself to Suchar after the meeting was over.

When the meeting was over I asked him [Mr. E.] how he felt about the evaluation. Mr. E. said, "She [Dr. J.] really pisses me off. She doesn't give me credit for knowing my own kid. That stuff about his use of language, words is bullshit. He does communicate and he means what he says." It is also important to note that in the official transcript or report of the meeting the counselor's objections to the evaluation were not recorded at all and the psychiatrist's evaluations became the official evaluation of the "clinical team." (p. 21)

Suchar concludes that the counselor trainee ran up against the "cult of expertise" and publicly acquiesced.

IMAGES AND AUDIENCES

Images of personal pasts in common usage in particular settings also enter into biographical work. When combined with audience considerations, the images construct circumstantially appropriate courses of experience. Consider images of treatment and the recovery process at Wilshire Hospital, a physical rehabilitation facility (Gubrium and Buckholdt 1982). Patients were admitted to Wilshire for a variety of problems falling broadly within physical medicine, including the bodily functions compromised by spinal cord injury, brain trauma, stroke, hip fractures, and amputations. Functional incapacities were treated, not the physical injuries themselves. Rehabilitation services included physical and occupational therapy, speech therapy, and counseling offered by rehabilitation psychologists and psychiatrists.

While, as in any treatment facility, there were many therapeutic strategies and complex apparatuses in place, staff members, families, and significant others did not interpret the parts they played in recovery strictly in relation to the technical side of treatment and recovery. In the course of the study, it became evident that the broad range of descriptions of the recovery process centered on either of two competing images—educational or medical—of what the process of recovery was "all about," as it was sometimes put. Some of the descriptions even referred to competing "models," as in the "medical model," although this was not a formal distinction.

In therapy, what was conveyed about recovery seemed uniform enough, framed as an educational process. One physical therapist after another informed patients that patients would not make progress in rehabilitation unless they put their minds to it. Therapists explained that rehabilitation was a matter of teaching and learning, that the therapists and other staff members could only inform and guide recovery. The therapeutic function was, in that sense, an educational one. It depended critically on the patient's attitude toward learning and his or her effort to put what was being taught into effect. Therapists repeatedly reminded patients that the staff could in no way cure their problems and that, if anyone was the doctor, it was the patient. The staff eschewed medical terminology as they cautioned patients not to think of being cured, referring to patients as good, average, or poor students, and, in turn, encouraging them to think of therapists as teachers.

This was not just a therapist's way of speaking about the process of recovery; doctors, too, used these terms of reference. At Wilshire, there were support groups for patients with particular types of rehabilitation problems. In the spinal cord injury group, for example, the physiatrist often discussed the physiology of paraplegia and quadriplegia. Especially noteworthy were sessions dealing with bowel and bladder control. The physiatrist highlighted the fact that patients would have to take cues from their bodies in adapting to paralysis. Cure was rarely part of the lesson, as learning and motivation were underscored, and the need to listen attentively and develop good habits was encouraged. Doctors also supported the educational efforts of therapists by conveying the need for hard work and self-reliance, confirming what patients repeatedly heard in their therapy sessions.

When the therapists were asked separately about the meaning of recovery, however, their answers were more diverse. On the one hand, teaching and learning were mentioned, as were the need to motivate the student-patient and the importance of good teaching skills. The comments coincided with what the working patient was said to "actually" be doing in the recovery process and how therapists and other staff members participated in it. On the other hand, therapists also stated that patients could remain inpatients only if they were benefiting from therapy, showing reasonable progress toward rehabilitation. It was noted repeatedly, especially by the utilization review coordinator, that if staff could not show effective medical treatment and the resulting patient progress, the patient had to be discharged.

In this context, recovery seemed to be something quite distinct from what was implied, if not claimed outright, in the context of staff relations with the working patient. In particular, there were more references to treatment and cure, less to teaching and learning. Indeed, especially in utilization review conferences (reviews of patient progress), there were clear and continuing statements of the need to show treatment progress, if not explicit directives to do so.

Need referred to the requirement of documenting for third-party payers such as insurance companies the success of therapeutic intervention as evidence of normal progress toward recovery. What was being said overlaid an entirely different sense of rehabilitation, one oriented more toward medicine than education.

The two images mediated interpretations of a variety of therapeutic activities. In this regard, for example, the cones stacked by patients in occupational therapy to help extend the range of motion of the upper extremities could mean either of two things. What was taking place was either the patient learning or the successful application of therapeutic skills. In an educational framework, every aspect of the recovery experience — including therapeutic apparatus, prosthetic and orthotic appliances, and physical assessment — were articulated in relation to teaching and learning functional skills. In a medical framework, the same features of the program were assembled into a different set of realities conforming to the contours of therapeutic intervention and doctoring.

The designation and assignment of educational or medical meaning to rehabilitation was not arbitrary. Audience was an important guide to articulation. Clinical staff communicated with three important audiences about the rehabilitative process: patients, patients' families, and third-party payers. Communication with patients about recovery was guided by the educational image and with third-party payers by the medical image, as suggested earlier. With patients' families, the image articulated depended significantly on how successful rehabilitation was said to be. Medical language typically was used to frame successes, claiming credit for Wilshire's special expertise and facilities. Educational terms generally were used to describe a patient's lack of progress; the patient's failure to work diligently at the learning process accounted for the lack of progress.

Patient biographies rose and fell in communicative significance depending on images, audience, and assessments of progress. In describing successful rehabilitation to families and in utilization reviews, the patient's personal past, including his or her motivation, took a distinct back seat to the language of treatment. Whatever was done to effect progress was communicatively underscored, with assessments of ensuing progress detailed. There were numerous references to what could be expected from continued treatment and estimates of when maximum benefit would be achieved. In this context, patients' pasts were hardly distinguished; descriptions of their biographical particulars were limited to their current responses to the clinical skills and efforts being put forth on their behalf. Mentions of such biographical matters as the patient's known need to achieve or his or her long history of overcoming major life challenges were likely to be supplanted by medical interpretations of recovery. If this was biographical work, it suppressed rather than constructed personal pasts.

When the audience was the working patient, as in therapy and group sessions, biography came to the fore. It was commonplace to hear staff members speak of the difference motivation could make in recovery. It was not unusual for a therapist to caution patients that some persons never made it in rehabilitation because of their overall attitude or the kind of person they were. Indeed, there were times when therapists pointed out that in rehabilitation, personality, if not motivation and attitude, was everything; the right person could do wonders in treatment while the wrong one got nowhere, notwithstanding staff efforts on his or her behalf.

Patients' pasts were used both retrospectively and prospectively in this regard. Therapists sought patients' life histories and used the information as part of their explanations for why progress was being made. For example, retrospectively, a therapist might account for the considerable increase in a patient's range of arm motion in terms of the usual "leaps ahead" characteristic of a person with this patient's track record, perhaps citing as a point of comparison what the therapist had learned about the patient's past business successes. Prospectively, a therapist might regularly remind a patient that a person "like him," referring to the patient's athletic achievements, could look forward only to rapid recovery.

Biography was also a significant reality in the communication of poor progress to families. When therapists had done all they believed they could do for a patient, personality might be used to explain why progress had not been made. As in staff's communication with the working patient, the person was separated from the patient, the former's biographical particulars treated as an explanation for the latter's apparent lack of success. While families were informed of the technical details of limited recovery, they also were told of the need for a positive attitude on the patient's part in order for there to be significant progress. Family members of course addressed biographical particulars in their own terms, agreeing or disagreeing with staff assessments, but nonetheless taking matters of the patient's past such as his or her known lack of motivation as sources of agreement or disagreement.

INTERVIEWING AS BIOGRAPHICAL WORK

As the life course grows in importance as a framework for research, even social and behavioral scientists become biographical workers, bringing us full circle to a commonplace method of the conventional approaches presented in chapter 1: the social science interview. With regard to life change, interviewers themselves often construct the life lines they ostensibly analyze.

Consider extracts from interviews presented in Douglas Kimmel's *Adulthood and Aging* (1974). Kimmel conceives of development as a lifelong process rather than confining it to the early years. His book's chapters trace life changes through young adulthood, marriage, family life, retirement, dying, and bereavement. Like most conventional researchers of human development, Kimmel conceives of personal pasts as objective and linearly organized. He describes his approach this way:

> Our approach will be to underplay individual variation
> and to emphasize the developmental theme. We argue
> that when the developmental theme is understood, one
> may then bring in the individual variations and examine
> a specific individual in a specific place at a specific time
> in life; however, if we do not understand the theme
> clearly, individual variations may be a confusing "noise"
> of idiosyncratic differences that make little sense.
> (Kimmel 1974:4)

Kimmel proceeds to explain how he will illustrate the developmental theme through his research:

> There will be several "interludes" of individual case
> histories interspersed between some of the chapters in

this book. We see these interludes as examples of individual variation in which both the general developmental theme as well as the interaction of this theme with idiosyncratic differences stand out. The interludes (and other persons we see around us) challenge our ability to understand the developmental theme in the midst of its variations; yet if we can understand the theme, the variations can be better understood. (p. 4)

He presents six interludes, extracts from transcriptions of interviews conducted with persons of various ages. The extracts present both sides of the data-collection process — Kimmel's questions as well as respondents' answers.

The interludes may be read in two ways, just as biography in general might be approached. Kimmel suggests that we orient to the interludes as reports of developing lives. What respondents say, and its nuances, represent the developmental logic operating *in* their pasts. From this point of view, Kimmel's side of the interview is less important than respondents' contributions; his talk is tacitly understood to be a neutral instrument for data collection. Apparent in the above quotation, Kimmel states that this approach is the only way to make general sense of the data, suggesting that ignoring the reality of the developmental theme leads virtually to nonsense — "noise," as he puts it.

There is, however, another way to read the interludes. If we set aside belief in the objective reality of development and stages, Kimmel's side of the interview conversations grows in importance, becoming as important as the respondent's contribution. Reading the interludes from this point of view shows how situated, constructed, and, in this case, conversational, the course of life is in practice.

In the following extracts from three interludes, note how Kimmel and his respondents interpret and converse themselves into developmental biographies, building linear order from what might might be alternatively organized. The first excerpt is from an interview Kimmel (K) conducts with George (G), a twenty-seven-year-old man. The selections display the interviewer's *constitutive* role in doing biographical work. Note how Kimmel immediately begins to typify the respondent's biography in developmental terms, using the terms "looking back," "milestones," and "turning points" as framing devices.

K: As you look back over your life, what are some of the milestones that stand out?

G: In terms of just profession, in terms of personal life? Do you want specifics?

K: Yes.

G: What made me choose my profession?

K: Was that a milestone?

G: It certainly was. . . .

K: And that was the turning point for you?

G: I look back and that's what I remember, so that's a milestone for me, what one would have to call a milestone. . . . Anyway, other milestones. Oh, I'm sure I have some. Oh! Telling my folks I was gay was a milestone. Partly because of the way they responded [*laughs.*]

K: When did that happen?

G: . . . Okay. More milestones. Can you think of some other areas maybe that would interest you? Or that would help me remember?

K: What about more recent milestones? Like coming to New York?

G: Well, coming to New York wasn't really a milestone for me because that was so planned, so matter-of-fact that I was going to do it that it wasn't really a milestone. . . .

K: It sounds like in a very real sense, once you made the decision to become a dancer, then somehow the rest of it is kind of an unfolding and fairly continuous.

G: Oh, yes; very much. . . .

K: We've been talking about milestones. What about crisis points? Have there been any crisis points that stand out?

G: Yes, I've had a lot of crises. Do you want some of them?

K: Yes. . . . Have there been any crisis points in your relationship with your family?

G: Not really. Some childish things. Nothing really recently. I've never run away from my family or anything like that as a child.

K: You said at one point when we didn't have the recorder on that your mother was in the hospital.

G: Yeah, she is.

K: Is this a serious matter?

G: It's not, now, as it's turned out, thank goodness. Oh, I see what you mean, a crisis in those terms. (Kimmel 1974:116–120)

The discussion produced a sense of development in George's past life—a string of milestones and crises. But consider how they materialized only in collaboration, indeed, at the interviewer's prompting. The structure of George's life course was supplied, at least in part, by the substance of the questioning.

The conversation between Kimmel and his respondent in a second interlude is similar. In this interview, note how life stages in the respondent's biography again "unfold" at the behest of the interviewer. The linear flow of this past is almost forced, as the respondent attempts to fit her story to the narrative framework presented by the interviewer. The following excerpts are from an interview with Theresa (T), a thirty-four-year-old woman, who also has been asked about "milestones."

K: Are there any other milestones that stand out to you?

T: I guess another milestone was moving to New York because I met my husband.

K: You met him in New York?

T: Right . . . another milestone? It's hard, you know, when you think back for milestones you can't think.

K: Anything more recently?

T: More recently. Not really. I guess my husband's business probably is a milestone. . . .

K: Are there milestones in terms of your career? Your occupation?

T: I guess so. . . .

K: Would you say that being married or the birth of your child was a milestone?

T: Oh, yes. It was. Getting married for me was especially a milestone.

K: No real crisis points in your marriage?

T: No, no, we have a pretty good life.

K: What about in terms of your job? Any crisis points there?

T: There was a crisis with Jan. (Kimmel 1974:177–78)

And finally, take an excerpt from the interview with Murray (M), the forty-eight-year-old vice president of a large organization who also teaches at a university. Note how Murray initially resists thinking of his past as a linear series of developing events. He is evidently more comfortable with the metaphor of life "pockets," at least at the beginning of the interview. Kimmel's continuing use of the "milestone" imagery, however, eventually shapes Murray's story into a developmental progression of milestone after milestone.

K: What are some of the milestones in your life? As you look back over it, what are some of the events that stand out?

M: . . . There are pockets. The third pocket of my life is my academic life, which I find probably the most rewarding of all my pockets. . . . Another milestone was deciding that I didn't want to be an accountant and starting a career in my present field. So these are the milestones; I never put them together. . . . Let me tell you something that just, you know, popped in and out of my head. I never had this feeling of desire for security until in the midst of my career there was a milestone. . . .[Murray describes certain events he experienced during the Depression.] So, I don't know how you put it together. I haven't thought about it enough. . . .

K: You fought in the second war?

M: Yeah, I was in the Navy. It wasn't really that bad.

K: But you indicated that it was one of the milestones for you.

M: Oh, yes . . . it was a milestone, being away from the protected environment very young, naive, traveling around the world for better or worse. That's certainly a milestone. And, wondering if your ship is going to get hit or not by a submarine. That's a milestone. Getting by it was a milestone also. [At this point, Murray begins to define all events in his past as milestones.] (Kimmel 1974:275–78)

Biographical construction occurs on many occasions, indeed, on every occasion when biography is a topic of consideration and conversation. This, of course, includes those occasions when researchers such as Kimmel speak of or inquire about past lives. Interviewers, like everyday conversationalists, interact with respondents in order to make sense of the things they ask about. In Kimmel's research interviews, the interviewer in collaboration with his respondents unwittingly generates the developmental sense of the past. Biography does not simply exist as a linear narrative. As in any interview, what comes to pass for a life is constituted in and through the interactional work of all its participants (Holstein and Staples 1992).

BIOGRAPHY AND POWER

Several areas of our discussion of biographical work imply that the work has political overtones. Recall, for example, the discussions in the psychiatric clinic between Dr. J., Mrs. Star, and Mr. E. The extracts give the impression that something we conventionally call "power" may be influencing what is being said and what the outcome will be. Position and power also seem to insinuate other realms of biographical work, such as the effect of accountability on how lives are interpreted. This poses an interesting theoretical problem for the social constructionist approach to the life course and for the constructionist perspective generally. Since the perspective considers the reality of the life world to be a product of interpretation and interaction, what does it make of circumstances that suggest that there is something "outside" the interaction that shapes the interpretation process? How does our approach propose that we understand aspects of the flow of talk and interaction, that, once known, might enable us to predict outcomes?

A social constructionist approach does not discount the possibility of power in social life. Although we have chosen for analytic purposes to set aside the objective reality of social structure, this does not mean that our subjects do likewise. People have a sense of social structure that is often "only too real." In part, this sense of the objective reality of social structure makes social structure seem external and constraining (Berger and Luckmann 1966). A shared sense of social structure does what it did for Dr. J., Mr. E., and Mrs. Star. It allowed Dr. J.'s invoked biography to predominate both in conversation and on record, as all three persons participated in and publicly accepted the legitimacy of the discourse of expertise (Foucault 1980).

Life course depictions are always rhetorical and political in this regard because they take place in settings in relation to such local interpretive conditions as professional standpoints and interprofessional relations. As far as biographical work is concerned, descriptions advocate as well as describe particular ways of understanding and acting on the past. Usage promotes versions of experience that both reflect and foster local concern. A social constructionist perspective can fully acknowledge both this micropolitics and the situatedness of discourse. In this sense, the shape and substance of personal pasts reflect the circumstances of biographical work as much as the personal pasts with which that work is ostensibly concerned.

We can think of power in terms of biography's descriptive organization, that is, the social distribution of ways that biography gets acceptably done. To the extent that settings provide preferred frameworks and vocabularies for describing personal pasts — local interpretive resources — the settings place a premium on constructing pasts in certain terms. Biographical workers who "speak the language" of the setting are likely to be heard at the expense of those who do not. In a setting where expertise or professionalism, say, is the preferred basis for interpreting the personal past, descriptive power revolves around expert or professional discourse and participation. Descriptive claims such as Mrs. Star's and Mr. E's claims to personal knowledge of a patient, are circumstantially weak challenges to Dr. J's more abstract and general, yet expert, claims. Resistance is possible, but formally designated interpretive cultures are difficult resources to surmount.

Still, power as a matter of descriptive organization does not determine biographical outcomes. It is entirely possible in practice for participants such as Mrs. Star and Mr. E. rhetorically to shift the preferred framework and vocabulary for describing the personal past — from the discourse of expertise to, say, a rhetoric of personal knowledge. Descriptive organization is a way of embedding power in the work anyone can, might, or might not do in relation to what is locally preferred. Biographical power, then, is a matter of practice and locale, situated at the border of individual agency and circumstance.

7   PROSPECTS AND IMPLICATIONS

The aim of this book has been to present a social constructionist approach to life course studies. The perspective offers an alternate way of conceiving of personal experience in relation to time that focuses on interaction and interpretive practice. From this viewpoint, the life course and its components are less objective features of experience than they are social forms interpretively constructed and used to make sense of experience. The meanings that are associated with time-related change are practical matters, articulated in and about varied settings of everyday life.

A RADICAL REFRAMING

While the perspective itself is not new, its introduction to life course studies is unprecedented. Construing the life world, the patterns, and the changes that comprise it as social constructions has radical implications — both theoretically and methodologically — for studying experience. It may be quite difficult to conceive of life course issues in the way we frame them, partly because the concrete is made transparent. To some, the approach may seem so incongruous that the initial reaction will be to resist, if not dismiss, it. Our hope is that the empirical evidence we offer provides the basis for rethinking old assumptions.

Conventional approaches to the life course view lives as moving through identifiably meaningful stages, phases, cycles and the like. Childhood, adolescence, and middle age, as well as the past, the present, and the future are components of lives that are encountered, experienced, or anticipated — more or less objective features of the life course. While we have shown throughout the book that persons talk and act as if life changes are concrete features of experience, we also have illustrated how persons, at the same time, are actively involved in formulating how their experience comes to have the shape it does in relation to time. If one person views life in terms of "turning points" and passing "milestones," another sees it as "pockets" of activity and experience. Some may describe life as a progression of "steps," each change being "the next move up the line," while others report that life is a "tangle." Of course background experience varies. The persons, circumstances, activities, and opportunities that confront one person are certainly different from those confronting another. But the way lives are experienced depends as much on what is *made* of daily encounters as it does on the things that are encountered.

The constructionist viewpoint specifies sources of experiential variation that are unacknowledged from a conventional stance. At the risk of oversimplifying, lives are what people make of them— descriptively, interpretively, interactionally. We can see this in the myriad ways that experience is interpreted and represented, by different persons, in diverse situations, using a variety of vocabularies and metaphors. Diversity in the meaning of experience, then, can be attributed as much to variation in interpretive practice as to variation in that which is experienced.

The point may be simple, but the analytic implications are profound. If lives are constructed, we must examine the *constitutive* practices that produce them. This requires us to refocus analytic attention onto the acts of interpretation that produce the meanings of experience in relation to the passage of time. Primary interest is in the practices through which the life world is given meaning. Thus, the emphasis is on the interpretive processes that produce reality, rather than on what are conventionally thought to be real, concrete features of the life course.

We are suggesting a shift in perspective, a radical reframing. But considering an alternate approach may be risky. In one respect, the choice of how to view life change is bound by the social organization of how we know the world in which we live. Knowledge is both practically produced and used. It emerges from commonsense reasoning, ordinary language use, and interaction, even (perhaps especially) in professional and scientific disciplines. To engage in a commonly shared discourse means to speak and otherwise interact with others in a familiar, conventional manner. Those involved with a discourse—whether it is scientific, disciplinary, or thoroughly ordinary—have sentimental, intellectual, and material investments in thinking about, conceptualizing, and reporting phenomena in the established ways. Investments may be threatened in the wake of new interpretive developments. To invoke an alternate discourse—to offer a competing "gaze" (Foucault 1975)—invites problems of both comprehension and reception. New ways of conceptualizing and communicating aspects of experience are not easily understood when one's view is grounded in the established way of thinking and talking. And even if the new way is understood, it is not likely to be tolerated, let alone embraced, in the face of conventionally conceptualized facts embedded in a prevailing community of understanding (Kuhn 1962).

Securing a practical as well as an intellectual niche for a constructionist approach to life change, then, is somewhat problematic. The constructionist approach raises fundamental questions about the empirical evidence of everyday life. It deliberately suspends belief in a priori behavioral constructs in order to make visible the practical side of things in the real world, as people enact them and make them real. The approach resists the usual analytic reliance on "mundane reason" (Pollner 1987) in order to see how the everyday practices of mundane reasoning and interaction in their own right produce a sense of objective or factual reality. In a sense, constructionist analysis objectifies the processes through which objective reality is created, as a way of seeing how lives are assigned organization in relation to time.

Because the approach is centered on practice, constructionism offers new ways of conceptualizing, observing, and reporting aspects of human development. This stands in marked contrast to the more conventional approaches that are concerned with discovering predictable relations between "fixed" variables, while they all but ignore the social dynamics of the world their variables ostensibly represent. If the life world is grounded in the artfully constructed, constantly emerging, yet circumstantially shaped environs of meaning, it seems imperative that we describe and analyze the procedures through which meaning is constituted. When we make the effort to notice this, it seems rather strange to see and hear all around us how people constantly describe, construct, and reconstruct the life world, yet simultaneously take for granted that the life world's representations are greater or lesser distortions of what is taken to be real.

The constructionist approach to the life course apprehends the life course in a way that seems to turn analysis "on its head." By making commonsense constructs and reasoning processes its *topics*, constructionism eschews their use as analytic *resources* (Garfinkel 1967: Zimmerman and Pollner 1970). This reconceptualizes those aspects of experience that conventional approaches treat as concrete variables. Rather than conceive of variables as components of the life world that explain or influence its objective conditions, we step back to examine how these components are themselves interpretively constituted. The analytic goal is to describe the constellation of practices used to assemble, recognize, and enact the realities otherwise treated as substantial and real. By making the construction of variables and other conditions into a topic, we set aside the causal or predictive role that they have traditionally been assigned in social scientific explanation.

This has clear implications for how the role of the human sciences and the human services is conceived. Generally, we think that the sciences and professions principally discern "what's there" and decide what to do about it. From this perspective, the human sciences and professions act upon aspects of life world. The constructionist approach, however, focuses on the role that scientists and professionals play in the *creation* and *maintenance* of personal realities, problems, and solutions in relation to time. The tenet that people construct reality applies to all persons without exception. Scientific, as well as commonsense, knowledge is constructed, all "artifacts" (Garfinkel et al. 1981; Lynch 1985) of interpretive work. The human services are no less constructive; they continually constitute clients and their organizationally relevant characteristics as part of the very process of assessing and addressing their needs and problems (Buckholdt and Gubrium 1985; Gubrium 1992; Holstein 1992; Loseke 1992; Miller 1991). A constructionist perspective thus provides an analytic, and potentially practical, awareness of the constitutive role that social scientists and human-service workers play in constructing and organizing lives from beginning to end.

CONSTRUCTION AND CONTROL

By maintaining the attitude that objects of the life world do, in fact, exist apart from interpretations or reports of them, everyday actors gloss over their own roles in creating the realities they encounter. Constraining forces appear to be outside their experience, controlling persons from afar. Because the mechanisms and dynamics of interpretation are obscured or ignored, persons are never fully aware of the sources of constraint. They neglect their own role in producing meaning just as they overlook their own authorship of the circumstances and forces that seem to control experience.

Interpretive practice does not just construct lives. By producing and managing meaning — organizing and manipulating the realities it constructs — interpretive activity exercises a subtle yet important influence over the lives and circumstances with which it is concerned. Viewing the life course from a constructionist perspective provides the opportunity to examine the ways in which representations of the life course are used as means of control. If we understand social control to involve activities through which lives are organized, rendered accountable, influenced, and made the objects of remedial or custodial attention, we can examine the ways that life course imagery is employed to influence and control the shape and substance of experience in time.

Images of the life course can be used both overtly or subtly to influence, motivate, and even coerce behavior, rendering some actions, occurrences, and characteristics accountable or acceptable while casting others as inappropriate. Their use as a means of interpretive control may be either formal or informal. Recall, for example, a story recounted in chapter 3 about some minor troubles between a mother and her thirteen-year-old son. The mother had been busily preparing the house for some afternoon guests while the son was constantly under foot, annoying her with one little thing after another. Fed up with her son's antics, the mother lost all patience and scolded the thirteen-year-old, saying "You are such a child!" While the correctness of the depiction was a matter of debate between mother and child, its correctness is not our analytic concern. Instead, we are interested in how the mother used related life-stage imagery, locating the thirteen-year-old in "childhood" to exert control over her misbehaving "child." Interpretively assigning the teenager the status of a child implied that he possessed an entire constellation of attributes—immaturity, dependence, and silliness among others. The mother's implicit denigrations were as rhetorical as they were descriptive. Her depiction called upon "what everyone knows" about children to provide a standard for assessing just where her son stood developmentally at this time in his life. To the thirteen-year-old, the life course location was none too flattering, a placement to be deflected.

The life-stage assignment was used to influence the circumstances it ostensibly described. By calling her son a "child," the mother implicitly challenged the boy to prove her wrong by acting in a way that belied the categorization. Her description could also be seen as an attempt to manipulate his conduct informally, indirectly. She demanded nothing of the boy, nor did she directly coerce him. But by casting his character and behavior in a fashion that was unbecoming, the mother provided an impetus for behavioral change. While informal, the technique is powerful. The admonition to "act your age," for example, is commonplace; its ubiquity testifies to its utility. Images of normal life course development as well as departures from the norm—such descriptions as being "on or off course," "on time," or "off time"—are continually used to incite or constrain behavior, interpretively invoking normative standards to assert control.

We can think of life course depictions as supplying working blueprints for directing lives. Descriptions of departures from the plan both interpretively constitute instances of deviance and encourage their correction. Normative standards regarding permission, proscription, and prescription (Hagestad and Neugarten 1985) are commonly invoked in terms relating to age or life course location. The standards even permeate our mechanisms of formal control. Legal statutes applying only to juveniles, for example, invoke images of childhood as a distinctive time of life and children as special kinds of people (Empey 1982). Claims about the normal course of development provide the warrant for juvenile laws as well as the motivation for creating a justice system that attempts to protect and rehabilitate, rather than punish, delinquent children. Even the terms "normal" and "delinquent" reflect distinctive understandings of, and attitudes toward, children, their behavior, and its management.

The actual application of law also responds to life course depictions. As a practical matter, the very definition of violations may be contingent on how putative violators are portrayed against the background of what is typical of persons their age. Recall our arguments in chapter 3 regarding the typification of the life course. Evaluations of one's character, we suggested, are often grounded in assessments of how well or poorly one is conforming to typified life course expectations. Emerson (1969) argues that this sort of character assessment is central to how juvenile courts process putative offenders. He reports that if offenders can be portrayed as typical "kids," with the traits and motivations common to most persons their age, the court is reluctant to invoke the most severe sanctions. But if putative offenders give the appearance of being atypical of children their age—acting beyond their years, say, in terms of criminal motivation or sophistication—they are likely to incur more drastic treatment.

Emerson recounts an instance where a juvenile court chaplain approached several court officials on behalf of a youth who had admitted to an offense and was about to be incarcerated. Referring to the boy, with whom he was apparently familiar, as a "good kid," the chaplain asked the boy's probation officer to "let him off." When the officer responded, "He pulled a knife on a teacher," the chaplain replied, "So what? That was a mistake. . . ." The chaplain's description did not deny the boy's wrongdoing, but offered a way of framing it that minimized its negative implications. Invoking the interpretive schema of the "good kid," the chaplain implied that the boy was basically like other boys his age, with basically good, if sometimes misguided, intentions. It provided grounds for interpreting an instance of bad behavior (i.e., the knife incident) as a "mistake," an exception to the normal pattern for "kids" like him. The use of a life stage in the description provided instructions on how to make sense of the boy's behavior, advocating a way of understanding and responding to the events in question. The implications for how this boy would be controlled were massive; the difference between supervised probation and long-term incarceration rested, in part, on the stage of life to which the offender would be interpretively assigned.

We can see the life course invoked throughout the judicial system with similar implications for the way laws are applied and sanctions determined. Extracts from conversations between prosecuting and defense attorneys, for example, show how references to a defendant's age figure in the resolution of criminal court cases in pretrial plea bargaining sessions (Maynard 1984). The conversations involved Public Defenders (PDs) appointed to represent accused offenders and representatives from the District Attorney's offices (DAs). In one instance involving an incident of shoplifting, a PD depicted the defendant in terms of her age, as well as several other personal characteristics.

> ... She's a sixty-five-year-old lady, Mexic- speaks uh Castillian Spanish. She's from Spain . . . for twenty years she's worked in the — in the Catholic Church of — at San Ramon as the housekeeper for the nuns 'n fathers 'n all this stuff (and uh) very religious well known . . . wonderful lady no problems sixty-five-years-ol' hhh sh- but on this particular occasion, she goes into Davidson's eghhh goes into a fitting room, takes two hundred dollars worth o' clothes, pins them under her dress and leaves. (Maynard 1984:126)

While it is not immediately apparent how the description is relevant to the PD's proposal that the shoplifting charges be dropped, the role of age in interpreting what "really" happened was made apparent as the PD continued his argument. He claimed that the defendant had taken two prescription medications that produced side effects leading to her uncharacteristic illegal behavior, actions that she was not even aware of committing at the time. These side effects, the PD argued, were especially serious for elderly persons like his client. Moreover, the woman's behavior in the incident in question was completely out of character for this lady, someone of advanced years and upstanding character.

While age was not the sole characteristic invoked in this defense, its utility in arguing for a lenient disposition is clear. Plea bargaining data also show how age — both old age and youth — can be invoked to argue for severe as well as mild sanctions. Consider, for example, another case involving a university student who was apprehended using an unauthorized parking sticker in a college parking lot. In his attempt to forestall a charge of theft, the PD referred to the student's age to argue the implications of a severe disposition.

> Uh you take a young student, I think he's eighteen or nineteen years old, he's uh just starting out, trying to get—you know, in college, uh and you lay larceny on him. Uh true he can come back in a year and get it taken off his record, but for many other purposes uh it's going to be known. . . . (Maynard 1984:228)

Among his counterarguments, the DA returned to the theme of the defendant's age:

> . . . You know they're all students, they all have futures before them. Which of course implies they also have or ought to have a heightened sense of responsibility and appreciation for the consequences of their acts, uh particularly with, you know a future beckoning before them and I- (pp. 228–29)

At this, the PD interjected:

> Uh, I don't think that's true, in fact I think maybe if you're oh about eighteen, nineteen, twenty, you're just not experienced enough. . . . (p. 229)

The meaning of the defendant's age was openly constructed, contested, and negotiated here as the PD and DA tried to decide reasonably what crime had been committed and what the disposition should be. It was not the defendant's age per se that was at issue. Rather, the case hinged on what was *made* of the fact that the defendant was eighteen, nineteen, or twenty years old. Arguments about what his age meant had ramifications for both how the defendant's actions would be understood as well as what particular punitive responses would represent for a person at his life stage.

Formal social control does not only involve defining and sanctioning criminals. All deviance designations and their accompanying responses conjure up some sense of control over person's lives. Chapter 3, for example, argued that aspects of a typified life course are used to establish symptoms of psychiatric disorder. If a person is, say, inexplicably "off course," the deviation may be interpretively constituted as a manifestation of mental illness. As we saw in chapter 3, a fifty-five or sixty-year-old man who brags of his insatiable sexual appetite may have this behavior labeled inappropriate for a man his age, and have this noted as pathological.

Life course imagery may be deeply implicated in what we do with, and for, so-called psychiatrically deranged persons. Consider how the meaning of fifty-one-year-old Lois Kaplan's age emerged in her involuntary commitment hearing, and what bearing it had on the outcome (Holstein 1990). Psychiatric testimony had established that Kaplan was severely mentally ill, but Kaplan's attorney argued that she did not need to be hospitalized.

> A woman her age should do just fine in a board and care facility because she's gotten to the point where she's not likely to be too difficult to look after. She seems to have stabilized and at her age she's not likely to go looking for trouble. The best part about Crestview [the board and care facility] is she'll be able to live on her own but there'll be someone there to look after her. She's at a point in her life where that won't take much. (Holstein 1990:125)

The judge, however, was skeptical:

> [To the PD] I'm not sure that I agree with you, Mr. Lyle. The problem with getting older is you sometimes need a little more attention. Little things seem like major problems. They seem to get out of hand a lot quicker. I know I have to do a lot more for my own mother now than just a couple of years ago. As far as I know, Crestview is a fine facility, but their policy is for residents to be able to pretty much do it on their own. I'm not convinced that Lois won't need more help than they can give her. (p. 125)

Note that there was no disagreement here about Kaplan's station in the life course. Everyone agreed that she was "getting older," although in other contexts fifty-one might be characterized quite differently. The judge and PD were at odds, however, about what this implied regarding Kaplan's manageability. The discussion continued through several exchanges concerning how well the board and care home could deal with problems that Kaplan was likely to encounter. The two perspectives on what Kaplan's age meant for the type of care she required were reiterated, interwoven with related arguments. Eventually, the judge took a different tack.

> You know what's bothering me? I think it's the fact that we're talking about letting an older woman live alone, even if there is someone looking in on her. I can't help but worry that she's going to do something and nobody's going to notice until it's too late. It's so easy for someone like her—mental problems, getting a little older, not able to do everything she once did—to do something that might really be dangerous, something that could hurt her real bad. (p. 126)

Here, the judge transferred his concern from how Kaplan would be "managed" to how "vulnerable" she was. In the process, he subtly transformed the meaning of Lois Kaplan's age. "Getting a little older" now meant that Kaplan was more susceptible to harm. As the discussion proceeded, the concern moved from one issue to another, with the judge and PD sometimes explicitly disputing and negotiating how Lois Kaplan's age was relevant to the decision under consideration. The reality of the life course and aging process, for the practical purposes of this commitment hearing, was an emerging product of the courtroom discourse. The interpretations that prevailed simultaneously constructed and controlled the life being discussed.

As practical activity, interpretation is implicitly purposeful. Life course depictions establish normative standards and instances of violation that can be used to exert social influence. The descriptive formulation of aspects of the life course may insinuate courtroom judgments, elementary school placement decisions, and myriad other circumstances of argument and choice. By simply calling a set of events a "midlife crisis," for example, we assign particular and familiar meanings and suggest ways of both understanding and reacting to those events and the life to which they apply. Saying that a teenager is "growing up too fast" or that a sixty-year-old executive is "past his prime" both describes and provides a warrant for reacting to or controlling the lives of those under consideration in distinctive ways. As part of interpretive practice, the control invoked is ubiquitous, suffused throughout the construction process, not limited to constraining forces outside of experience.

RATIONALIZATION AND REPRESENTATION

Understanding the life course clearly involves more than sorting and articulating a sequence of events over time. If sorting and articulating were all there was to the matter, accuracy and authenticity would be primary concerns. It would mean that the facts of a person's life course would be best discerned by those most capable of making precise, authoritative, and objective reports of the life in question. Close proximity and clear vision might be prerequisites for factual accounts. The person whose life was under consideration could be the best source to consult. Who would better know his or her personal experiences?

Of course, on occasion, the person might be "too close" to, or "too involved" in, life to see things as they are. One might not see the forest of one's life because the trees of individual events were in the way, so to speak. Accuracy and authenticity then become the responsibility of others who are either close to the life in question but objective or who are specially trained to discern life patterns and variations. A mother, for example, could be consulted about the details of how her daughter negotiated adolescence to grow into mature and capable adult. Or professionals such as psychotherapists, social workers, and counselors might offer a clearer picture of a client's life than the client himself by virtue of the expertise that allows professionals to penetrate obfuscations. Psychoanalysts, for instance, offer ways of seeing through the confusions of conscious everyday thought and action to the deep meanings attached to individuals' psychosexual pasts and interiors. Similarly, family therapists are trained to discern signs that family members are failing to carry out the ostensibly requisite roles of parents and children that make for a stable and functioning domestic life. Their ability to identify inappropriate behavior in relation to persons' ages and role expectations makes the therapists' insight regarding the life course particularly valuable. The presumption behind the various searches for authenticity is rather straightforward: experiential "reality" is available for accurate description by those best trained and situated to see and convey it.

In the constructionist approach, however, interpretation of any kind *constitutes* experience; the notion of truly authentic reporting is practically, as well as theoretically, untenable — an impossible goal. Each act of interpretation constructs or reconstructs meaningful experience. One version is not more objectively authentic or accurate than another; no version can claim privileged access to the truth. While an expert's versions might carry more persuasive currency in real-life situations, his or her life course depictions are not taken a priori to be more authentic than others as constructions. Diversely situated constructions, expert or otherwise, produce an array of divergent interpretations that reflect the different circumstances of their communication. The "same" life might thus be cast quite differently by different interpreters, on different occasions.

In a sense, this makes what have conventionally been thought of as private lives into decidedly public matters. The meaning of experience in relation to time is not inherent in private, firsthand encounters with events and occurrences. Instead, it emerges out of *social* formulations of what is taken to be personal. In this context, the life course is not simply an identifiable path that an individual follows; it is a pattern that interpreters superimpose on experience to make a coherent life line apparent. Explication of the life course therefore requires us to *de-construct* depictions of the life course into the diverse social practices and discourses through which they have been constructed. Analysis works backward from the commonsense, everyday realities of life change and development to the interpretive process and circumstances that produce them. Our focus is on the public practices of interpretively "doing" the life course.

Objects like the life course are also public in another sense. If interpretive practice continually constitutes everyday life, it does so in a fashion that produces things that generally appear to be quite familiar. Despite its "artfulness," the construction process does not build meaning and coherence uniquely from the ground up on each interpretive occasion. When someone describes his current state of depression as part of a "midlife crisis," for example, the description strikes a familiar chord. Others appear to understand, or at least let the description pass until further notice. The evidently shared meaning is taken for granted as part of "what everybody knows," or so it seems (Garfinkel 1967). While life's meaning, form, and pattern are continually emergent, they are also grounded in generalized, unspecified, yet known-in-common stocks of knowledge (Schutz 1970). The construction process thus utilizes a more or less shared set of interpretive resources — collective representations — from which realities are fashioned (Durkheim 1961).

Interpretive practice is shaped by social context and representational resources. As lives are considered, the interpretive process comes under the purview of the circumstances at hand; it is embedded in local interpretive orientations, conventions and discourses. This does not suggest that situations dictate interpretation, but it does mean that organized settings provide familiar, normative ways of communicating and representing experience in locally recognizable and useful ways. Consequently, depictions of the life course — its progressions, changes, and phases — tend to reflect the contingencies of interpretive occasion as much as the objects and events that they represent. Once again, we see a public side of interpretive practice, a side that deprivatizes personal experience.

This has important implications for what we have otherwise come to know as personal or private lives. Contemporary life is carried out more and more in organizations and bureaucracies that process and channel lives. Indeed, lives often seem to be virtually turned over to organizations. We might say that experience is increasingly "professionalized" and "institutionalized." By this we mean that people are likely to call upon professionals and formal organizations to interpret and respond to personal questions, dilemmas, and troubles. Human service agencies abound, offering help and advice seemingly at every turn. Schools and churches socialize the young, while support groups see us through mid- and later-life changes and crises. Mental health specialists deal with our sentiments, obsessions, and confusions. As these proliferating institutions and agents make their contributions — assessing and processing lives — the life course increasingly becomes a bureaucratic and professional accomplishment.

There is a growing concern about what some say is a public intrusion into private matters. Lasch (1979), for one, decries the extent to which public institutions have invaded the private side of contemporary domestic life, undermining the family's privacy and ability to function in the process. While his argument specifically addresses incursions into the domestic realm, it raises the more general issue of the pervasive bureaucratization of experience.

Max Weber (1958, 1968) referred to "formal rationality" as the organization of conduct according to calculated principles, explicit rules, and institutionalized procedures. He argued that rationalized social relations adhere to generalized principals that promote the sort of predictability to which contemporary organizations and bureaucracies aspire. Weber believed there was a certain cost to this. As modernization brought aspects of life under formal and official auspices, the meaning of self and other experiential domains was increasingly fixed within the "totalizing" tendencies of organizational business, rationalizing their representation and homogenizing personal differences. Rationalization, he suggested, promotes a growing reliance upon expert knowledge and authority, especially scientific knowledge. That expertise comes to be embodied in organizations, their procedures, and the ways that members typically practice interpretation.

The more fully rationalized an organization becomes, Weber argued, "the more completely it succeeds in eliminating from official business love, hatred, and all purely personal, irrational and emotional elements" (Weber 1968:975). Rationalization thus undermines long-cherished values in Western culture—spontaneity and individual autonomy among others—thus diminishing the importance and appropriateness of nonrational factors such as intuition, sentiment, and emotion (Giddens 1971).

Weber's assessment is undeniably dour (Bendix 1960). In his view, the "voicing" of experience in modern times is progressively subject to organizational categories, definitions, and mandates. Institutions seem to think and speak for their participants, as Mary Douglas (1986) puts it, shaping the very worlds that the participants occupy. Participants, in a sense, cease to think and act as their own agents as they defer to organizational conventions. According to Weber, life is "disenchanted" in that there is no space or role left for personalized, spontaneous thought and action.

If we temper Weber's "totalized" characterization, his analysis can resonate with our less pessimistic arguments regarding the public constructions of the life course. First, Weber's argument presages the notion that life course depictions reflect their organizational embeddedness. Second, with the ideological diversification of organizations, it can suggest a multiplicity of life constructs. As diverse organizations and/or professionals engage and assess the features and events of a particular life, their separate outlooks and diverse interpretive resources cast the life in a fashion distinctive to their organizational circumstances. Put simply, a life course may be portrayed one way in one setting and organized differently in another. One's life or life course can be repeatedly enacted, constructed in terms of, and to the specifications provided by, the circumstances of its interpretation. Instead of a single, coherent entity, the life course as a social object can be written, say, as "the-life-course-according-to-this-person" or "the-life-course-from-that-organizational-standpoint." Each representation is authentic to the extent it conscientiously reflects an institutionally defined reality. At the same time, each life can be variously yet authentically reconstructed as it passes from one socially organized setting to another.

The picture may be unsettling from the standpoint of the modern cultural belief in object constancy. Indeed, the multiplicity of experience we have depicted is part of what is being described as the postmodern condition of "de-differentiation" of objects and their representations (Lash 1990). From this perspective, experience cannot be separated into differentiated signs and their meaningful referents. Consequently, the life course, as it is constructed, is not an object apart from acts of interpretation. It is bound up with interpretations, the myriad occasions of representation producing a multiplicity of potential lives for any particular person.

This characterization seems to relativize and depersonalize the life course as an aspect of human experience. But let us not forget that the constructionist perspective also provides a way to "see through" the hegemony of rationalization. Indeed, it is by understanding the interplay between interpretive structure and practice that we might account for, if not fully integrate, the diversity and deprivatization of organizationally structured life worlds with the familiarity and seeming uniqueness of commonsense understandings.

Organizationally embedded rationalization is not a fully structured enterprise. Its apparatus is neither monolithic nor totalizing. Instead, rationality is locally enacted, relying on delimited interpretive cultures that are diversely and artfully articulated with, and attached to, experience. Local culture—whether it is characteristic of an organization, profession, ethnic or gender group, or of any other organized collectivity or setting—supplies orientations and resources for interpretation, not irresistible injunctions or directives. Organized settings may have familiar, conventional ways of representing experience, but they do not force them into any particular interpretation. Social organization may help give voice to experience, but it is always *some* voice that engages organizational discourse. As such, voice is partially separate from culture, even if representation is contextually provoked, facilitated, and embodied.

By deconstructing the voicing of life change, we make visible both structure and inventiveness. We reveal how interpretation responds to the multiple settings, organizations, and orientations in which persons participate in the course of everyday life, again detotalizing rationalization. While lives described in a particular organization or setting may take on the general orientation to experience that the organization or setting promotes, description also reflects the variety of settings, organizations, and circumstances in which a person participates, as well as the multiple orientations that may exist in a single setting. People are not "organizational dopes," mere extensions of organizational thinking. They exercise discretion, conditioned by complex layerings of interpretive influence.

While persons may be "incited to speak" (Foucault 1978) in organizationally preferred ways, their incitements are practical. A psychologist, for example, may engage in interpretive work in a behavior modification program for emotionally disturbed children based on principles of operant conditioning. Her associate may be a practicing psychoanalyst, trained in Freudian techniques. Their work may be done in consultation with a teacher or counselor who has little concern for "psychologizing" when the problem at hand is getting the child to behave properly in class or at meal times. Any interpretation may thus be subject to several situational and perspectival influences, none of which straightforwardly speaks for the psychologist. She must sort through and inventively combine in her terms the variety of available resources in such a way as to accomplish what needs to be done in relation to these varied voices.

Whereas individuals bring multiple influences to any interpretive occasion, any local culture is also likely to be multifaceted, layered with interpretive resources and possibilities that often complement, but sometimes contradict, each other. For example, as staff members of a treatment center for emotionally disturbed children consider a client's progress, disciplinary orientations (say, psychological versus educational), professional background, training, therapeutic philosophy (behaviorism versus psychoanalysis), and practical relationships to the case at hand (staff member versus outside consultant) may all be asserted as ways of understanding what the child's life course is, and will continue to be. The prevailing interpretation will emerge as a provisional adaptation of diverse local voices, until further notice.

Whereas interpretation will always be *of* something, we must remember that what is selected for interpretation is always problematic, and what is made of it is always interpretive. Culture orients and equips the selection and definitional process, while individual inventiveness and serendipity intervene. The "raw" experience itself is but one of several resources used in constructing meaningful reality. The process repeatedly and reflexively turns back on itself, as substance, structure, and practice are enmeshed in the ongoing production of the reality of a life course. The process is unavoidably paradoxical: practice sustains spontaneity, while structure promotes pattern. Antithetical as the two may be, each simultaneously contributes to the complexity of life construction. If persons engaged in interpretation are provided with institutionally formulated scripts, they still enact them, recognizably, yet extemporaneously de-totalizing rationalized constructions.

AGENCY, ORDER, AND DISORDER

The life course is a product of human discretion and interpretation, even as it reflects the rationalizations of modern society. There is, however, a certain tension regarding agency in this imagery. In one respect, we have argued that the meaning of life experience is always "under construction." Interpretation constitutes and reconstitutes the life world to yield a more or less unique, constantly emergent reality. At the same time, our arguments suggest a "radical situationalism." Circumstances provide the interpretive resources for life construction so that the constitutive work done under their auspices yields distinctive, organizationally embedded realities. Interpretive practice links the two in constant interplay. The result is a richly textured, dynamic yet familiar, social world for which working agents are always responsible—even in the presence of seemingly concrete social objects and forces.

Locating agency in practice provides a measure of relief from the specter of bureaucratic tyranny that preoccupied Weber. Our constructionist approach reasserts an agency that others portray as lost to a constellation of all but irresistible or constraining factors. To the extent that our approach highlights the role of local interpretive practice and organizational embeddedness in an increasingly bureaucratized society, it invites the imagery of lives that are diversely constituted in the myriad interpretive arenas of the contemporary world. A person may, for example, know and describe his or her life in linear, developmental terms in one setting, but understand and represent it as a tangle of experiences in another. Any one person can have as many life courses as his or her course of life has occasions for formulation.

Diversity—or diversification—of experience may be the defining characteristic of postmodern society. Understandings of life change reflect the varied and numerous circumstances of their construction. In particular, the structure and meaning of lives seem to change as considerations of those lives circulate through organizations. In practice, experience is a kind of living script—one written, produced, and enacted under changing institutional auspices. There is no fixed text, so to speak, only practical renderings and ultimately occasioned versions.

While people generally gloss over disjunctures between occasioned constructions of their lives, they may still experience a sense of disorder. The human-service professions have been increasingly attracted to developmental models of human behavior as resources for dealing with such problems. The notion that patterns have been established that continue to cause problems is central to many of the technologies of the "helping" and therapeutic professions. In the process, the notion of a life course or linear pattern is often invoked as the basis for suggesting ameliorative change. Most forms of counseling and therapy rely, at least implicitly, on contrasts between models of pathological or dysfunctional life patterns and those of normal, healthy persons. Recommendations for change are often based on the desire to bring a life that is characterized as disordered into better conformity with the healthy model—to get the unhealthy life "back on track." As Emerson and Messinger (1977) suggest, however, troubles and their remedies are simultaneously produced, so that the history or pattern of a trouble is as much a consequence of the remedy that is under consideration as it is a precipitant of that remedy's use. Life course depictions, then, may suggest particular remedies, but they are also used to justify and account for treatments.

The model of a life course or cycle appears to be quite useful for the human services. Consider, for example, how treatment and self-help programs like Alcoholics Anonymous build off the notion of a linear pattern of experience and change. On one level, the treatment paradigm posits a deep-seated and almost irreversible pattern of addiction—obsessive pathological behavior that cannot be shaken. A person is an "alcoholic" for life; the underlying condition is immutable. Having this pattern as a basis from which to work, intervention concentrates on resisting the manifestations of the pattern "one day at a time." The pattern may not be eliminated, but it might be disrupted or suppressed so that its effects on the life in question are contained or minimized. The "recovering alcoholic" is still involved in the addictive life course, but its surface manifestations can be incrementally resisted, breaking its "lifetime" into manageable single-day challenges to the addiction. A string of so-called sober days may be linked into years, then into a lifetime of sobriety, thus using the linear life model to display the ongoing mastery, if not elimination, of the problematic underlying pattern.

The familiar metaphor of the life cycle may be similarly useful in addressing perceived problems of daily living, providing the basis and rationale for intervention. The idea of a "cycle" of violence or domestic abuse (Windom 1989), for example, is currently widely cited as a model of the transmission and perpetuation of violent, abusive behavior. Commonsense and professional theories have converged into the belief that parents transmit violent and abusive behavior to their children by modeling the behavior. The children then perpetuate the "cycle" when they become adults by modeling the behavior for their own children. An intergenerational transmission pattern is used to explain why individuals repeat even those behaviors that they have themselves experienced as harmful. By metaphysical implication, the solution to the problem, of course, is to somehow "break" the cycle, thus ending both the present and future violence. Again, a model of how lives are structured in some continuous fashion underpins both the diagnosis of, and solution to, the problem. Disorder is interpretively produced—as a form of order—to establish the basis for remedial action, linking the generally shared with the practical.

The practical utility of the constructionist perspective has recently been recognized by the therapeutic community, family therapists in particular (see *The Family Therapy Networker*, 1988, v. 12, n. 5). Indeed, "constructivist" therapies are claiming a good deal of success at improving the quality of people's experiences by literally constructing lives, problems, and solutions as part of therapeutic regimes (deShazer 1985; deSchazer and Berg 1988). Miller (1987), for example, describes how family life—its history, patterns, and problems—is rhetorically constructed during the course of therapeutic interactions. He argues that the course of a problem may be formulated and reformulated explicitly for the purpose of suggesting a workable solution to the problem *as it is interpreted*. In this regard, reality construction becomes the therapist's manifest function, a way of producing a set of circumstances that are amenable to remedial change. "Disorder" is constructed—but according to a discernibly organized model—in order subsequently to "repair" lives otherwise "out of control" (Gubrium 1992).

The concepts of a "disordered" life course and lives "out of control" are popular interpretive resources for organizing experience. Indeed, the concepts of disorder and lack of control are frequently used to make sense out of situations where other forms of order are not apparent. While any number of constructions might be available as ways of organizing persons' understanding of experience, it seems likely that the underlying metaphor of a singular, coherent, normative life course will persist, even though different conventional approaches to life change may serve to explain empirical variation. Within the rationalized bureaucracies that consider and manage human lives, the pattern of linear progression through stages or phases provides a useful way of characterizing change, allowing for predictable outcomes if particular interventions are completed.

To the extent that organizations continue to find the image of the life course helpful in accomplishing their objectives, the metaphor will be diffusely reified. Even as persons confront almost infinite interpretive possibilities for constructing the meaning of life change, the institutionally prevalent linear imagery will be widely reproduced. It is likely to become an increasingly compelling depiction of experience in relation to time as rationalization settles on the stagelike developmental model as the "reality of choice" for accomplishing organizational business.

REFERENCES

Altheide, D. 1985. *Media Power*. Beverly Hills: Sage.

Aries, P. 1962. *Centuries of Childhood: A Social History of Family Life*. New York: Vintage Books.

Ayllon, T., and K. Kelly. 1972. "Effects of Reinforcement on Standardized Test Performance." *Journal of Applied Behavior Analysis* 5:477–84.

Bandura, A. 1969. *Principles of Behavior Modification*. New York: Holt, Rinehart and Winston.

Baratz, S.S., and J.C. Baratz. 1970. "Early Childhood Intervention: The Social Science Base of Institutional Racism." *Harvard Educational Review* 40:29–50.

Becker, H.S. 1960. "Notes on the Concept of Commitment." *American Journal of Sociology*. 66:32–40.

———. 1964. "Personal Change in Adult Life." *Sociometry*. 27:40–53.

Becker, H.S., and A.L. Strauss. 1956. "Careers, Personality, and Adult Socialization." *American Journal of Sociology* 62:253–263.

Bendix, R. 1960. *Max Weber: An Intellectual Portrait*. New York: Doubleday.

Benedict, R. 1934. *Patterns of Culture*. Boston: Houghton Mifflin.

———. 1938. "Continuities and Discontinuities in Cultural Conditioning." *Psychiatry* 1:161–167.

Berg, I. 1971. *Education and Jobs*. Boston: Beacon Press.

Berger, P.L., and H. Kellner. 1970. "Marriage and the Construction of Reality." Pp. 49–72 in *Recent Sociology, No. 2*, ed. H.P. Dreitzel. New York: Macmillan.

Berger, P.L., and T. Luckmann. 1966. *The Social Construction of Reality*. Garden City, N.Y.: Doubleday.

Berger, R.J. 1991. *The Sociology of Juvenile Delinquency*. Chicago: Nelson-Hall.

Bittner, E. 1967a. "Police Discretion in Emergency Apprehension of Mentally Ill Persons." *Social Problems* 14:278–92.

———. 1967b. "The Police on Skid Row: A Study of Peace-Keeping." *American Sociological Review* 32:699–715.

Blacking, J. 1990. "Growing Old Gracefully: Physical, Social and Spiritual Transformation in Venda Society, 1956–66." Pp. 121–30 in *Anthropology and the Riddle of the Sphinx*, ed. P. Spencer. London: Routledge.

Blumer, H. 1969. *Symbolic Interactionism: Perspective and Method*. New York: Prentice-Hall.

Bordieu, P. 1977. *Outline of a Theory of Practice*. Cambridge, England: Cambridge University Press.

Bruner, J. 1986. *Actual Minds, Possible Worlds*. Cambridge, Mass. : Harvard University Press.

204

Buckholdt, D.R., and J.F. Gubrium. 1985. *Caretakers: Treating Emotionally Disturbed Children*. Lanham, Md. : University Press of America.

Carlson, R. 1965. "Stability and Change in the Adolescent Self-Image." *Child Development* 36:659–66.

Charmaz, K. 1991. *Good Days, Bad Days*. New Brunswick, N.J.: Rutgers University Press.

Cicourel, A.V. 1968. *The Social Organization of Juvenile Justice*. New York: Wiley.

―――. 1974. "Some Basic Theoretical Issues in the Assessment of the Child's Performance in Testing and Classroom Settings." Pp. 1–17 in *Language Use and School Performance*, ed. A.V. Cicourel et al. New York: Academic Press.

Cicourel, A.V., K. Jennings, S. Jennings, K. Leiter, R. Mackay, H. Mehan, and D. Roth. 1974. *Language Use and School Performance*. New York: Academic Press.

Cicourel, A.V., and J.I. Kitsuse. 1963. *The Educational Decision Makers*. Indianapolis: Bobbs-Merrill.

Cohler, B. 1982. "Personal Narrative and the Life Course." In *Life-Span Development and Behavior*, vol. 5, ed. P. Baltes and O. Brim. New York: Academic Press.

Cole, M., and P. Griffin. 1987. *Contextual Factors in Education*. Madison, Wis.: Center for Education Research.

Coleman, J., E. Campbell, C. Hobson, J. McPartland, A. Mood, F. Weinfeld, and R. York. 1966. *Equality of Educational Opportunity*. Washington, DC: Government Printing Office.

Collins, J. 1986. "Differential Instruction in Reading Groups." In *The Social Construction of Literacy*, ed. J. Cook-Gumperz. Cambridge, England: Cambridge University Press.

Collins, R. 1979. *The Credential Society*. New York: Academic Press.

Coontz, S. 1988. *The Social Origins of Private Life*. London: Verso.

Couch, C. 1982. "Temporality and Paradigms of Thought." *Studies in Symbolic Interaction* 4:1–24.

Coulter, J. 1979. *The Social Construction of Mind*. London: Macmillan.

―――. 1989. *Mind in Action*. Atlantic Highlands, NJ: Humanities Press.

Cumming, E. 1963. "Further Thoughts on the Theory of Disengagement." *International Social Science Journal* 15:377–93.

Cumming, E., and W.E. Henry. 1961. *Growing Old*. New York: Basic Books.

Darrough, W. 1990. "Neutralizing Resistance: Probation Work as Rhetoric." Pp. 163–88 in *Perspectives on Social Problems*, v. 2 ed. G.Miller and J. Holstein. Greenwich, CT: JAI Press.

Degler, C. 1980. *At Odds: Women and the Family from the Revolution to the Present*. Oxford, England: Oxford University Press.

Derrida, J. 1977. *Of Grammatology*. Baltimore, Md.: Johns Hopkins University Press.

deShazer, S. 1985. *Keys to Solution in Brief Therapy*. New York: Norton.

deShazer, S., and I.K. Berg. 1988. "Constructing Solutions." *Family Therapy Networker* 12:42–3.

Douglas, M. 1986. *How Institutions Think*. Syracuse: Syracuse University Press.

Dumont, L. 1965. "The Modern Conception of the Individual." *Contributions to Indian Sociology* 8:13–61.

———. 1986. *Essays on Individualism*. Chicago: University of Chicago Press.

Durkheim, E. 1961. *The Elementary Forms of the Religious Life*. New York: Collier-Macmillan.

Eder, D. 1981. "Ability Groupings as a Self-Fulfilling Prophecy." *Sociology of Education* 54:151–61.

Elder, G.H. 1974. *Children of the Great Depression*. Chicago: University of Chicago Press.

———. 1979. "Historical Changes in Life Patterns and Personality." In *Life-Span Development and Behavior*, vol. 2, ed. P. Baltes and O. Brim. New York, Academic Press.

Elkind, D. 1967. "Egocentrism in Adolescence." *Child Development* 38:1025–34.

Emerson, R.M. 1969. *Judging Delinquents*. Chicago: Aldine.

Emerson, R.M., and S. Messinger. 1977. "The Micro-Politics of Trouble." *Social Problems* 25:121–34.

Empey, L.T. 1982. *American Delinquency*. Homewood, Il.: Dorsey.

Entwisle, D.R., and M.J. Webster. 1974. "Expectations in Mixed Racial Groups." *Sociology of Education* 47:301–18.

Erikson, E.H. 1950. *Childhood and Society*. New York: Norton.

Erikson, K.T. 1962. "Notes on the Sociology of Deviance." *Social Problems* 9:307–14.

Fortes, M. 1984. "Age, Generation, and Social Structure." Pp. 99–122 in *Age and Anthropological Theory*, ed. D.I. Kertzer and J. Keith. Ithaca, N.Y.: Cornell University Press.

Foucault, M. 1965. *Madness and Civilization*. New York: Random House.

———. 1975. *The Birth of the Clinic*. New York: Random House.

———. 1978. *The History of Sexuality*, vol. 1. New York: Random House.

———. 1980. *Power/Knowledge*, ed. C. Gordon. New York: Pantheon.

Freud, S. 1933. *New Introductory Lectures on Psychoanalysis*. New York: Norton.

Friedman, N. 1968. *The Social Nature of Psychological Research*. New York: Basic Books.

Friedrichs, R.W. 1970. *A Sociology of Sociology*. New York: Free Press.

Garfinkel, H. 1967. *Studies in Ethnomethodology*. Englewood Cliffs, N.J.: Prentice-Hall.

Garfinkel, H., M. Lynch, and E. Livingston. 1981. "The Work of a Discovering Science as Construed with Materials from the Optically Discovered Pulsar." *Philosophy of the Social Sciences* 11:131–58.

Garfinkel, H., and H. Sacks. 1970. "The Formal Properties of Practical Actions." Pp. 338–66 in *Theoretical Sociology*, ed. J.C. McKinney and E.A. Tiryakian. New York: Appleton-Century-Crofts.

Geertz, C. 1973. *The Interpretation of Cultures*. New York: Basic Books.

———. 1986. "Making Experience, Authoring Selves." In *The Anthropology of Experience*, ed. V. Turner and E. Bruner. Urbana: University of Illinois Press.

Gergen, K. and K. Davis, eds. 1985. *The Social Construction of the Person*. New York: Springer-Verlag.

Giddens, A. 1971. *Capitalism and Modern Social Theory*. Cambridge, England: Cambridge University Press.

Goffman, E. 1963. *Stigma*. Englewood Cliffs, N.J.: Prentice-Hall.

Gouldner, A.W. 1959a. "Organizational Analysis." Pp. 400–425 in *Sociology Today*, ed. R.K. Merton, L.S. Cottrell, and L. Broom. New York: Basic Books.

— — —. 1959b. "Reciprocity and Autonomy in Functional Theory." In *Symposium on Sociological Theory*, ed. L. Gross. New York: Harper & Row.

— — —. 1970. *The Coming Crisis of Western Sociology*. New York: Basic Books.

Grusky, O., K. Tierney, J. Holstein, R. Anspach, D. Davis, D. Unruh, S. Webster, S. Vandewater, and H. Allen. 1986. "Models of Local Mental Health Delivery Systems." Pp. 159–95 in *The Organization of Mental Health Services*, ed. W.R. Scott and B.L. Black. Beverly Hills: Sage.

Grusky, O., K. Tierney, R. Anspach, D. Davis, J. Holstein, D. Unruh, and S. Vandewater. 1987. "Descriptive Evaluations of Community Support Programs." *International Journal of Mental Health* 15:26–43.

Gubrium, J.F. 1975. *Living and Dying at Murray Manor*. New York: St. Martin's.

— — —. 1980a. "Doing Care Plans in Patient Conferences." *Social Science and Medicine* 14a:659–67.

— — —. 1980b. "Patient Exclusion in Geriatric Staffings." *Sociological Quarterly* 21:335–48.

— — —. 1986a. *Oldtimers and Alzheimer's*. Greenwich, Conn.: JAI Press.

— — —. 1986b. "The Social Preservation of Mind: The Alzheimer's Disease Experience." *Symbolic Interaction* 9:37–51.

— — —. 1988a. *Analyzing Field Reality*. Beverly Hills: Sage.

— — —. 1988b. "The Family as Project." *Sociological Review* 36:273–95.

— — —. 1989. "Local Culture and Service Policy." Pp. 94–112 in *The Politics of Field Research*, ed. J. Gubrium and D. Silverman. London: Sage.

— — —. 1991a. "Recognizing and Analyzing Local Culture." Pp. 131–41 in *Experiencing Fieldwork*, ed. W. Shaffir and R. Stebbins. Newbury Park, Calif.: Sage.

— — —. 1991b. "Problems in Conceptualizating 'the' Care Receiver." Paper presented at the Annual Conference of the Gerontological Society of America, San Francisco.

— — —. 1992. *Out of Control: Family Therapy and Domestic Disorder*. Newbury Park, Calif.: Sage.

Gubrium, J.F. and D.R. Buckholdt. 1979. "Production of Hard Data in Human Service Organizations." *Pacific Sociological Review* 22:115–36.

— — —. 1982. *Describing Care: Image and Practice in Rehabilitation*. Boston: Oelschlager, Gunn and Hain.

Gubrium, J.F., and J.A. Holstein. 1990. *What is Family?* Mt. View, Calif.: Mayfield.

Gubrium, J.F., and B. Wallace. 1990. "Who Theorizes Age?" *Aging and Society* 10:131–49.

Gutmann, D.L. 1967. "Aging Among the Highland Maya: A Comparative Study." *Journal of Personality and Social Psychology*. 7:28–35.

— — —. 1987. *Reclaimed Powers*. New York: Basic Books.

Hagestad, G.O., and B.L. Neugarten. 1985. "Age and the Life Course." Pp. 35–61 in *Handbook of Aging and the Social Sciences*, ed. R.H. Binstock and E. Shanas. New York: Van Nostrand Reinhold.

Hamblin, R., D. Buckholdt, D. Ferritor, and M. Kozloff. 1971. *The Humanization Process*. New York: Wiley.

Hareven, T. 1978. "The Dynamics of Kin in an Industrial Society." In *Turning Points: Historical and Sociological Essays on the Family*, ed. J. Demos and S. Boocock. Chicago: University of Chicago Press.

Havighurst, R.J. 1951. *Developmental Tasks and Education*. London: Longman.

Hazan, H. 1980. *The Limbo People: A Study of the Constitution of the Time Universe among the Aged*. London: Routledge and Kegan Paul.

— — —. 1990. *The Paradoxical Community*. Greenwich, Conn.: JAI Press.

Heath, D.H. 1965. *Explorations of Maturity*. New York: Appleton-Century- Crofts.

Heritage, J. 1984. *Garfinkel and Ethnomethodology*. Cambridge, England: Polity Press.

Hewitt J.P., and R. Stokes, R. 1975. "Disclaimers." *American Sociological Review* 40:1–11.

Hochschild, A.R. 1973. *The Unexpected Community*. New York: Prentice-Hall.

Hogan, D.P. 1989. "Institutional Perspectives on the Life Course: Challenges and Strategies." Pp. 95–106 in *Age Structuring in Comparative Perspective*, ed. D.I. Kertzer and K.W. Schaie. Hillsdale, N.J.: Lawrence Erlbaum Associates.

Holstein, J.A. 1983. "Grading Practices: The Construction and Use of Background Knowledge in Evaluative Decision-making." *Human Studies* 6:277–92.

— — —. 1984. "The Placement of Insanity: Assessments of Grave Disability and Involuntary Commitment Decisions." *Urban Life* 13:35–62.

— — —. 1987. Producing Gender Effects on Involuntary Mental Hospitalization. *Social Problems* 34:141–55.

— — —. 1988a. "Court Ordered Incompetence: Conversational Organization in Involuntary Commitment Hearings." *Social Problems* 35:442–57.

— — —. 1988b. "Studying 'Family Usage': Family Image and Discourse in Mental Hospitalization Decisions." *Journal of Contemporary Ethnography*. 17:261– 84.

— — —. 1990. "The Discourse of Age in Involuntary Commitment Proceedings." *Journal of Aging Studies* 4:111–30.

— — —. 1992. "Producing People: Descriptive Practice in Human Service Work." Pp. 22–39 in *Current Research on Occupations and Professions*, v. 7, ed. G. Miller. Greenwich, Conn. JAI Press.

— — —. 1993. *Court Ordered Insanity: Interpretive Practice and Involuntary Commitment*. Hawthorne, N.Y.: Aldine de Gruyter.

Holstein, J.A., and W.G. Staples. 1992. "Producing Evaluative Knowledge: The Interactional Bases of Social Science Findings." *Sociological Inquiry* 62:11– 35.

Holt, J. 1964. *How Children Fail*. New York: Dell.

Hunt, J. 1961. *Intelligence and Experience*. New York: Ronald Press.

Ichheiser, G. 1970. *Appearances and Realities*. San Francisco: Jossey-Bass.

Jackson, P. 1968. *Life in Classrooms*. New York: Holt, Rinehart and Winston.

Jencks, C., M. Smith, H. Ackland, M. Bane, D. Cohen, H. Gintis, amd B. Heyns. 1972. *Inequality*. New York: Basic Books.

Kardiner, A. 1939. *The Individual and His Society*. New York: Columbia University Press.

———. 1945. *Psychological Frontiers of Society*. New York: Columbia University Press.

Karp, D.A., and W.C. Yoels. 1982. *Experiencing the Life Cycle*. Springfield, Il.: Charles C Thomas.

Kertzer, D.I., and J. Keith, eds. 1984. *Age and Anthropological Theory*. Ithaca, N.Y.: Cornell University Press.

Kieth, J. 1985. "Age in Anthropological Research." Pp. 231–63 in *Handbook of Aging and the Social Sciences*, ed. R.H. Binstock and E. Shanas. New York: Van Nostrand Reinhold.

Kimmel, D.C. 1974. *Adulthood and Aging: An Interdisciplinary, Developmental View*. New York: Wiley.

Knorr-Cetina, K., and M. Mulcay, eds. 1983. *Science Observed*. London: Sage.

Kohl, H. 1968. *36 Children*. New York: New American Library.

Kohlberg, L. 1984. *The Psychology of Moral Development: The Nature and Validity of Moral Stages*. San Francisco. Harper & Row.

Kozol, J. 1967. *Death at an Early Age*. Boston: Houghton Mifflin.

Kubler-Ross, E. 1969. *On Death and Dying*. New York: Macmillan.

Kuhn, T.S. 1962. *The Structure of Scientific Revolutions*. Chicago: University of Chicago Press.

Lakhoff, G., and M. Johnson. 1980. *Metaphors We Live By*. Chicago: University of Chicago Press.

Lannoy, R. 1971. *The Speaking Tree: A Study of Indian Culture and Society*. London: Oxford University Press.

Larson, M.S. 1977. *The Rise of Professionalism*. Berkeley: University of California Press.

Lasch, C. 1979. *Haven in a Heartless World*. New York: Basic Books.

Lash, S. 1990. *Sociology of Postmodernism*. London: Routledge.

Lee, D. 1949. "Being and Value in Primitive Culture." *Journal of Philosophy* 46:401–15.

Leiter, K. 1974. "Ad Hocing in the Schools: A Study of Placement Practices in the Kindergartens of Two Schools." Pp. 17–75 in *Language Use and School Performance*, ed. A.V. Cicourel et al. New York: Academic Press.

LeVine, R.A. 1973. *Culture, Behavior, and Personality*. Chicago: Aldine.

Linton, R. 1936. *The Study of Man*. New York: Appleton-Century-Crofts.

———. 1945. *The Cultural Background of Personality*. New York: Appleton-Century-Crofts.

Lofland, J. 1969. *Deviance and Identity*. Englewood Cliffs, N.J.: Prentice-Hall.

Loseke, D.R. 1992. *The Battered Woman and Shelters*. Albany: SUNY Press.

Luborsky, M. n.d. "In Whose Image Does the Life History Empower?" Philadelphia: Behavioral Research, Philadelphia Geriatric Center.

Lynch, M. 1983. "Accommodation Practices: Vernacular Treatments of Madness." *Social Problems* 31:152–63.

————. 1985. *Art and Artifact in Laboratory Science*. London: Routledge and Kegan Paul.

McHugh, P. 1968. *Defining the Situation*. Indianapolis: Bobbs-Merrill.

MacKay, R. 1973. "Conceptions of Children and Models of Socialization." In *Childhood and Socialization*, ed. H.P. Dreitzel. New York: Macmillan.

McKinney, J.P. 1968. "The Development of Choice Stability in Children and Adolescents." *Journal of Genetic Psychology* 113:79–83.

McLuhan, M., and Q. Fiore. 1967. *The Medium Is the Message*. New York: Random House.

Maines, D. 1983. "Time and Biography in Diabetic Experience." *Mid-American Review of Sociology* 8:103–17.

Marlaire, C.L. 1990. "On Questions, Communication, and Bias: Educational Testing as 'Invisible' Collaboration." Pp. 233–60 in *Perspectives on Social Problems*, ed. G. Miller and J. Holstein. Greenwich, Conn.: JAI Press.

Marlaire, C.L., and D.W. Maynard. 1990. "Standardized Testing as an Interactional Phenomenon." *Sociology of Education* 63:83–101.

Marsella, A.J., and G.M. White eds. 1982. *Cultural Conceptions of Mental Health and Therapy*. Boston: Reidel.

Maynard, D.W. 1984. *Inside Plea Bargaining*. New York: Plenum.

Mead, G.H. 1934. *Mind, Self, and Society*. Chicago: University of Chicago Press.

Mead, M. 1928. *Coming of Age in Samoa*. New York: Morrow.

————. 1930. *Growing Up in New Guinea*. New York: Morrow.

————. 1935. *Sex and Temperament in Three Primitive Societies*. New York: Morrow.

————. 1954. "The Swaddling Hypothesis: Its Reception." *American Anthropologist* 56:395–409.

Mehan, H. 1973. "Assessing Children's School Performane." In *Childhood and Socialization*, ed. H.P. Dreitzel. New York: Macmillan.

————. 1974. "Accomplishing Classroom Lessons." Pp. 76–142 in *Language Use and School Performance*, ed. A.V. Cicourel et al. New York: Academic Press.

————. 1979. *Learning Lessons*. Cambridge, Mass.: Harvard University Press.

————. 1992. "Understanding Inequality in Schools: The Contribution of Interpretive Studies." *Sociology of Education* 65:1–20.

Mehan, H., A. Hetweck, and J. Meihls. 1985. *Handicapping the Handicapped*. Stanford: Stanford University Press.

Mehan, H. and H. Wood. 1975. *The Reality of Ethnomethodology*. New York: Wiley.

Miller, G. 1987. "Producing Family Problems: Organization and Uses of the Family Perspective and Rhetoric in Family Therapy." *Symbolic Interaction* 10:245–65.

————. 1990. "Work as Reality Maintaining Activity." Pp. 163–83 in *Current Research on Occupations and Professions*, v. 5, ed. H. Lopata. Greenwich, Conn. JAI Press.

————. 1991. *Enforcing the Work Ethic*. Albany: SUNY Press.

Mills, C.W. 1940. "Situated Actions and Vocabularies of Motive." *American Sociological Review* 5:904–13.

Mintz, S., and S. Kellogg. 1988. *Domestic Revolution: A Social History of American Family Life*. New York: Free Press.

Myerhoff, B. 1984. "Rites and Signs of Ripening: The Intertwining of Ritual, Time, and Growing Older." Pp. 305–34 in *Age and Anthropological Theory*, ed. D.I. Kertzer and J. Keith. Ithaca, N.Y.: Cornell University Press.

Neugarten, B.L. ed. 1968. *Middle Age and Aging*. Chicago: University of Chicago Press.

— — — . 1974. "Age Groups in American Society and the Rise of the Young-Old." *Annals of the American Academy of Political and Social Sciences* 415:187–98.

— — — . 1978. "The Future and the Young-old." Pp. 137–52 in *Aging into the 21st Century*, ed. L.F. Jarvik. New York: Gardner Press.

Oakes, J. 1985. *Keeping Track: How Schools Structure Inequality*. New Haven: Yale University Press.

Ostor, A. 1984. "Chronology, Category, and Ritual." Pp. 281–304 in *Age and Anthropological Theory*, ed. D.I. Kertzer and J. Keith. Ithaca, N.Y.: Cornell University Press.

Parsons, T. 1951. *The Social System*. New York: Free Press.

Perrucci, R. 1974. *Circle of Madness*. Englewood Cliffs, N.J.: Prentice-Hall.

Piaget, J. 1947. *The Psychology of Intelligence*. New York: Harcourt Brace Jovanovich.

— — — . 1952. *The Origins of Intelligence in Children*. New York: Norton.

— — — . 1957. *The Language and Thought of the Child*. New York: Meridian Books.

Piliavin, I., and S. Briar. 1964. "Police Encounters With Juveniles." *American Journal of Sociology* 70:206–14.

Pollner, M. 1975. "'The Very Coinage of Your Brain': The Anatomy of Reality Disjunctures." *Philosophy of Social Sciences* 5:411–30.

— — — . 1987. *Mundane Reason*. Cambridge, England: Cambridge University Press.

Pollner, M., and L. McDonald-Wickler. 1985. "The Social Construction of Unreality: A Case Study of a Family's Atrribution of Competence to a Severly Retarded Child." *Family Process* 24:241–54.

Rist, R.C. 1973. *The Urban School: A Factory for Failure*. Cambridge, Mass.: MIT Press.

Rogers, C. 1964. "Toward a Modern Approach to Values: The Valuing Process in the Mature Person." *Journal of Abnormal and Social Psychology* 68:160–67.

Roheim, G. 1950. *Psychoanalysis and Anthropology*. New York: International Universities Press.

Rose, A.M. 1965a. "Group Consciousness Among the Aging." Pp. 19–36 in *Older People and Their Social World*, ed. A.M. Rose and W.A. Peterson. Philadelphia: F.A Davis.

— — — . 1965b. "The Subculture of the Aging: A Framework for Research in Social Gerontology." Pp. 19–36 in *Older People and Their Social World*, ed. A.M. Rose and W.A. Peterson. Philadelphia: F.A Davis.

Rubinstein, R.L. 1990. "Nature, Culture, Gender, Age: A Critical Review." Pp. 109–28 in *Anthropology and Aging*, ed. R.L. Rubenstein. Dordrecht, The Netherlands: Kluwer Academic Publishers.

Sacks, H., E. Schegloff, and G. Jefferson. 1974. "A Simplest Systematics for the Organization of Turn-Taking in Conversation." *Language* 50:696–735.

Sampson, E., S. Messinger, and R. Towne. 1962. "Family Processes and Becoming a Mental Patient." *American Journal of Sociology* 68:88–96.

Sanders, W. 1976. *Juvenile Delinquency*. New York: Praeger.

Sankar, A. 1984. "'It's Just Old Age': Old Age as a Diagnosis in American and Chinese Medicine." Pp. 250–80 in *Age and Anthropological Theory*, ed. D.I. Kertzer and J. Keith. Ithaca, NY: Cornell University Press.

Saussure, F. 1960. *Course in General Linguistics*. London: Owen.

Schegloff, E.A. 1982."Discourse as an Interactional Achievment." Pp. 73–91 in *Georgetown University Roundtable on Languages and Linguistics*, ed. D. Tannen. Washington, D.C.: Georgetown University Press.

Schultz, T.W. 1962. "Reflections on Investment in Man." *Journal of Political Economy* 70:1–8.

Schutz, A. 1967. *The Phenomenology of the Social World*. Evanston, Il.: Northwestern University Press.

———. 1970. *On Phenomenology and Social Relations*. Chicago: University of Chicago Press.

Schwendinger, H., and J.S. Schwendinger. 1985. *Adolescent Subcultures and Delinquency*. New York: Praeger.

Scott, M.B., and S.M. Lyman. 1968. "Accounts." *American Sociological Review* 33:46–62.

Segalen, M. 1986. *Historical Anthropology of the Family*. Cambridge, England: Cambridge University Press.

Silverman, D. 1987. *Communication and Medical Practice*. London: Sage.

Singer, M. 1961. "A Survey of Culture and Personality Theory and Research." Pp.40–59 in *Studying Personality Cross-Culturally*, ed. B. Kaplan. New York: Harper & Row.

Smith, D.E. 1987. *The Everyday World as Problematic*. Boston: Northeastern University Press.

———. 1989. "Women's Work as Mothers: A New Look at the Relation of Class, Family, and School Achievement." Pp. 109–28 in *Perspectives on Social Problems*, vol. 1, ed. J. Holstein and G. Miller. Greenwich, Conn. JAI Press.

Smith, L.M., and W. Geoffrey. 1968. *The Complexities of an Urban Classroom*. New York: Holt, Rinehart and Winston.

Strauss, A.L. 1959. *Mirrors and Masks*. New York: Free Press.

Suchar, C.S. 1975. "Doing Therapy: Notes on the Training of Psychiatric Personnel." Paper presented at the Annual Meeting of the Midwest Sociological Society, Chicago.

Sudnow, D. 1965. "Normal Crimes: Sociological Features of the Penal Code in a Public Defender Office." *Social Problems* 12:255–76.

Sykes, G. 1958. *The Society of Captives*. Princeton, N.J.: Princeton University Press.

Thompson, S. 1990. "Metaphors the Chinese Age By." Pp. 102–20 in *Anthropology and the Riddle of the Sphinx*, ed. P. Spencer. London: Routledge.

Unruh, D.R. 1983. *Invisible Lives: Social Worlds of the Aged*. Beverly Hills: Sage.

Weber, M. 1958. *The Protestant Ethnic and the Spirit of Capitalism*. New York: Scribner.

———. 1968. *Economy and Society*. New York: Bedminster Press.

Wheeler, S. 1969. *On Record: Files and Dossiers in American Life*. New York: Russell Sage Foundation.

Whorf, B.L. 1956. *Language, Thought, and Reality*. New York: Wiley.

Wieder, D.L. 1988. *Language and Social Reality*. Lanham, Md.: University Press of America.

Wilcox, K. 1982. "Differential Socialization in the Classroom." In *Doing the Ethnography of Schooling*, ed. G.D. Spindler. New York: Holt, Rinehart and Winston.

Windom, C. 1989. "The Cycle of Violence." *Science* 244:160–66.

Yarrow, M.R., C.G. Schwartz, H.S. Murphy, and L.C. Deasy. 1955. "The Psychological Meaning of Mental Illness in the Family." *Journal of Social Issues* 11:12–24.

Zigler, E. 1970. "The Environmental Mystique: Training the Intellect Versus Development of the Child." *Childhood Education* 46:402–412.

Zimmerman, D.H., and M. Pollner. "The Everyday World as a Phenomenon." Pp. 80–104 in *Understanding Everyday Life*, ed. J.D. Douglas. Chicago: Aldine.

Zurcher, L. 1983. *Social Roles*. Beverly Hills: Sage.

AUTHOR INDEX

SUBJECT INDEX

217